WELCOME BACK, CONNIE!

With outstretched arms I circled the theater, embracing the audience and they me, ending seven agonizing years of self-doubt and heartbreak. There was the same old love affair between us, just the way it had always been since my career began a millenium ago. It was a night of never-before-felt exhilaration—of coming home again—of reaching out almost desperately to touch the hands and hearts of the people.

Then I sang my final song: "If I Never Sing Another Song."

"I guess you've probably suspected by now that tonight is a very, very special night for me," I said, with bouquets in both arms and tears streaming down my face. "I'm proud to call you my friends. I told you to hang in there, guys. Thank you for waiting."

WHO'S SORRY NOW?

Raves for Connie's Moving and Memorable Story:

"Where most performers are evasive about their early lives, Francis is nuttily specific and bursting with comic enthusiasm. . . . Worthwhile in this age of throwaway show business memoirs."
—*Washington Post*

"This is not just another name-dropping, kiss-and-tell show business autobiography. . . . A bittersweet story of personal triumph and tragedy. . . ."
—*Columbus Citizen-Journal*

"Destined to shock . . ."
—*New York Daily News*

"An effervescent and humorous Connie Francis bubbles up from the pages of *Who's Sorry Now*."
—*Cedar Rapids Gazette*

Who's Sorry Now?

CONNIE FRANCIS

ST. MARTIN'S PRESS / NEW YORK

I would like to dedicate this
book to my brother, Georgie.

As a public figure, I was the
greater success. As a human
being, Georgie was. For the rest
of my days, I will aspire to become the warmhearted and loving person he was. For the rest
of my life, I hope the things I do
with mine will make him proud
of me.

ST. MARTIN'S PRESS TITLES ARE
AVAILABLE AT QUANTITY DISCOUNTS
FOR SALES PROMOTIONS, PREMIUMS OR
FUND RAISING. SPECIAL BOOKS OR
BOOK EXCERPTS CAN ALSO BE
CREATED TO FIT SPECIFIC NEEDS. FOR
INFORMATION WRITE TO SPECIAL SALES
MANAGER, ST. MARTIN'S PRESS, 175
FIFTH AVENUE, NEW YORK, N.Y. 10010.

ISBN-0-312-90386-3

Contents

PART TWO

PART THREE

Acknowledgments

I WOULD LIKE to thank the many fans and friends who supplied me with their own painstakingly-cared-for and chronicled accounts of my career in the form of scrapbooks. I would also like to thank Barbara Clarke for helping me with the tedious chronology needed for the accuracy I insisted upon; Karen Martylewski for typing the manuscript of the book; and Pat Niglio for supplying me with so many pictures, scrapbooks, dates, and events, all of which I had lost in two floods in my basement. I would like to thank Hank Weiland as well, for supplying all the fan magazine stories that I had also lost. Without their dedication and the many hours they invested, it would have been virtually impossible for me to write this book with any degree of accuracy.

Introduction

I DON'T have a lot of personal friends . . . Connie Francis is one of them. When you've known and loved someone for as long as I have known and loved her, objectivity goes out the window. Without trying to color my feelings . . . here goes.

Obviously, *Who's Sorry Now?* is the story of a girl who grew to womanhood and international stardom. Fame, fortune, and all those things we read about in stories and see in films became hers. Unfortunately, one thing kept eluding Connie . . . personal happiness. Everyone's life is a book. We all have hopes and dreams . . . successes and failures . . . happy times and moments of despair.

Who's Sorry Now? isn't just a story of one woman's career and her personal ups and downs. It's inspiring and touching. It will warm you . . . it will frighten the daylights out of you . . . it will amuse you. Probably, it will cause you to come up with an observation similar to mine.

Connie Francis is special! No one questions her remarkable talent or professional success. More importantly, she is proof that strength and personal character will get you through the most difficult moments life presents.

DICK CLARK

In this business that we call "show," there are certain words and phrases that are used with a great deal of frequency. For example: "sweetheart" as in a "'sweetheart' of a deal," "you'll love it," "above the titles and below the lines," "Have I ever lied to you before?" And of course "Trust me," and then there's the declension of the verb "to owe" as in "he owes her one," "you owe me one," "we owe them one," "they owe us one," "I don't owe you anything." But of course that last one you can't use until after you've paid your dues. But there are also words we use with less frequency, words like "courage," "guts," "perseverance," "talent," "comeback." We have with us tonight someone who is all those very rare words. Ladies and gentlemen: CONNIE FRANCIS . . .

—ROBERT PRESTON speaking at the Golden Globe
Awards, 1981

PART ONE

1

Smile (for Daddy)

Daddy always said I wasn't pretty
Unless I'd SMILE
He said SMILE, SMILE, SMILE

I was Daddy's smilin' girl
And I always tried to please
I could make him happy
And put him at his ease

I would SMILE for Daddy
And sing a little song
And Daddy would take care of me
That's how we got along*

August 1943
Olympic Amusement Park
Irvington, New Jersey

"MOMMY, why is Genevieve crying?" I asked my
mother, puzzled. Why was my twelve-year-old cousin

running so frantically from the giant open-air stage with that great big accordion strapped to her back?

What's going on? This is the fourth kid today from my accordion school who did that!

"She's just scared, honey. She's got stage fright, that's all."

"What's that, Mommy?"

Many years would pass before I'd ever know that feeling. Fear of any kind simply played no part in my young life.

Mom jokes that I was always in show business—that when I entered the world on that snowy December morn, I was belting out "Al Di La." (Impossible, Ida. The song wasn't even written then.)

So naturally, on this hot, special August day, the only emotion filling my four-year-old heart was happy anticipation. I just couldn't wait to dash up to that big old bandstand and begin playing my twelve-bass accordion.

Daddy, holding my plump baby brother Georgie, waited eagerly, too. My mother was fidgety and nervous. She kept fussing with my hair, turning the fat hot-dog curls around her finger and fixing the bow at the top.

At last, when Teresa Masciola, my accordion teacher, announced my name, I leaped from my mother's arms and, dwarfed by my accordion, I quickly scaled the steps, unassisted. I didn't need anyone to hold my hand to get me on stage then, and I never have since. I grinned confidently at the orchestra leader, Joe Pasile, and he grinned back. Then I began playing "Anchors Aweigh."

After the first few bars of the music, I could hear the audience chuckling and applauding. It was a new and truly heavenly sound, and it made my heart smile.

I curtsied, just the way I'd practiced every day in the mirror behind Mommy's bedroom door. And when I did, my pink lace panties peeked out from under my pink and white lace pinafore.

What a day to remember! Not only did I get to per-

form! Not only did Mommy and Daddy take Georgie
and me on all the rides! But I knew from the gleam in
my father's eye that I'd made him very proud of me.
And *nothing* was ever more important to me than
that! I was clearly the apple of Daddy's eye, and I was
always made to feel very safe, very loved, very protected and very, very special.

It was my father, George Franconero, who introduced me to his first love—music—and forever after,
music became my life. Every evening Daddy would
come home weary from a day of back-breaking labor;
but after dinner he always managed to play for us on
the tiny out-of-tune concertina *his* dad had brought
with him to Ellis Island, New York, when he arrived in
1905—an Italian immigrant from Reggio di Calabria.

That was the time of the greatest mass migration to
America; and they were lean days indeed. There was
no welfare, relief, or federal assistance of any kind;
but the city of Newark, New Jersey, gave each immigrant family a ton of coal to keep them from freezing
and a small plot of farmland, out of necessity. Here in
this new *terra straniera* (strange land) where the
streets, they'd heard, were paved with gold, many of
these industrious people simply couldn't find work, so
at least they were able to raise their own food.

It was here, on this small piece of farmland where
Newark Airport now sits, that my paternal grandfather, Frank Franconero, and then later my grandmother, Maria Concetta, and their thirteen children
would settle in a humble hovel. Grandma and the
older children grew vegetables and raised chickens,
nanny goats, and pigs. Daddy, at age eight, even
skinned the pigs and made his own sausages. What
stock these people were made of! At ninety-one, my
grandmother, all alone, would still be tilling, planting,
and seeding her own tiny bit of farmland on Astor
Street in Newark, New Jersey.

My grandfather worked two long jobs as a street
cleaner and a night watchman in a coffin factory. He

adored music; so among the meager possessions he brought with him across the Atlantic were some bag-pipes, an ocarina, a bamboo reed instrument that he called a sweet potato, and of course, the out-of-tune concertina.

It was a tough life. From the age of seven, Daddy worked very hard shoveling coal and chopping trees for firewood, and he was forced to leave school before the seventh grade. Although insensitive in most mat-ters, he is an innately intelligent man, and with any real opportunity I'm sure he would have made a very successful professional or businessman.

As it was, each night by a gasoline lamp (they had no electricity) he would read anything and everything he could get his hands on till the wee small hours of the morning.

The immigration to America of my mother's family almost parallels that of my father's. My maternal grandfather, Antonio Ferrari, and my grandmother, Maria di Vito Ferrari, also arrived in 1905 from Mondo Virginina, Italy, a province of Naples, and set-tled in that same Italian ghetto they call the Iron-bound section of Newark.

My grandmother, Maria di Vito, was a tall, strong-willed, sturdy woman who bore sixteen children. When the midwife failed to arrive on time, she deliv-ered two of those children at home alone, cutting the umbilical cord herself. Her husband died at the age of forty-two. Widowed, and with all those children, she *had* to be shrewd in order to survive, and that she was!

Once a week, she would go to a different market where live chickens were sold, and while the pro-prietor wasn't looking, she would wring some poor chicken's neck. Then, in very broken English, she'd demand: "Look-a-mister, for dis-a chicken, I give-a you ten cents. She's-a-half-a dead *now*. And you lucky I give-a you dat much."

In order to exist, she took ten boarders into her tiny

two-family wood-framed house at 228 Walnut Street in Newark—cooking, washing, ironing, and cleaning for them. I remember the day Grandma, at age ninety-three, took a bus ride with a few girlfriends to take in the sights of Washington, D.C. I remember still another day seeing her run down the narrow alley of our house, hitting her upstairs tenant over the head with a giant broom for not paying his rent on time.

Here in Newark's Little Italy, very typically, none of my grandparents ever learned to speak more than a few words of English. It wasn't necessary; if you weren't Italian, *you* were the foreigner. Besides, survival was more important.

There's one thing I know for certain. Both my grandparents and my parents are the last of a breed. If necessary, they definitely would have made it—without too much pain or strain—clear cross-country on the Oregon Trail in a covered wagon.

When my father was fourteen, he worked in an envelope factory for twelve dollars a week, and it was there that he met my mother. They were childhood sweethearts. (Today he says he "fooled around a lot, though—*all* us guys did"—but never, of course, with the person you loved.)

It wasn't your average whirlwind courtship, but it was well worth the waiting and the planning. They married seven and a half years later with quite a nest egg—a whole sixty dollars. At the time, Daddy was putting in a ten-hour day shoveling coal off barges for four dollars per day, and Mom wrapped gifts at Woolworth's on Broad Street.

There was no honeymoon in Niagara Falls—just the nervous car ride to the small Jewish neighborhood on Dean Street in Brooklyn where they made their first home.

Daddy worked at the Brooklyn Navy Yard. I was born almost five years after they married, not because my father didn't want children, but because the times were so hard. When my mother told him about the future blessed event, he didn't speak to her for three months. (This is shocking only if you are a non-Italian.)

And, he didn't pick me up from the crib either, until I was six months old. (We had nothing in common yet.) It was only when I began showing an avid interest in music, that I became the center of Daddy's universe—to the exclusion, I'm afraid, of everyone and everything else.

If my folks were living in Brooklyn, why, you may ask, was I born in Newark? Well, it was on a visit—one of those weekend visits my parents made to Grandma Ferrari's house. So, it was there that I was born Concetta Maria Franconero, on December 12, 1938.

It seems that my very pregnant mom got word of a big shindig that night at the VFW Hall near Grandma's. My mother simply loves to dance, and she's phenomenal at it. How could she possibly resist dancing the night away to the Charleston with her brother, Uncle Ray (also a smoothie on the dance floor), at one of those grueling marathons that lasted a year and a half. (You remember *They Shoot Horses, Don't They?*)

Right smack in the middle of "You Must Have Been a Beautiful Baby," Mom and Uncle Ray made a hasty, but predictable, exit from the dance floor of the VFW Hall directly to the maternity ward of St. James Hospital a mere block away. Daddy stayed away that night.

When I was born, we were living on St. Mark's and Utica Avenues in Brooklyn, and Daddy was working for a Jewish man, a plumber. One day the Jewish man said, "We've gotta find a job." (It seems there was a wartime shortage of the materials needed to furnish homes. He was out of business, and they were out of work.) But the Jewish plumber reassured Daddy: "Don't worry. We'll go down to the shipyard. I've heard there's plenty of work there."

Week after week they went together to fill out the job applications. One day a political ward leader advised: "Don't knock your brains out. They don't hire Jews or Italians." (This was not the policy of the federal company, Daddy says, but of the hiring bosses.)

He borrowed the identification papers of his sister's Irish husband, and overnight George Franconero became Frank Conners. As an Irish fellow, he sailed right through—no tests, no interview, no nothin'!

A year and a half later, shortly after my brother arrived, my father had an accident. Some coal fell and split his head wide open. The company gave him a fat seven hundred dollars, but he suffered from headaches for years afterward. For a while he couldn't work, so we moved from Brooklyn back to my maternal grandma's home in Newark.

How I loved that crowded, friendly neighborhood with its tree-lined streets and its poor but happy first- and second-generation Italian families! On hot summer nights we would sit outdoors on our stoops laughing and singing Neapolitan songs. I remember so well the sounds and smells and sights of men selling chestnuts, sweet potatoes, and big old-fashioned salted pretzels on their pushcarts.

There was a life all its own to this neighborhood— an intangible pulse—but more than that, there was a sense of belonging, of roots, of total safety.

In my neighborhood if you weren't Italian, not only were you a *foreigner*, but worse yet, you were American. (It's comical, but even today many Italian people still think this way. One can be anything—Polish, Greek, Spanish—but anybody non-Italian is considered American.)

To this day, my ethnic heritage and roots are a very real and fundamental part of my life, and they have served me well. I'm so proud of this group of people into which I was born, and I'm very, very grateful for all the special and wonderful things they are.

They're warm-hearted and happy, vibrant and proud, industrious and passionate. They make the most devoted parents and the most loyal of Americans.

*   *   *

We were a close-knit family. My father was far from demonstratively affectionate, but I was secure in my parents' love. Georgie and I were listening to Daddy play the "squeeze box" one night, when suddenly Daddy asked me: "Do you wanna take music lessons?" I nodded yes; I was three.

"Okay. Do you wanna take accordion lessons or piano lessons?"

I didn't know which was what. Accordion just sounded more exotic. (Go know, right? What a dope *I* was!) Eventually, I grew to despise that rotten accordion. When it finally died in a flood in our basement in '67, I threw a real big party.

Sometimes I think my father wanted me to be an accordion player so much because it was second only to the bassoon as the most asexual instrument ever known to man. Just think about that a minute. Would anyone have ever caught Jean Harlow or Marilyn Monroe strapped to an *accordion*? Aha! That's it! That's the answer right there! Strapped! And trapped!

My father wanted Georgie to take music lessons, too, but he wasn't interested.

The day after I made that dumb choice, my mother took me to Teresa Masciola's Accordion School on Elm Street. Miss Masciola said that at age three, I was simply too young to read music, but that Mom should leave me with her anyway for an hour or so. When Mom returned, Miss Masciola said I was "a natural."

I had a golden childhood; I was everybody's little princess, always dressed in something new and starched. To my everlasting regret, I was also a perfectionist. It is a most painful style of living for *everybody* involved. Even then, if there was a spot on my shoe, I made a federal case out of it. Nothing changes.

All Italian girls who had Italian fathers who were living played the accordion, but *I* played the accordion the way I did everything else—with a vengeance! Music became my obsession in life. Who had time for hopscotch, hide-and-go-seek, or even dolls, when I had discovered the very best way to gain Daddy's instant and undivided attention and approval?

To be sure, I inherited my passion for music from my father and my voice from my mother. She used to sing in the school choir, but by sixth grade, she was forced to leave school and go to work, just as Daddy had. But my sense of drama—that was all mine.

My *father's* dream was that one day I would open an accordion school in Newark. (I humored him.) *My* dream, all my life, was to take bows. It didn't necessarily have to be in show business, but there simply would have to be a place and a reason to take a few bows!

I got my first chance to be the ham I would always be before my third birthday—it was a milestone in my life. Uncle Ray was marrying Aunt Marie Maccione and I was Aunt Marie's darling little flower girl.

Two adoring neighborhood ladies, Lil and Mary, made me a pinafore every week. But, for this special occasion, they made me an olive green velvet strapless gown—with a long train, just like the bride's. (Even with all the baby fat, I still don't know exactly *what*, besides gravity, held it up.) My hair was in those same hot-dog curls, this time with an olive green plume sticking out of the top of my head. I felt like the Italian Shirley Temple.

Before I left for church, I planted a big fat kiss right on my baby brother's chubby hand so that I could leave the imprint of my first lipsticked lips somewhere. When the priest saw me walking down the aisle, he was convulsed in laughter; Aunt Marie had convulsions, too. She says that choosing me for her flower girl was the worst mistake she ever made. (I don't agree.) How could anybody concentrate on the bride when they were so busy watching the pudgy little girl who kept winking at the priest and everyone else there that day?

Yes, it was a golden childhood for *me*. But as an adult, I've thought so often of how awful it all must have been for my brother, Georgie. We loved each other dearly; rarely was there evidence of the usual sibling rivalry.

We were poor, and Mom rarely bought a stitch for herself. But she saved every cent she could to buy matching outfits for Georgie and me. "Ida's kids" always looked as if they'd stepped out of a bandbox. Her son was her favorite, of course. Italian sons *always* are. Yet even with all the love she showered upon my brother, in the end, it simply wasn't compensation enough.

Our family did everything together. I remember so well the trips to Riverhead, Long Island, where my Aunt Rose, Daddy's sister, owned the general candy store, and those camping trips there, in the creaky little rowboat we rented for fifteen dollars a weekend. (We did an outdoorsy thing like camping in those days only because, at age two, I still had no veto power. Even though I'm a Sagittarian, until recently I could never stand the discomforts of nature. "Just give me the pool at the Fontainebleau in Miami Beach any day of the week," was my motto. But then, I'm not tall, either.)

I remember too, those trips to my Aunt Lizzie's house in Union Beach, on the Jersey shore, where the merry-go-round in the penny arcade played the hottest hits like "Peg o' My Heart" by the Harmonicats, and the rides in my Uncle Joe's car with the rumble seat in back.

I especially remember that night in August of '45 when everybody got so excited—just 'cause a man named Gabriel Heatter said on the radio that A Big War was over. And I remember too, that same night and the drive back to Newark, where there was dancing, laughter, and rejoicing in the streets. Men in uniforms twirled girls around, and the people seemed a little wide-eyed and scary to me. Yes, it was a real funny night.

What carefree, simple, happy days they were! My young world was a safe secure place, indeed. I remember one hot summer night when I was going on five. With the nickel Mommy gave me, I walked down the street alone in my pajamas to the corner candy store.

I said to my friend, the store owner, "Hey Luigi, can I have a double-decker strawberry ice cream cone?" He handed me the cone, and I gave him my nickel. "Hey Luigi, what happened? You forgot my jimmies? Please, Luigi, put some chocolate jimmies on top."

"Okay, Concettina. *Ma*, that's-a one more penny."

"I don't have a penny. C'mon, Luigi, put the jimmies on anyway."

"Okay. Okay. Okay. Here's-a you jimmies. Who wants-a hear you grandma if I no give-a you jimmies. Now, go home! *Buona notte. Ciao*, Concettina."

2

Happiness

July 1944
Belmont Avenue
Newark, New Jersey

"How much, mister?"

"It's a nickel a pickle," said Mr. Goldberg, the delicatessen owner. My mouth was watering as I peered into the big vat filled with those delicious Jewish pickles and their great big seeds swimming all around them. When I found the biggest and fattest one, Mr. Goldberg placed the pickle on a piece of wax paper.

I strolled leisurely down the street eating the pickle with gusto. What a treat! I'm sure gonna like it here in this new place.

When I was five Daddy managed to save up the $1,200 necessary for the down payment on a $4,800, three-family house, our first very own house in Newark. And so we moved away—twenty-five minutes and a world away.

Everything was different here, but nice, too. Almost everybody spoke English and something funny called Yiddish. There were people running around with strange names like Metzger and Weinberg—all *kinds* of names that didn't have *o*'s and *a*'s at the end of them.

I loved our house; I especially loved my very own bedroom painted pink with its Early American maple furniture. Mommy even took an old table and, with thumbtacks, covered it with a pretty pink eyelet skirt; above it hung a mirror—a great big mirror I could practice in front of.

Our hearts, though, were still back in the old neighborhood with our friends and relatives, and we went back to visit each weekend and often more than that. This gave me a chance to play my accordion and even to sing along sometimes at Uncle George's butcher shop on Jefferson Street.

And each time I did, Uncle George gave me a bottle of green olives with little red pimientos sticking out. Imagine that! A whole bottle of green olives— just for a couple of songs! For a really special treat, Mommy and Daddy took Georgie and me to see grown-up stars like Frankie Carle play the piano at the Adams Theater in downtown Newark.

I played my accordion everywhere anybody would pay attention—at all the church socials at Our Lady of Mt. Carmel and St. James and at veterans' hospitals— anywhere they'd listen to a chubby little Italian kid play an accordion.

And I soon found out that there were lots of other songs people wrote besides "Anchors Aweigh," because every time Daddy had thirty-five cents he'd buy me a musical lead sheet to a new song.

This is as good a time as any to thank, from the bottom of my heart, my third-grade teacher at Bergen Street Elementary School for contributing so very little to my singing career; to be more precise, for nearly sabotaging it before it ever got off the ground.

I never could sing "The Star-Spangled Banner"; you see, Francis Scott Key wrote it in Somebody Else's Key, probably for some massive Italian lady soprano at the Milano opera house.

My third-grade teacher, Mrs. Nye, a thin redhead
with horn-rimmed glasses who resembled Eve Arden,
never realized this fact of life. She was under the distinct impression that every woman born in America is
born a soprano. One day, while the class sang that
miserable song, Mrs. Nye stood behind me.

I'm not unpatriotic, but let's face it, gang! My apologies, Mr. Key, but it's a bad song. Didn't anybody
ever consider "America, the Beautiful" or Mr.
Berlin's "God Bless America" as our national anthem? Anyway, I couldn't reach all those high notes
Mr. Key wrote. So that day Mrs. Nye, in her infinite
wisdom, instructed:

"Connie Franconero, please move up to one of the
front seats; I'll need to work with you a lot. You're
just not hitting any of those high notes. Stay after
class, will you?"

I'm so glad Mrs. Nye and my fourth-grade teacher,
Mrs. Ida Charles, went to different music academies.

"Connie Franconero, you have a lovely voice," said
Mrs. Charles one day. "I've never heard a student sing
"America, the Beautiful" so well before. Stay after
class, dear, will you?"

"Connie, how would you like to be Gretel in our
annual auditorium musical? We'll be presenting
Hansel and Gretel this semester," said Mrs. Charles
encouragingly.

"Well, Mrs. Charles," I hesitated, "I really am an
accordion player, but . . . I guess I could *try* to be
Gretel."

Thus began my merciful, but gradual, transition from
accordionist to vocalist, and I owe it all to Mrs. Ida
Charles. Many years later, I would have a chance to
thank that great lady when NBC-TV put her on a train
(she was afraid to fly) and shuffled her off to Hollywood, California, the night I was honored on "This Is
Your Life." She even skipped me a whole grade so
that I got to graduate at sixteen. All this, because of
one chorus of "America, the Beautiful"!

After Mrs. Charles discovered me, I realized there was a whale of a difference between singing songs like "Prisoner of Love," "Jezebel," and "That's My Desire" and playing "Lady of Spain" and "The Flight of the Bumble Bee."

Playing the accordion was much harder work! Singing was a real piece of cake—a total snap! No practicing, no sore fingers or shoulders, no nothin'!

But play I did—sometimes up to six hours a day. Even Daddy would sometimes say: "Cut it out, will ya? Go out 'n' play." But who listened to him? I knew he'd have a fit if someday I didn't have my own Accordion School of Music just like Miss Masciola's. (Sorry I loused up your big plans, Daddy!)

The first time I told Mommy about the fresh boy in the neighborhood who pulled my long pigtails every day, she warned, "Don't make me nervous. This is a new neighborhood—don't start! You know somethin', you're a real troublemaker!"

But when I came home from school with two scraped knees and the shiner Ronnie Turner planted on my left eye, Ida changed her mind. "The next time that jerk does that, you knock his block off!"

The words were music to my ears, and it was well worth the waiting. They say every dog has his day. Well on *my* day Ronnie Turner got his comeuppance all right. He came home from school in real grave condition after we had gone a couple of rounds. Come to think of it, Ronnie looked something like Leroy Brown after he messed around with Doris—"like a jigsaw puzzle with a couple-a pieces gone!" Remember?

Ever since Ida gave me the go-ahead and I had that match with Ronnie, it's a tough contract for anyone to get me to walk away from a worthy brawl; I always have to suppress that inner urge to get myself involved. And I try very hard at all times, even under the worst of circumstances, to be a lady. But it doesn't always work.

For example, I'll conduct a negotiation between half a dozen gentlemen and myself (sometimes that "gentleman" comes with a real small "g"). "Hello, gentlemen," I'll begin with style, aplomb, and charm. "I'm so glad we could meet today; I hope you guys are all well. And now for the matter at hand. . . ."

Then, little by little by little, if in the course of these negotiations I discover that someone I trusted turns out to be an empty suit (a fake person) or worse, a phony or a cheat, and I get real, real frustrated . . . I'm a heck of a lot better now than I used to be, but my family and friends still have to listen to a lot of stories.

Aunt Marie says that as a very small child I was forever sitting on her living-room floor surrounded by a ton of books and papers. Ha-ha! That's what *Aunt Marie* saw!

After school, I was always surrounded by a bunch of boys. I don't know why that is; I was certainly no beauty. But each day I was followed home by a legion of boys, all of whom had a lot of fun teasing and flirting with me.

It would always make me feel very feminine and very girlie-girlie; and it always made me blush, too. It's comical, but whenever I was singing and playing my accordion—especially on stage—I came on like Gangbusters, but in real life, it was very different; I was always very, very shy with boys.

In our newfound Jewish neighborhood, my brother Georgie's best friend was Farrell Fand. Farrell Fand's grandparents, two very orthodox Jews, lived with him. It seems that every other night Farrell Fand was eating dinner at our house—the food was better.

His Yiddish grandma became crazier by the hour about the whole situation. One day she asked Farrell, "What kinda food are you eatin' all the time at the Franconeros' house? I'll kill you if it's not good kosher food!"

"No, *Bubba*, I swear! Mr. Franconero said, 'Tell

your grandma she's got nothin' to worry about—everything I cook in this house is kosher!'"

"So then, tonight, Farrell, what did you eat?"

"Tonight—lemme see—we had shrimp!" confessed Farrell.

"Shrimp!" his *bubba* shrieked like a maniac.

"Yup! And Thursdays, it's Virginia ham!"

Georgie and I attended catechism classes at Blessed Sacrament Church on Wednesdays. On that first harrowing day, I noticed something mighty unsettling: whenever they meant God, they wrote "He"—with a capital "H." It really got me shook up, and with good cause; you see, I'd always believed God was a woman.

I was always extremely modest and self-conscious about my body—even my less-than-remarkable seven-year-old body. So, for a whole week, I found myself dressing and undressing in my bedroom closet.

My mother happened to notice this. She looked at me curiously and asked, "Connie, are you nuts or what? Why are you gettin' undressed in your closet?" From the closet I shouted, "Today in Lesson One at Blessed Sacrament, I got a big shock, Mommy! Sister Mary Claire told me that God's a man!"

"Then read Lesson Two," she advised me. "You'll find out God's everywhere! So He's in your closet, too! Get outta there, you dopey kid."

In retrospect, I don't think I was so dopey at all; I'm thoroughly convinced I was right in the first place—even more now than I thought back then. Sorry, you guys! But God's a woman, all right! And, don't try to confuse me with the facts.

Saturdays and Sundays at the movies had to be the Hottest Ticket in Town; it was always a big production number. My mother would stuff milk, sandwiches, bananas, and lots of goodies in two brown paper bags from the Food Fair, and send Georgie and me off to the Avon, Roosevelt, or Cameo Theater.

We sure got our quarter's worth! It was a double

feature—two movies, ten cartoons, a short, and a weekly serial like *Hopalong Cassidy* or *Captain Marvel*, to say nothing of my most favorite thing, the Coming Attractions—Wednesday through Saturday, Sunday through Tuesday.

Sometimes Mommy would let me go to the movies on both Saturday *and* Sunday, but only when Alan was in town. Even my mother and father tolerated my obsessive behavior, 'cause they knew how totally flipped out I was over Alan Ladd.

The whole Alan Ladd Affair was the cause of an awful lot of trouble between me and my very best friend, Roberta Linker. It was tragic, but both of us were hopelessly in love with the same man; it was a triangle in the grand and true Hollywood tradition.

But, Roberta and I loved each other a lot, so we made a real important compromise—we *shared* Alan. Each day we played house, dressing up in our mothers' dresses, jewelry, and high heels, stuffing them with tissue paper so they'd fit our feet; and every *other* day one of us would land Alan—as a husband, of course. But there was always a big beef.

"Connie, *you* had Alan yesterday—he's *my* husband today!"

"Oh, no you don't, Roberta! Don't give me *that*! *You* had Alan yesterday! If we're gonna be friends forever and ever, Roberta, I think we'd better start keepin' a calendar right away! We'll just mark the days in red ink when you get Alan and blue ink when it's my turn!"

My other best girlfriend, Phyllis Lynch, couldn't care less if Alan Ladd turned into a tree trunk. I don't know why—Phyllis was straight—but she had this real weird obsession about an older woman, Hollywood's hottest child star, Miss Margaret O'Brien; O'Brien was Phyllis Lynch's whole life. (Maybe it had somethin' to do with them both being Irish 'n' all.)

Whenever Alan was out of town or whenever I wasn't surrounded by my accordion or my books, I was surrounded by Margaret O'Brien's everything—

her photo album, her cut-out dolls, her diary, her scrapbook, her little doll house—the works. It was a real pain!

All three of us, Margaret, Phyllis, and I, celebrated the Big Birthday when Margaret reached puberty—with a cake, no less. It was a very important day for my girlfriend, Phyllis Lynch. The whole thing made me nauseous; I got to hate Margaret O'Brien.

Later on, my best friend became Connie DiCepoli; we were the perfect couple, a match made in heaven. The reason we got along so well was because whenever Connie's mom ordered pizza, Connie wanted only the crispy fat crust while I waited on the hot spicy mozzarella cheese on top.

Daddy always worked very, very hard for us; when I was nine he became a roofer. One day he came home from work, his hands covered with tar, suffering from third-degree burns. Another day, he came home in even worse shape. Even though he was badly injured after falling off a second-story roof, he refused to go to the hospital for treatment. (Even when they move to a Jewish neighborhood, Italian people from Calabria still have hard heads.)

And an Italian home, even in a Jewish neighborhood, is still an Italian home. The hub, the very pulse beat and life of that home revolves around the kitchen or, to be more precise, around food. For Italians, food is a pagan ritual—in most cases, the reason for one's existence.

The main staple for any Italian household is the "gravy," or tomato sauce for the pasta. The most vile crime an Italian wife can ever perpetrate upon her husband is to burn the sauce or to overcook the pasta.

In more conservative jurisdictions I'm certain it's a capital offense. When an Italian wife *does* commit the unpardonable and burns the tomato sauce, you're sure to overhear her wail in fear, "Oh my God! Who wants to listen to my husband when he comes home?"

Anyone under eleven whose weight is below 192

pounds is emaciated by my mother's standards. To this day, I can telephone anyone from anywhere in the world and the first thing a normal person will say is, "Hi, Connie. How are you?"

But not when I call Ida. "Did you eat?" always comes first and foremost.

Italians are the only people who can be devouring a seventeen-course meal—they can be in the midst of a Roman food orgy like in one of those scenes from *Tom Jones*—and be discussing something "beautiful" they ate last week, or something "beautiful" they're planning on eating next week.

Italians rarely fail to refer to food as "nice" or "beautiful." My mother says, "Sit down—eat! You look like you're dyin'. I'll make you a nice sandwich." My father gleefully announces, "Hey, Jitters! Did ya see this beautiful piece of butt pork? Only eighty-nine cents a pound!" (For as long as I can remember my father's name for Mom has been "Jitters," and with good reason.)

I was delighted when God made somebody else Julia Child—better her than me. As a child I *never* wanted to be Julia Child; she can keep hangin' on to the job like a Pope if she wants it. I don't dine—I'm not interested; I just eat and get it over with. My oven could double as a planter; I serve ketchup as a vegetable (thanks, Joanie Rivers), or in a pinch as a main course.

I was always receiving conflicting signals from the people in my young life. Domesticity was one feminine virtue my father never tried to nurture in me. Whenever my mother asked me to do even the slightest household chore, my father would say: "Leave 'er alone, will ya? She's gotta practice."

Every *normal* person in my little world placed tremendous emphasis on the need to be a good Italian girl, wife, mother—everyone except Daddy. Even idle chatter about my one day becoming a wife or mother was virtually banned on Belmont Avenue—or in my house, at any rate!

But Mom gave it the ol' college try, anyway. She'd send me laden with gigantic brown bags all the way up and down that great big hill to the A&P to do the weekly food shopping. She'd attempt to teach me those very valuable culinary skills; and every night I'd wash dishes and Georgie would dry, unless Daddy caught me, that is.

Very early in life I discovered that you get no points for doing dishes or washing floors. I learned that because my mother did all those things and many, many more, but like many Italian wives of her generation, she was, at best, unappreciated. She was simply taken for granted. And to be taken for granted is simply not to be seen.

My mother is the A-1 Certified World's Greatest Cook! And those lazy Sundays when we'd sit in the kitchen, read the funnies, and tell stories to the delicious aroma of the great tomato sauce Mom made and that great homemade Italian sausage Daddy made, are among my happiest memories.

In my young life, there were at least two family members who thought I'd be better off dead than in the seamy world of show business; Grandma Franconero was one of them. She'd direly warn Daddy, "It's-a no good, all-a dis music! When-a she grow up, you make-a her go work at the factory like-a nice Italian girl, you hear me!"

Her very religious daughter, my Aunt Tessie, a direct descendant of St. Francis of Assisi, guardedly cautioned him, too. "What you crazy, George? Why are you makin' her sing in all those wild places?" (She was referring to the church socials.) "Connie could wind up in show business! God forbid! With all those tramps and bums!"

A thousand-year generation gap existed between my grandparents' world and mine—astoundingly different worlds, when you came to think of it. Oh, the many contrasts!

Years later, when we gave my grandma and Aunt Tessie things like color TVs and air-conditioning units, they were always enshrined beneath a cloth, never utilized. They refused to waste money on electricity for "unnecessary" things. My grandma never once saw me perform, in person or on TV; she couldn't have cared less.

But she loved me and my brother dearly. Many years later, the first time she came to see my grand, new house in Essex Fells, New Jersey, she looked around, saw the grandeur of it all, and exclaimed in horror to my father, "She spend-sa too much-a money on dis-a place. For what-a she needs it! It must-a cost-a twenty thousand dollars!"

One Christmas I decided to postpone a Las Vegas engagement in order to be with my family. I had given Grandma a brand new handbag with five hundred dollars in it. When she heard about Vegas, she returned the five hundred dollars to Daddy saying, "She needs-a the money now; she's outta work."

I remember the first time I ever felt pretty; I was nine, and it was at Irwin Levine's Halloween party. Irwin was my first little boyfriend, and I was a gypsy. I wore a gaily flowered skirt with a wide red sash, a white peasant off-the shoulder blouse, and big gold hoop earrings. And for a change, my hair wasn't in pigtails. It was real long, black and flowing, very Yvonne de Carlo. And Mommy even let me wear a little rouge and lipstick 'cause I told her, "All gypsies do that."

I'll never forget that first Halloween party, when I felt so pretty and feminine. All the little boys in my neighborhood surrounded me and planted little butterfly kisses upon my cheeks. It made me feel just like Cinderella, all warm inside. It was super fun, almost as special as singing. But not quite, not ever.

A few years later I got to stay up very late one night (2:00 A.M.) all because I was invited to Irwin Levine's

Bar Mitzvah by his folks. Many years later Irwin would write a few fair-sized hits like "Tie a Yellow Ribbon 'Round the Old Oak Tree," "Sweet Gypsy Rose," "Candida," and "Knock Three Times," to name but a few. For a poor girl from a poor family from Newark, as a child and as a teenager, I knew any number of people who went on to become famous.

Aunts are very important people. At least to me, they've always been. I have a ton of them—one hundred aunts, uncles, and cousins in all. But two of them were very close to me and very special. Neither of them was a blood relative. My Aunt Marie was married to Mom's brother, Ray; and my Aunt Rose wasn't even an in-law of the family.

My Aunt Rose and her husband and Mom and Dad went to kindergarten together. And for many years no two couples could have been closer, spent more time together, or loved each other more. When I was a child, Aunt Rose was my second mother.

She was a gentle soul and very beautiful, with a face like a Madonna. And she was very religious—not fake-religious, but pious and pure in her heart. She was my godmother, and to Italian people that is a very important thing.

And when I received confirmation, as is the custom, I took her name as my middle name (Connie Rose Marie Franconero). My Aunt Rose also dug drinking beer, rooting at the most gruesome boxing matches, and eating anything that crawled on the bottom of the sea—with red-hot sauce on it.

Friday nights were really fun, because whatever Aunt Rose and Daddy ate on those meatless nights was the subject of eager anticipation for all the kids on Belmont Avenue. They'd gather faithfully at my home, just to gaze in wonder at the weird, grotesque, crawly things—things like octopus, squid, *scungilli* (conch), or *escargots* (snails). Once I opened the freezer door and discovered the two eyes of a lamb's head (*cappucella*) staring back at me. (Cannibalism died a slow death in my family.)

Aside from my two neighborhood friends, Lil and Mary, my Aunt Rose was the first person who told me that I was pretty. She said that, because Aunt Rose looked only into people's hearts. And if she truly loved you the way she did me, then you were beautiful in her eyes.

On February 13, 1967, my Aunt Rose was brutally strangled and bludgeoned to death in her home. By "person or persons unknown," said the official Newark police report. Unknown, that is, except to me and a few influential people in high places. Organized crime played no part in her untimely and tragic death. I love you, my Aunt Rose in Heaven.

3

Daddy's Little Girl

You're the treasure I cherish
So sparkling and bright
You were touched by holy and beautiful light
By angels that sing a heavenly thing
And you're DADDY'S LITTLE GIRL *

> January 1949
> Belmont Avenue
> Newark, New Jersey

FORTY-NINE will always be known as the year the "boob tube" came to Belmont Avenue; that's when our neighbor, Mrs. Seaman, got the first TV set on the block.

I think Mrs. Seaman was very sorry she ever got that 13-inch Emerson set (which was an eye test), because each afternoon every kid on the block could be found at her home watching Buffalo Bob, Clarabelle, and Howdy Doody.

Before long we had our own TV, and shortly thereafter, all the kids on the block were watching "Howdy Doody" and *me*.

A nice, rotund, blond lady from New York called Marie Moser was hosting a local show on Channel 13 from Newark; it was called "Marie Moser's Starlets." When I was ten, Daddy entered me in a talent contest she ran. I played and sang "My Happiness," a big hit by Jon and Sondra Steele. As a result, I won a one-year scholarship to Miss Moser's Talent School to study—would you believe it?—dancing! There's little justice in this world.

Marie Moser recognized right off the bat that, as a dancer, I was pitiful. But she invited me anyway to be one of her starlets each week for a year, as an accordionist and a singer. And what invaluable experience it was!

"The Starlets" also toured what was probably one of the last vestiges of what was once called vaudeville, the RKO theater circuit. It was great fun, 'cause in between the four shows a day we could watch super films like *She Wore a Yellow Ribbon* with John Wayne.

Nobody at Bergen Street School seemed much impressed by my new career. Particularly unimpressed was a kid named Eugene Lieberman. Actually, that statement is inaccurate. Eugene was impressed, all right—but not by my accordion. Let me take this one from the top.

I should preface this story by mentioning that for half a year before it happened, my mother kept bugging me to buy my first bra.

"Connie, for godssake, *look* at you! You *have* to wear a bra! It's embarrassin'! Everybody's talkin' about it!"

But I cast her advice to the wind; I guess I just didn't like any evidence which pointed to the fact that I wasn't Daddy's Little Girl anymore.

"Your Aunt Rose will take you shoppin' for a bra. Even she says you should be wearin' a bra!" But I stood fast; I wasn't interested.

Aunt Rose wasn't the only person who noticed; Eugene Lieberman did, too. And I guess he liked what he saw, the prurient worm! Because he did the most horrific thing anybody had done to me in my entire life.

It happened in the cloakroom at Bergen. I was wearing my phys-ed apparel that day—you know, one of those dreadful short blue gym suits with the elastic bottoms that bloom out around your thighs. (My not-so-petite body needed something that bloomed out at the thighs like Bangladesh needs Diet Delite.)

So far in this book no names have been changed to protect the innocent *or* the guilty, and I don't intend to start now. And Eugene Lieberman was guilty, all right! He had the unmitigated gall to touch one of my developing breasts—sans the bra I'd refused to wear.

What followed made the War Between the States seem like an Italian picnic in Philadelphia! I was outraged by the temerity of this lascivious preteen Jack the Ripper! I made such a hullabaloo! I wailed and I whined so much that by the following morning, all the players in this drama—Eugene, his mother and Mom and I—were gathered together at the behest of the principal of the school, Mrs. Anna O'Keane, for a Summit Conference in her office.

I took great pains to describe the whole sordid scenario in explicit detail. And, believe me, Mrs. O'Keane had some harsh words of warning, via his mother, for Eugene!

"Mrs. Lieberman, if this occurs again," she said sharply, "I'm afraid I'll have to take serious action!"

As we were leaving her office, Mrs. O'Keane asked to see Mom privately in order to offer *her* a few sage words of advice, as well.

"Eugene was out of order, Mrs. Franconero, I grant you that. But do all of us around here a big favor. Buy your kid a bra, will you?"

"I know. It's a sin, isn't it?" despaired Mom. "She's got a head like a rock, my daughter."

The whole affair was revolting. It seemed that from

birth I was always strapped into something or other—
first the accordion and now, a brassiere. Who *needed*
this? I did! Because both my career and my chest were
developing quickly.

Twice I auditioned and appeared on the Horn and
Hardart (Less Work for Mother) "Children's Hour."
Now is as good a time as any to thank still another
booster of mine—the people at "The Ted Mack Amateur Hour"—also for doing so little for my career. I
passed the audition for radio's "Amateur Hour," but a
couple of years later flunked the audition for the TV
show. (This gives you an idea of where my career was
headed.)

On the day of the radio show, at the Mosque Theater in Newark, Mr. Mack told me: "Little girl, why
don't you lose that accordion somewhere, and just
sing 'St. Louis Blues'?" (To my father that would have
been tantamount to pulling the plug on his life-sustain-
ing machine.)

"Please, Mr. Mack! My father will *die!*" I pleaded,
in a frightful dither. Mr. Mack was very understand-
ing, so I played *and* sang "The St. Louis Blues." And
still, I rated third in the call-in/write-in vote! And in
Newark, my own home town, to boot!

At age nine or ten, I could always be found performing tunes like "Frankie and Johnnie" or Mr.
Handy's:

> St. Louis Woman, wid her diamon' rings
> Pulls dat man round—by her apron strings
> 'Tween't for powder an' all that store-bought hair
> Dat man I love, he wouldn't have gone nowhere. *

* "St. Louis Blues" © copyright MCMXIV by W.C. Handy. © copyright
renewed MCMXLI by W.C. Handy. Published by Handy Brothers Music
Co., Inc., New York, New York. All rights reserved including the right of
public performance for profit. Francis, Day & Hunter, Ltd., 138 Charing
Cross Road, London W.C.2, England, European Representatives. International copyright secured.

All this, in white anklet socks, yet.

It was television that caused the only significant confrontations between my brother Georgie and me. And it happened like clockwork, every Tuesday night just after Texaco's "Milton Berle Show." My bedtime was 9:30 P.M., when "Suspense" went off the air. Georgie, who was younger, was supposed to go to bed by 9:00 P.M. So, each week on the dot of 9:00, the harangue began. Georgie balked so much that not *once* did I get to see what all the "Suspense" was about.

Later on, for one week each summer, Aunt Marie and her son Anthony and Mom, Georgie and I went on vacation to the boardwalk in Atlantic City. We stayed at the Greater Pittsburgh Hotel—ten dollars a week per family, which included the community bathroom down the hall.

What fun we had walking the boardwalk, enjoying the amusement rides and watching the many attractions like the Diving Bell and the woman who jumped into the water atop a horse on the steel pier! At ten, as usual, I turned fun into work, because work has always been my fun. There was a man there who adored kids, and he produced a kiddie show called "Tony Grant's Stars of Tomorrow."

It was on that show that Daddy first had me sing foreign songs like "La Vie en Rose" in French and "Siboney" in Spanish; I grew to love foreign languages. Years later, this suggestion by my father contributed greatly to my internationalizing American music; every time I recorded a single or an album, I'd automatically record it in at least six languages—sometimes thirteen.

Coming from Belmont Avenue didn't hurt my Hebrew, either. I sang "Hatikva," the Israeli national anthem, like a native. I accompanied my friends to synagogue on all the High Holy Days and to their

Passover *seders*. I developed a deep and abiding respect and an affinity for the Jewish people.

Most Jews have a strong sense of family and tradition, and their sense of humor, their love of good food, music, fun, and the good life remind me of similar qualities I love in Italian-Americans.

It always amuses the parents and grandparents of the Jewish fellows I date to hear me use Yiddish expressions as easily as I use Italian ones. Just as I sometimes think in Italian, I sometimes think in Yiddish. I believe I know more about the Jewish language, protocol, and traditions than all those Bar Mitzvah boys I ever dated; and shame on them, too. That kind of heritage and tradition—no matter what the religion or nationality—should never be allowed to die. It's just too much fun, and it gives one a sense of history—an added perspective on life. It's truly a special experience for people to know where they originated. And all those who don't remember where they came from, whether they be Jewish, Italian, English, or whatever, are what I refer to as the WASPs of this world.

Years later I introduced my first Jewish LP (again, my dad's idea) on "The Ed Sullivan Show." Shortly thereafter, I appeared at the Concord Hotel in the Borscht Belt (the Jewish Catskills), where my mother overheard two Jewish women talking.

"You know, Shirley, don't you, that Connie's father was a rabbi."

"You know from nothin', Sadie!" her friend contradicted strongly. "She's not Jewish at *all!* She was just *raised* by a rabbi and his wife!"

They could've fooled Mom. But that's not a very difficult thing to do. My mother is very naive, very unassuming, very basic and very down to earth; show business has never changed either of my folks one iota.

Mom treats everyone she meets alike, and she still cuts out coupons to save a dime on a can of coffee. And when she thinks I'm not looking she buys generic (no-brand) products at the supermarket—it's cheaper.

She's the most selfless and soft-hearted woman I've ever known; and without meaning to be, she's a very humorous lady.

In every way my parents are prototypes of the typical Italian husband-wife mentality of their generation. The Italian husband was The Boss! Period! End of story! The Italian wife was, with rare exceptions, subservient. Even if she wasn't she *pretended* to be, if she was smart, which I never was. One of the prerequisites for being a good, old-fashioned Italian wife was that you were compelled to relinquish all rights to a mind of your own.

One graphic example: Not long ago I observed my parents as they watched an old movie on "The Late Show" on TV. They call it "The Late Show" because the average age of the actors is deceased. (Thanks, Gabe Kaplan.) My mother was very excited about the movie, reveling in every moment of it, because it starred Ann Sheridan, her favorite.

"George, this is some movie, isn't it?" she asked Daddy eagerly. There was only silence (a very common thing in my house).

"Hey, George! They sure don't make movies like *this* anymore, do they?" More silence.

"Hey, George! That Ann Sheridan was some star, wasn't she?" You guessed it.

"George, you *like* the movie—doncha?"

"It stinks," Daddy responded graciously. (Let's hear it for brevity, anyway.)

Then something curious happened (not curious to *me*, of course—I was used to it—but to any normal observer). When Mom answered the phone, it wasn't necessary to hear what Aunt Marie was saying in order to get the gist of the conversation: "Oh, nothin', Marie. We're just watchin' TV," Mom told her.

There was a pause. Then, "No, Marie, nothin' good's on; just some crummy picture with Ann Sheridan in it." 'Nuff said?

My father, when he's home alone with his immediate family, is what some Italian people refer to as a

"Turk." My apologies to the Turkish people, because I really don't know where this expression originated. But it means in essence that one is expressionless, uncommunicative, and sour, at best—a true graduate of the Richard Speck School of Charm. But when my father leaves the house—aha! An astounding transformation takes place right before your eyes.

Without so much as a sip from Dr. Jekyll's smoking vial, the man becomes a totally different personality—gregarious, charming, high-spirited and humorous—the life of everybody's party. He flirts with every waitress and takes all the lady bank tellers to lunch—in Nashville, the Bahamas, and even in Japan. He is a most popular fellow, my daddy. He becomes Art Linkletter, Johnny Carson, and Noel Coward, all rolled into one neat little package.

Every time someone enthusiastically tells me, "Connie, your father has a personality second to none," I respond, "Really? Tell me all about it."

My father can also do or fix *anything*. Each and every time I'd hire a workman to do a job at my home, Daddy would call the person a "thief," whether it was the gardener, the pool man, the plumber, the painter—or anyone else. The truth is, he hates to pay anyone for something he knows he can do himself, so he merely fires even the honest thieves at will.

"You didn't need 'em, anyway—those goddamned crooks with their Connie Francis prices!"

Two summers ago, the pool was a disaster area—a pipe had burst somewhere and the first estimate was $30,000—just to repair the pool. Because my father knows of all the idle time I have on my hands, he demanded that I look in the Yellow Pages in order to get three comparative estimates from pool maintenance firms. Naturally, I disregarded his gentle instructions.

"Get rid of 'em all!" he ordered sweetly.

He went to Channel Lumber, a hardware store plus, and bought something plastic and small.

"Here," he said flatly, handing me a plastic tube of some kind. "Your pool's fixed."

"How much did it cost, Daddy?"

"A dollar ninety-six," he said. "You don't wanna listen to me, sister, but these guys see you comin'."

Next to my Olympic-sized swimming pool, Daddy still covered the fig trees in the winter and grew tomatoes and basil (*basilicola*) plants close by—but hidden from sight by me. The press would never have understood.

I will always credit my father for any professional success I enjoyed. Daddy was just a poor laborer, but for his daughter, he was a man with a dream. And he obsessively devoted his entire life to making that dream come true.

He didn't always do it in the most diplomatic manner—I still call him Tommy Tact. But because of Daddy, one of the things I learned very early in life was to confront criticism.

To this day if I get a less-than-favorable review, I'll ordinarily call the critic and ask what he or she thinks I can do to improve my act; sometimes their criticisms are valid.

Unlike many performers, I am able to view my career, my performances, my marketable value or lack of it, as objectively and as dispassionately as I suppose any human being can.

If, at age eleven, I could ask my father what he thought of a show and have him answer: "It stunk," any review Gene Shalit could dish out would be, by comparison, a twenty-one-gun salute. Whenever I wanted the real low-down, Honest-Injun brutal truth, I asked Daddy.

When I was eleven, the whole family drove to Philadelphia where I performed on TV's "Paul Whiteman Show." It was there that I received my very first anything for performing. It was a Bulova twenty-one-jewel Spandex watch.

On the show, as a "regular," was a girl singer about my age, named Kathy Keegan; she was sweet, pretty, and Irish. Each week when Daddy saw her on TV, he raved about what a super talent she was. But on this particular day, the sweet young thing chose to become Judy Garland live-and-in-person.

At the camera rehearsal Daddy watched her intently as she sang both her songs, and casually said, "Now *that* kid can sing!" (It made me a little irritated.) Then he asked me a question and answered it himself.

"Know why? 'Cause she sings from her heart—*that's* why!" (Now I was more than a little irritated!)

"That kid makes you believe every word she sings!" (At this point, I was fit to be tied, but I uttered not a single word.)

Then—are you ready for this?—the little darling began crying during her last song. Real, mammoth tears! Daddy was sure impressed with Kathy Keegan.

"Say, how come *you* can't do that? This kid is the best yet!" Now Daddy was really pressing his luck!

"There'll never be another kid who can sell a number like this kid!"

That did it! Overnight, I became Sarah Bernhardt, Bette Davis, and Tallulah Bankhead all rolled into another neat little package. Okay, Daddy! You want tears? *I'll* show you tears! I'll cry you a river, pally!

Each Christmastime, instead of the usual four unknown professional performers, "The Arthur Godfrey Talent Scout Show" showcased four child performers.

My favorite uncle, Uncle Gus, truly believed in me, so when I was twelve, he saw no reason why his niece, whom he thought was the greatest thing to hit the East Coast since Eva Tanguay, shouldn't perform for Mr. Godfrey. He wrote requesting an audition, and I was told by letter to come in for an audition (I still have that letter from the Godfrey show.)

Mom and I took the bus to the Port Authority building and then a bus to the gigantic CBS building.

We took one look at that enormous room spilling over with boisterous, precocious kids, and were so turned off we nearly took the bus back to New Jersey. But if I didn't make the Godfrey audition, who wanted to listen to Daddy? So for a l-o-o-o-ng while, we sat there—but definitely not in silence.

"Why do these kids brag so much about themselves, Mommy? I wonder where they're from?"

"From hunger," Ida decided.

A fat, cocky boy about my age struck up a most informative, but ego-deflating conversation with me. In fact, he asked so many questions, Mom said: "You sure he's not Edward R. Murrow, this kid?"

"What's your name?" the boy Seymour asked me matter-of-factly.

"Connie Franconero."

"What kinda name is *that*, girlie?"

"It's Italian."

"Never heard of it. So whadda ya do?"

"I'm an accordion player."

"You're kiddin' me! *You* play the *accordion*!" he roared in a fit of laughter. "That's a riot! You gotta look like a *man* playin' an accordion!" (Obviously, he didn't come from Grandma's neighborhood, where all Italian girls played the accordion, or he would've known better.)

"Well," I offered apologetically, "sometimes I sing a little, too, when I play."

"Yeah, very, very little, I bet. I suppose you do tap, modern, and ballet, too. What about a little magic and comedy—do you do that, too?"

"No. . . ."

"Well, which one of these talents are you gonna show us today?"

"Your fist, you're gonna show him!" murmured Ida.

"Well," I continued undaunted, "the reason I wanna sing *and* play the accordion, is so I'll have a better chance of makin' the show."

"*This* show!" Seymour exploded in peals of laughter.

To be more exact, I thought he'd die laughing, but unfortunately, he lived—and talked on and on and on.

"It's all who you know, girlie. You gotta have connections in this business. Now take my father—he knows the producer of this show *real* well!"

Where was *I* going, anyway? The only producers my father knew were on Grandma's farm—those hens that occasionally produced a few good eggs.

By the time my name was called, I was so drained of confidence that when I played and sang "Daddy's Little Girl," I felt more like somebody's little ant that just got stepped on—hard.

How I was called back for three more screening-out auditions, I'll never know. But the next time we went to that audition, three-quarters of the kids had vanished—along with my fat friend, Seymour.

I was selected as one of the four kids that Christmastime to appear on Mr. Godfrey's show. (He let all the kids win.) When the big day arrived, Mr. Godfrey called me over to him during camera rehearsal.

"How do you pronounce your last name again, little girl?"

"Frank-oh-near-oh," I said distinctly, as if teaching him a foreign language.

"Whew! That's a toughie!" Mr. Godfrey whistled. The stage crew laughed. "Why don't we give you a good ol' easy-to-pronounce Irish name like—let's see—Francis. That's good—Francis!"

"My father will have kittens, Mr. Godfrey!" I whispered, my hand cupped over my mouth. "Would it be okay if you tried real hard just this once to say Franconero? Tomorrow I'll talk to Daddy, and then maybe he'll let me be Connie—what did ya say?—Francis? Okay?"

He nodded and winked okay.

4

The Startime Kids

STARTIME, yes this is your time
To meet your favorite personality
STARTIME, yes this is your time
To meet and greet and say hello to:

Lenny . . .
Angel . . .
Kenny . . .
Rosalie . . .
Joey . . .
Connie . . .
Vinnie . . .
Barry . . .
Sharon . . .
Bobby Appell . . .
Lonny Starr . . .
The Kaye Sisters . . . *AND*
Charlie and Lillian*

EACH Saturday for two years, Daddy and I faithfully watched "The Startime Kids" TV show from Manhattan.

"You're just as good as any one of them kids,"

* © George Scheck. Written by George Scheck. Used by permission.

Daddy observed modestly. And from the safety of our very small living room, I agreed, just to humor him.

As far as I was concerned, these kids and I weren't even in the same league! They were the livin' end, that's all—sophisticated, versatile, polished—all kinds of fabulous things I was never gonna be.

One May day in 1951, time ran out for me; Daddy insisted we drive into Manhattan in an attempt to meet the show's producer, George Scheck.

"The Godfrey Show you did will at least get our foot in the door," he predicted with lots of confidence. And that was that! Period! End of subject! Stage fathers are the worst!

I took one look at the infantile boop-boop-de-boop jumper and blouse my mother selected for me to wear—with white anklets yet—and I nearly barfed.

"But it's a kiddie show!" she implored. "You're only thirteen! Who do you wanna look like—Sadie Thompson?"

"No, not like Sadie Thompson, Ma," I sulked, "just like myself!"

"So?"

"So—so far I don't know who myself is."

"Well, when you find out, let me know. Then we'll go out and buy her some clothes, too!"

"Real cute, Ma—who writes your material?"

How could my own mother *do* this to me? Today of ALL days!

Someone pointed out "Startime's" producer, George Scheck, as he dashed out the door of Nola's rehearsal hall studios. He was very dapper, indeed, and very light on his feet. He tiptoed like the dancer he once was; he wore a pin-striped charcoal gray suit with a deep burgundy tie; he had dark wavy hair. Next to him, Daddy looked like a sharecropper.

"Hello, Mr. Scheck. I'm George Franconero," Daddy said, offering his laborer's hand. "Could you give a listen to my daughter, Connie?"

"What does she do?" Mr. Scheck asked inattentively, flagging down a taxi.

"She's a singer, Mr. Scheck."

"*Gevalt!* Not another singer! I'm up to here with singers," he said, looking up at the sky and slicing himself off at the neck with the side of his palm. He wasn't able to look *down*, not at *us*, anyway, because he was just as statuesque as we were—all five foot one inches of him.

"Well, she's really an accordion player," Daddy ventured.

George Scheck had started to enter his cab, but when he heard "accordion player," his face seemed to brighten a bit. He spun around delicately like a ballet dancer.

"An accordion player! Say, that's different! I don't have one of those!" he said brightly, slipping Daddy his card. "Go inside. Have a seat. I'll be back in an hour."

Well, finally! All the years of sweat and toil practicing that lousy ol' squeezebox might just pay off, after all. We entered the large rehearsal studio where the show's piano player, Nat Brooks, sat at a black upright, a cigarette dangling from his lips. He was playing something foreign, like jazz. The whole thing reminded me of a sleazy scene from a George Raft movie.

Daddy and I sat in one of those folding chairs you see in auditoriums. I was so awestruck by the mere prospect of seeing in person some of the big stars I'd watched religiously week after week on the tube, that I thought I was going to pass out. I was perspiring, my hands were cold and clammy, and my stomach took a nose dive.

"I wanna go home, Daddy!" I cried desperately. "Right this *minute*, Daddy!"

"What for? You sick or somethin'?" I couldn't tell him I was dying of fear. "So then don't be so stupid!" counseled Daddy tenderly.

I glanced up and saw my most special TV idol, Lenny Dale, the big *macher* of the show. Sometimes he even got production assistant credits. He was such a sexy person that my heart did acrobatic flips every time I saw him on the ol' Philco. It was a first for me—I'd never felt so funny before.

Sure, he was a kid, but he did *everything*! He choreographed all the dance routines to songs like "Slaughter on Tenth Avenue" and "Autumn Nocturne." (Step aside, Gene Kelly.) He sang hits like "Because of You" and "Rags to Riches." (Tony Who?) He did tasteful impersonations of Eartha Kitt and James Cagney. (Eat your heart out, Sammele Davis.)

In addition, he did off-the-cuff introductions of all the other acts on the show in a suave, impromptu style. (Move to the back of the bus, Georgie Jessel!) I just knew he had to be in the business at least thirty-seven years, but he was only fourteen.

Suddenly the door to the rehearsal hall flew open. In slithered a girl about twenty-five (I learned later she was thirteen), carrying one of those round models' hat boxes. She sauntered over to my idol; she was wearing spiked heels, and she'd stuffed herself into one of those black Apache dancer satin skirts with a long slit clear up the side. To top it off, her sweater was so tight, it was enough to cut off her air supply. The whole *megillah*.

She was somethin' else, all right. She had a certain strut, a confident, sexy wiggle that made me want to regurgitate. I'd never seen anything like it except on Saturday afternoons with Georgie at the movies.

To make matters worse, the girl didn't travel alone; every female person on the show, except for the three-year-old kids, looked just like her. Involuntarily, I ran my moist hands over my blouse with the asinine Peter Pan collar.

"Lenny, dahling," the sexy girl squealed, tossing both her arms casually about my idol's neck. She kissed him, too—of all places, smack on the lips! I was stunned. These kids were just too chic for this universe! And there *I* sat, dumbfounded, pathetic, and pitiful in my Mammy Yokum dress.

"Let's get outta here, Daddy, *please!*" I yowled once more. Simon Legree refused once more. So I was compelled to gaze star-struck at the wonder of it all: those slim, disgustingly perfect little bodies clad in black leotards and black fishnet hose and those cute little ponytails held up by those gaily colored ribbons.

I mean, what did these girls *eat?* Forget about the daily kosher salami sandwiches I put away with discouraging ease. Forget about that pasta every Tuesday and Thursday night and Sunday afternoons. On these girls, a chocolate-covered ant would show! What was *I* doing here, anyway!

"Daddy," I implored, in vain, "how can I play the accordion in front of *these* kids? Please, Daddy—let's go home!"

"Wise up, will ya? You been playin' in front of *grown-ups* since you're two months old! What the hell's the matter with ya?" he asked again, bewildered. "You sick or somethin'?"

The man must have been mentally arthritic! (Thanks, Neil Simon!) Where were his eyes? Couldn't he see the pitiful difference between me and these "peers" of mine? Some peers!

Just then, Mr. Scheck entered the hall. Now it was too late. I was trapped again. Like a reluctant robot, I climbed the steps to the stage, my ugly Nunzio accordion strapped to my chest.

My legs felt like linguini as I played "Bonaparte's Retreat." I'd've chosen *any* retreat over this—even Sing-Sing.

After my number, George Scheck said, "Okay, Connie, now put the accordion down and let's hear you just sing a number."

Oh, no, I mourned. Not him, too. Not this man who let me in the door only because of the lousy accordion. Even *he's* saying: "Get rid of the thing!" One hundred and sixty million Americans can't be wrong!

And thus began an experience worth a million and then some—my colorful four-year run as one of the Startime Kids.

*   *   *

My debut on "The Startime Kids" was calm indeed in comparison with my debut at Arts High School in Newark.

"Arts" was a marvelous special school for students interested in pursuing art or music as a career. The music courses were practically college level, lasting two-and-a-half hours a day. Many people from the school went on to become very successful in the world of music: record producer-arranger Charlie Calello; singers Melba Moore, Sarah Vaughn, and Dionne Warwick; and Merv Griffin's orchestra leader, Mort Lindsey, to name but a few.

At any rate, talk about repulsive milestones!

Every young person who registers for high school feels some awkwardness, some trepidation, that first day. It means an awful lot to us to make a favorable impression on our classmates—the people with whom we'll spend most of our time in the next four years.

And I made an impression, all right, but it was surely not really favorable. What I did was unforgiveable, outrageous, it was that ol' impatience and rotten temper again.

There I stood in the long line at the registration hall, lost in a sea of strangers and hoping for just one familiar face. There weren't any, though, because all my elementary school friends had gone to schools where normal kids go.

That loathsome day, I had a "Startime Kids" rehearsal in New York and I was carrying in my pocket an "excuse" from the principal giving me special permission to leave early.

As the time dragged on and on, I fidgeted, tapping my foot with increasing frequency and looking at my watch, which is never set, anyway. I worked myself into such a fevered pitch that finally, in desperation, I made what turned out to be a fatal error in judgment.

I bolted directly to the front of the line where I came face to face with a boy named Charlie, a Very

Big Fat Boy with Tough, Unfriendly Kid written all over him.

I began as usual in my little-girl-Scarlett-O'Hara voice which was very alluring. (I *always* start out that way.)

"Hi, there. Excuse me a moment, please," I purred with a slight southern drawl. "Could I just get in line here? You see, I've gotta go to New York, and I'm kinda late, because . . ."

"Get to the back of that line, girlie!" he growled. I knew right off the bat that this kid was gonna make some mighty big waves.

"Please," I cooed persistently, batting my long brown lashes. It always worked, but Charlie had an attitude that was making my voice rise—always a bad sign.

"Please! You *must* let me in—you don't understand! I'm half an hour late for . . ."

"You heard me, girlie," he barked, with minimal finesse. And he remained fixed, his arms folded, like an implacable piece of granite.

"Look fella . . ." I croaked. "If I don't get . . ."

"Just keep it up, girlie, I'm tellin' ya! You know somethin', you got a lotta guts! Now just ask me one more time, and I'll . . ."

That's when I demurely gave him the old one-two—which turned into the old one-five. Two, three, and four, *I* got. (Thanks, Jackie Mason!)

I should've stayed down the first time I landed on the floor, but I was dumb enough to visit the same place twice. Then I rallied long enough to land my Rocky Graziano right hook, which knocked Fat Charlie three feet clear into the air.

With an SRO audience, all chuckling and gloating, Charlie rammed into my stomach like a bull with its head bent downward. I tried to shriek as my body slammed into the wall of the corridor, but I didn't have enough breath left. Charlie, on the other hand, had enough for both of us.

"You big cow!" he bleated, his lips snarling.

Charlie went a little too far with that one, so daintily I yelled back, "Big, fat, pimply jerk!"

At this point, my mind became non-functional, and I was seized by an overwhelming desire to obliterate Fat Charlie completely. Before I could reach my goal, however, a teacher managed to tear us apart.

I was limp and crimson as Charlie and I were led down the corridor—like The Last Mile on Death Row—straight to the principal's office. (I'm surprised Pat O'Brien didn't show up.) I never did get to New York the day of that hideous confrontation; I was in no condition. Instead, both Charlie and I went to the nurse's office for first-aid treatment.

In the two long years I remained at Arts High, Charlie and I took great pains to ignore each other. Wordlessly, we'd pass each other in the school corridors like two shipwrecks that pass in the night. I'm sure the kid must've gone on to become somebody like Charles Bronson.

Meanwhile back at "Startime," sing I did—and solo, if you please, without my odious accordion! Great tunes like "Rag Mop" and "On a Slow Boat to China." But Mom still had me in anklets, although with flat gold sandals now. The other girls, of course, still wore their sexy four-inch spiked heels.

There were two little black girls on the show, a Polish kid, several Jewish kids, a few Italians, and a Hungarian thrown in for good measure. On broadcast day, each mother would bring a tray of exotic ethnic foods, so show day was a gastronomic extravaganza. *My* mother, whose mission in life is to feed the whole world, would bring at least five or six trays.

The normal girls on the show would poke and pick in a blasé manner at the food, as if it were a chore. One look at those Sunday feasts and I picked, too—with a spear! I devoured everything that didn't devour me first. And even during the week I still continued to bring to rehearsals my two elephantine kosher salami sandwiches on rye—with the big juicy pickles, yet.

One day, Mr. Scheck warned me: "Look, Connie, between us girls, you're eatin' yourself out of a career. Even a train stops!"

But I *didn't* stop; not until the fateful day when I had that cataclysmic conversation with Lenny Dale that changed my world.

I had such a giant crush on this larger-than-life individual that it was moronic. Ida watched the whole scene in total amazement.

"You're actin' like a real jerk," she said with diplomacy. "Over what, I'd like to know! Some of the mothers even told me he's a sissy! Now get that lovesick look off your face! You look like an idiot!" But who listened to her? *I* knew what I liked when I saw it.

One rehearsal day My Dreamboat told me charmingly, "Lemme talk to you a sec, sweetheart."

"Of course, Lenny," I managed with feigned composure.

"Now don't get me wrong, sweetheart—this is just my unsolicited, professional opinion. But for what it's worth, I think you oughta start playin' your accordion again on the show."

"Gee, Lenny, do you really think so?" I gasped, thrilled to the marrow of my bones. "You're the first person in my whole life who didn't say: 'Get *rid* of the accordion!' Do you really mean it, Lenny? 'Cause if you do, I'll ask Mr. Scheck if I can start playin' it again, okay?"

"That's a good career move, believe me, sweetheart. The accordion is a godsend for you. It hides your shape completely on camera." I was destroyed.

"Let's face it, little girl. You're not exactly petite to start off with. But that bad camera adds fifteen pounds to the ol' bod *you* sure can live without! Listen to an old pro!"

Then the boy's criticism became even more constructive. "Hey, I got another good idea, sweetheart. It's cute. You've met Godfrey before. You did his Christmas show, right? Okay! So on the next show, why doncha just play and sing his new hit, 'Too Fat Polka'?"

I was pulverized, ground into teeny-weeny granules. But Lenny Dale's sage counsel turned the tide for me. I had myself a little project now, and as usual I tackled it with operatic fervor.

With military discipline and no cheating whatsoever, it was yogurt, cottage cheese, and every other disgusting food you can name for the fat little Italian kid from Jersey. Farewell, fellow gourmands—you'll have to carry on without me! Farewell, rigatoni! Farewell, kosher salami sandwiches! Farewell, to all the beautiful things in life I'd come to love!

Right before the wondering eyes of Lenny Dale and the rest of the "Startime" cast, my weight plummeted from 135 pounds to 102 pounds; I lost about a third of a person, or thereabouts. (My arithmetic's the worst.)

Okay boys! Line up on the left! No more room, you say? Okay, then, fellas! Line up on the right, too! Too bad, boys, you should've asked sooner! My date book's all filled up!

Did I say "date?" Did I actually utter the word "boys?" For a split second there, I almost forgot about someone named George Franconero, Sr. To him, every boy who came within a 700-mile radius of my body was an insidious threat to be avoided at any cost. Sex, to me, was some fancy store on Fifth Avenue.

That's the way it was when you were an Italian girl with an Italian father who was living. My mother, as usual, took her cues from her Italian master. The woman is an ambulatory talking Xerox machine. To most Italian women of my mother's generation, sex is a spectator sport. It's often considered the "high price" they have to pay for that life of indentured servitude they call marriage.

I often say to those women: "You guys don't know

it, but Lincoln freed the slaves!" Grow up—and fast—
Italian women of the world!

Case in point: Recently I was on my way to Las
Vegas to join a friend, Dennis Rappaport, who man-
ages another friend, Gentleman Gerry Cooney, the
kindest man in boxing I've ever known. It was the day
of Gerry's ten-million-dollar fight with Larry Holmes,
a special day for all of us who'd been rooting for
Gerry from the beginning.

As usual, I was late. As I dashed out of the house in
a mighty big hurry, my mother noticed the book I was
carrying.

"What the hell are you readin' now?" She knew
very well what I was reading (the name was on the
cover in big bold print), but Italian and Jewish mothers have the market cornered on guilt. And they're
very clever about it! They know it makes you feel
even guiltier if they can make you answer a question
to which both of you already know the answer.

"Don't be cute, Ma. You see the cover." (She knew
I was wise to her a long time ago.) "C'mon, Ma, let
me go. I'll miss my plane."

"Don't tell me you have the *nerve* to walk all over
the airport readin' that disgusting book! Everybody
can see what you're readin', you know. Don't you
have any shame? What's the name of it, anyway?"

"Okay, I'll make you feel better, Ma. It's called
How to Make Love to a Man," I said defiantly. "Are
you happy now?"

"What the hell are you—*stupid*, or what? You don't
know by *now*?"

"You know, Ma, you're right. I'm a jerk. After all
the data on the art of love making you've shoved
down my throat since puberty, for me *still* to be in the
learning stage—I must be a jerk!"

At the very beginning of my career, my parents
weren't as crazy about restricting my "personal" life as
they were to become. But it all changed dramatically

and unpredictably on that wretched night when the Kids were appearing at Charles and Lillian Brown's Hotel.

When I opened the door to the room I was sharing with another "kid," I discovered her and a male "kid" on my bed "wrestling" passionately. That's what they tried to make me believe, anyway. But I was no dope, because I knew better from personal experience.

One New Year's Eve when I was nine, I caught two of my parents' friends, a married couple, doing the exact same thing on the living-room floor. They were house guests, and there was no guest room. Even back then, I surmised the sordid truth. I wasn't *that* stupid.

I knew just what the Dynamic Duo were doing in my hotel bed, all right. For a split second I gazed at them in horror; then, involuntarily, I shrieked and, like a dope, ran to report them to the next-to-the-last person in the world I *should* have reported them to— my mother.

Mom was busily chatting and joking, and playing her usual illegal Saturday night poker game with the rest of the mothers.

"Hurry up, Mommy! Get a load of this one! What a shock! You should see what _____ and _____ are doin' in my bed!" Go know, right? Who ever said I was smart?

Forgetting all about her precious poker game, my mother grabbed me by the hand and raced to the den of iniquity, where she discovered the pair dressing frantically. She said a prayer in Neapolitan asking God to forgive them, called the girl a *putana* (a tramp), and wailed, "*Che disgraziata!* Your father will have a stroke!" (No news to me.)

That was a pivotal night for me. And I blame no one but myself. Ida and George suddenly became my two "wardens." It would have been easier on me if I had been a ward of the state. Vigilant is not the word! My father's new obsession in life was to prevent me from becoming The Swinging Singer.

I needed some kind of outlet from all this tension,

so I bought myself my first diary. But even that source of privacy proved to be a dead-end street—I was in a no-win situation.

Every night of the week I'd furtively conceal The Daring, Deadly Diary in a different location. On Mondays, it went under the bed; Tuesdays, it was under my slips in the drawer; Wednesdays, under the shoes in the closet, etc., etc., etc.

But somehow Ida always managed to know some very private tidbits of information I'd told to only *one* other person in the whole wide world—my best friend, Joanie Weintraub. And *she* wouldn't tell my mother a blessed thing. Not Joanie—not on pain of death!

My mom snooped so much that it wasn't long before she had my whole game plan down pat. So for a while there, I even had to relinquish Diary Rights; that is, until I sent away for the *Gregg Book of Shorthand*. It was purely and simply a case of survival.

I was taking a CP (College Preparatory) course in high school, and stenography wasn't on the curriculum. But it was so important to me to have *some* kind of privacy that I mastered shorthand in about five weeks. Finally, I was able to hide the truth about my "decadent" life. Some decadence.

As you might expect, the worst subjects in school for me were in descending order:

> A. Gym/Math (a toss-up)
> B. Cooking
> C. Home Economics
> D. Sewing
> E. Music

Why, you ask, did I get a D in music—my life's work? I found Dr. Peck's music class to be sleep-inducing, so one day, in order to alleviate my boredom, I became a wise guy, and began crawling on the floor on my hands and knees.

"Connie Franconero!" said Dr. Peck sternly, "why are you disrupting my class! Why on God's good earth are you on the floor on your hands and knees?"

"I just lost my voice, Dr. Peck, and I'm looking for it."

Dr. Peck was not pleased. Hence the D.

One day in sewing class I was cutting out the pattern for a two-piece outfit I was making. I had saved two months' allowance to buy the material. Quickly and deftly, I cut out the pattern for the skirt just like that—a snap! I made only one mistake, however: I had cut out the pattern for my blouse first, and it was lying just beneath the pattern for the skirt.

The results were unsalvageable. I didn't want my mother to learn that all the money I'd blown on that material had gone down the drain. So I took my "project" home and hid it in the cellar.

There's one thing I'll never be able to hide, even from someone who's not too bright: Aside from dancing, when it comes to any activity that involves body movement, I'm not interested.

I am an athletically declined person, and I really don't want to change that. Why should I force myself to do something I hate, like exercise or sports, even if it will allow me to live a few years longer? They wouldn't be happy years, anyway. To this day, the only pleasure I derive from sports is buying sports clothes.

In gym, I was the world's worst! In fact I became co-editor of both my high school newspapers for only one reason (later, in Belleville High School, there were two): It was any excuse to get out of phys-ed. I'd always have a deadline to meet for the newspaper, and I always used gym time to meet that deadline.

This ploy worked about once a week; another day, I'd forget the sneakers I'd taken home to wash; another I'd feel faint and have to go to the nurse's office; yet another I'd forget the key to my locker. I'd alternate the alibis, however, so as not to raise too much suspicion. One day a week I'd show up, just so everybody would remember what I looked like.

In gym I was always afraid I'd be hit by the ball, so instead of catching it, I'd run away from it. If the ball hit me, how would I edit the newspaper? There was no doubt about it—I was a liability to any team.

But that still wasn't reason enough for Martha, one of the gym captains, and Roz, the other one, to treat me the way they did. (Female gym captains are the worst, anyway; they always look like boys.)

Each day Martha and Roz would take turns selecting their teams. They'd alternate until no one was left. I was always the last to be picked.

One day after they'd gotten down to me again, Martha said magnanimously, "Okay, Roz, there she stands. She's all yours!"

"Oh, no, you don't, Martha! Don't pull *that* one on me again! *I* had her yesterday!" It was downright demoralizin'.

It's a good thing I got out of that school when I did; I was going nowhere in a hurry. Even the gym instructor was beginning to catch on to me when, just in the nick of time, we made the big move to suburbia and Belleville, New Jersey.

5

You're Gonna Hear from Me

Fortune smiles on this road before me
I'm fortune's child; hey, listen world
You can't ignore me

I've got a song that longs to be played
Lift up my flag, begin my parade
And watch the world over start turnin' up clover
That's how it's gonna be, you see
YOU'RE GONNA HEAR FROM ME *

February 1954
Belleville, New Jersey

To me, our new $15,000 home in Belleville was the
Taj Mahal. It rested atop a grassy hill on the corner of
Greylock and Forest. It had a rock garden with a little
fountain and goldfish in it that the cats always ate.

Even though we couldn't afford to decorate it—
only two rooms were carpeted—to me, it was the ulti-
mate in living splendor. We even had a "spare"

room—my very own music room along with my first piano.

Our move to Belleville also meant a change of high schools for me, and I was absolutely mad about Belleville High. It wasn't a special school like "Arts" with special, talented kids; it was a real high school with normal kids.

There was a varsity football team with cheerleaders, special clubs that met after school, like the Dramatic Club and the Debating Club, and even sororities. Girls got pinned and went steady just like other people—normal girls, that is.

Everybody wore plaid accordion-pleated skirts with turtleneck sweaters, bobby socks, and loafers with pennies in them. We wore neckerchiefs at our necks, or through our belts. There were a lot of cardigan sweaters with one big initial on them. I even began wearing a ponytail like everyone else.

I told you that I had two reasons for wanting to join the school newspaper at BHS. The first, as I mentioned, was to get out of gym. The second was the verrry cute editor of the BHS school newspaper, one Nick LaPara. Shortly after I arrived at BHS, he personally interviewed me for the school newspaper, *The Spotlight*, and wrote:

> A welcome addition to BHS' student body is Connie Franconero, a verrry cute junior whose claim to fame (rather, one of her claims; extremely talented, this kid) is that she's already a veteran in show business. She makes appearances on the "Startime Revue" on NBC-TV as a featured singer (if you haven't tuned in and heard her yet, please do so, if she doesn't curl your hair she'll at least broil the rug under the TV set; hot, man, just hot), and has appeared often on TV and in personal appearances. But enough statistics; how about Connie herself? She really is quite an interesting person. (Connie is the kind of person I love to interview; beauty and brains, if you know what I mean.) About Belleville, "the only thing I didn't

like," she goes on, "was the second or third day I got a zero in gym class." It seems there was a mix-up on lockers.

(I guess I was back to my old tricks again.)

As you can see, Connie takes marks very seriously. In Arts High she was on their newspaper, *The Scope*, was a member of the National Honor Society, and a member of the All-City Chorus of Newark.

Nick LaPara was the only boy I was allowed to go out on a truly legitimate-like date with in high school. It wasn't all that legitimate either, because my father never knew of it.

I don't know what form of sanity possessed my mother, but for once she defied my father, said I could go, and kept the entire matter hush-hush. I still have the foil bag of popcorn from that movie date—with butter still in it. I hope I haven't revealed something that could cause a divorce between my folks after forty-eight years of marriage.

I performed on other TV shows, too, besides "Startime," talent shows like "Battle of the Ages" with Morey Amsterdam. On "Startime" we sometimes had big stars who appeared with us; that's how popular the show was in New York! I earned twenty-five dollars a week on "Startime;" two years later, it was upped to fifty dollars—a 100-percent raise!

The week Milton Berle appeared on the show with the kids, Mom spent the unusually exorbitant sum of eighteen dollars for me, on a dress at Klein's in Newark. It was a small fortune. It hurt me that she'd spent all that money for just one dress, so I went back to the store and bought three for the price of one. (Sometimes if you knew how to shop there, you could really get a bargain at Klein's.)

The performers on "Startime" were versatile and very talented. There was singer-dancer Rosalie Mann, who taught me a lot; she came on like Ethel Merman. There was seven-year-old Joey Sheptock, who did Jimmy Durante impersonations. Joey stuttered, but only when he wasn't on TV. There was six-year-old Sharon Wright Porter, a little black girl with long curls, who sang songs with lines like: "You fill me with extra-sy!" (Ecstasy.) All kinds of good talent! I've left out a lot of people like Angel, Kenny Sharp, Vinnie Monte, Bobby Appell, the Kaye Sisters, etc., and so many other marvelously talented kids, but space doesn't permit.

We also did lots of benefits. One day I met a lady blues singer who was appearing with us somewhere. She was really a favorite of mine; I used to buy all her records. I had even sent for a photo of her once from one of those big ads in *Photoplay Magazine* that lists all your favorite stars. I'd never asked for anyone's autograph before, but Mom said, "You're meetin' all these important people, and nobody believes you." So I mustered up all the courage I possessed, timidly handed the lady my brand new autograph book, and asked her if she'd sign it for me.

Not only did she refuse to do so, but in so many words, she told me to get lost. What a twirp! She made me feel so unimportant and low; it taught me a mighty big lesson in life.

I've never, to this day, turned down an autograph seeker. No matter how pressed I am for time—I've missed planes because of it—I've never refused. It takes courage and a lot of self-assurance for the average person to approach a celebrity and ask for an autograph, and I still get a thrill each and every time someone asks for mine. To me, it's a very special honor, and it's always like the very first time.

It bugs me when I hear a celebrity "does not sign autographs" or "speak to his fans" in a public situation. These same people will pay public relation firms $2,500 a month to get their names and faces in the press. Then, when people *do* recognize their faces, they get their backs up and resent it. "After all," they say, "I have to have a private life of my own!"

To these performers I say: It would be wise for you to consider another occupation—one in which, perhaps, you will not be so extravagantly rewarded, but one in which you could retain your anonymity, which is obviously paramount to you. There is always more privacy and safety in obscurity.

A friend recently told me this definition she'd heard of a celebrity: "A celebrity is a person who breaks his butt to be recognized and then wears dark glasses so he won't be." The inconveniences these poor souls endure—all for a lousy fortune!

Whenever I step out of my home—whether it's to go to a department store, a supermarket, or the hairdresser's—to me, that constitutes a personal appearance, because I'm a public figure. If someone I'm dating resents this, the relationship usually comes to a fast end. It's part of my life—the fun part—making people happy.

For the two years I was at BHS, my life was frenetic. Three days a week I took the bus to the Port Authority bus terminal in New York City and then a bus to Nola's rehearsal hall for "Startime." (Today I wouldn't go to the Port Authority alone without a full Marine divison.) I belonged to the Debating Club and the Glee Club, and was co-editor of *The Spotlight*.

There was another boy at BHS that I had a crush on. I believe he was captain of the football team. His name was Stevie Cohen and he had a Reputation. One sunny Sunday afternoon Stevie asked me to go to the Milk Bar in Belleville for an ice cream soda. I planned an elaborate explanation for Daddy: "Daddy, can I go to the Milk Bar for an ice cream soda?"

"What are you askin' *me* for? You want an ice cream soda, go get an ice cream soda."

"Ah . . . well . . . uh . . ." I stammered, "Stevie Cohen wants to come with me. . . . We'll only be gone—"

"You're cute, you know? Okay, I got the picture. You want an ice cream soda? I'll tell ya what. Go to the basement. You'll find a whole case of Bolla soda—there's every flavor you like. Then go to the kitchen. In the freezer there's your favorite ice cream—cherry vanilla. Get a big glass and a long spoon. You mix 'em together and ya got yourself your soda. Forget about Stevie Cohen."

Every Friday night at the school auditorium they had dances called "Beehives." It was *the* social event of the week. At one of the "Beehives," in the middle of a merengué, I got Lipstick on the Collar of Stevie Cohen's new white sport jacket—The Truth! (Talk about fate.)

All the kids, including me, would go; after the "Beehive" all the kids, *excluding* me, would go for pizza. My father's car would always be waiting just outside the auditorium door to take me directly home without passing Go and collecting two hundred dollars. But who could blame the man? One never knows what earth-shattering catastrophe could befall me with forty-nine other kids in a pizza parlor? Talk about humiliation! What a joke!

No one ever believed me when I insisted that my father didn't "just get off the boat" from Palermo. It was difficult to conceive that the man was actually made in America.

Meanwhile, when I was fourteen, I saw the inside of a recording studio for the first time. It was the most exciting experience of my life until then. I was hired to make demonstration records—"demos"—for music publishers.

A music publisher would hire a singer like myself and a couple of musicians in order to demonstrate his newest, yet-unrecorded songs. Then, the demo would be brought to the top artists in order to solicit their recording of that song. Sometimes the publisher would have a particular singer in mind for a certain song. In fact, in most cases it happened that way.

At a demo session a publisher would say to me: "Connie, try to give us a little more of that great Patti Page sound, will you?" Another day, he'd want me to sound like Teresa Brewer, another day like Joni James, or Kay Starr, or Jo Stafford, or Kitty Kallen, or Rosemary Clooney, ad infinitum.

I began to sound like every female singer in the world. I wouldn't have minded, except that I didn't have a style of my *own* yet—and didn't even know where to find one. But I *did* earn ten dollars a session, and that went a long way.

Very often I'd have one stupendous, pie-in-the-sky dream. I guess you could call it a secret wish, but it was a dream, nevertheless.

I would be sitting in the control room of a recording studio next to THE PRESIDENT OF THE BIG-GEST RECORD COMPANY IN THE ENTIRE WORLD. Invariably, there'd be a lead sheet before me. THE HOTTEST PUBLISHER IN THE EN-TIRE WORLD would keep pleading with me to re-cord his song, written by THE VERY HOTTEST SONGWRITER IN THE ENTIRE WORLD. It was the lead sheet to THE NEXT NUMBER ONE SMASH HIT RECORD OF THE ENTIRE WORLD. I would always be most gracious, agree to give him a break and listen to his hit tune.

The president would say to the demo vocalist in the sound booth:

"Miss Clooney? Do me a favor, will you?"

"Yes, Mr. So-and-so," Miss Clooney would respond politely. "What can I do for you?"

"I'm really dyin' to get Connie Francis, THE WORLD'S BIGGEST FEMALE RECORDING ARTIST, to cut my song. Give us a little of that great Connie Francis sound, will you, Miss Clooney?"

"Well, that won't be easy," Miss Clooney would apologize, "but I'll give it the ol' college try, anyway."

It was a silly dream, I know, but everybody has the right to dream a little. And if you do, sometimes you can make the most impossible things come true.

6

Freddy

FREDDY I know that you've been seeing Daisy
Freddy you drive me absolutely crazy
Lovin' you the way I do
You're gonna break my heart in two—Oh, Freddy *

January 1955
New York City

NINETEEN fifty-five was a very good year. The country was relaxed, complacent, and optimistic; prosperity was already a matter of course. Business was booming and there was plenty of extra folding money in the pockets of Americans. The so-called working class was now the middle class, and we were living better than ever before in the nation's history.

The tenth year of the atomic age was coming to a close. If a few dissenting voices called out words of warning, no one seemed to be listening. Yes, it was still our parents' world. But the young and old were fast becoming polarized as never before.

We gals wore bobby socks, ballerina slippers, and strapless prom dresses. We set our hair in pin curls.

* Used by permission of MCA Music.

Some of us even went to pajama parties and talked all
night about the dreamiest boys (I wasn't one of them).
Our fellas wore dirty buck shoes. And the black
leather jackets and DA (ducktail) haircuts they
sported became the symbols for a new kind of teenage
rebellion.

Nineteen fifty-five brought the advent of rock 'n'
roll. The first teen-oriented movie was released in the
hot summer of that year. It was called *The Blackboard
Jungle*. And, even though *Billboard* magazine (the Bi-
ble of the music industry) begged us weekly "Keep
Pop Music Alive in '55," two elderly men, Freedom
and DeKnight, one of them a postman, wrote a song
called "Rock Around the Clock." The first rimshot of
"One o'clock, two o'clock, three o'clock, rock" was
the shot heard round the world.

A disc jockey out of Cleveland, Alan Freed, culled
a line from "Rock Around the Clock," coining the
phrase "rock 'n' roll."

Where did it all start? The roots of rock 'n' roll
reach back to the late forties and early fifties when
two giant musical forces—Country and Western (hillbilly) and Rhythm and Blues (race music)—collided.
It was created by southerners who had grown up with
country and black music all their lives.

Back in Philadelphia, the baseball games sponsored
by Tastykakes featured a young M-O-R (middle-of-
the-road) disc jockey (DJ) named Dick Clark, while a
veteran, Bob Horn, hosted a show called "Bandstand."

In 1955, "The Startime Kids" went off the air, and
George Scheck became my personal manager—a relationship that has lasted almost thirty years. A family
friend was able to change my date of birth at the Hall
of Records, so that I could obtain a falsified police
card and work in real night clubs on weekends and
during the summers. And so Mom and I hit the road,
and I began to do the thing I would always love doing

most in this world—entertaining people live-and-in-person.

Mom and I took the lonely train from Boston to the Frolics in Revere Beach, Massachusetts. Closer to home, I sang at the Rustic Cabin in Englewood, New Jersey, where Frank Sinatra got his start. Then it was Long Island's Casa Seville in Franklin Square. (I still have all those contracts.)

The Seville's read: "Vocalist, three days. Two shows Friday, three Saturday, two Sunday—$150 for three days." The Rustic Cabin: same deal—$150! How could I spend it all?

On my first engagement in an important supper club, the El Morocco in Toronto, Canada, Edith Piaf had just closed the previous evening. It was awesome that I would be performing in the exact spot where the Great Piaf had sung.

A very gracious but poor Canadian family, who were distant relatives of Aunt Rose's, met Mom and me at the airport. It was our first trip to a foreign country, and we'd have been lost if it weren't for that wonderful family. They escorted us everywhere and couldn't do enough for us.

One Sunday, however, they made the unfortunate mistake of inviting Mom and me to the usual big Italian Sunday dinner. At the dinner table, after the father said grace, the hostess served us a salad and pasta. Then she placed a soup-sized bowl of assorted meats directly in front of me; it contained a meatball, braccioli, and a piece of sausage, covered with mounds of tomato sauce. In comparison to the truckdriver portions Mom served each of us at home, to me, it looked like a child's portion.

Everything looked so scrumptious that I devoured that bowl of meat in ten seconds flat. When my mother saw the empty bowl, she gritted her teeth and gasped, "What happened to all the meat in that bowl?"

"I ate it," I said matter-of-factly.

"You ate *what? All* of it? Oh my God! How embarrassin'! I wanna die! That meat was for *everybody!*" What could I do? I couldn't return it.

I played another supper club outside of Buffalo with an up-and-coming singer, Johnny Mathis. After seeing me do my first show, the irate club owner called George Scheck and growled, "What the hell are you tryin' to get away with? You stuck me four hundred bucks for an amateur!"

My brother began working with Daddy on the roofs, because Daddy wanted Georgie to know, at an early age, what hard manual labor was really like, so that Georgie would be persuaded to become a professional man.

One day Mr. Scheck told me that a music publisher, an amiable man named Lou Levy who was once married to one of the Andrews Sisters, was willing to put up half the money necessary for me to record four of his songs. And so, together with George Scheck putting up fifty percent, I did my first very own recording session.

Their plans were to sell these "masters," as they are called in the record business, to a major record company. Lou Levy and George Scheck took a big risk, because girl singers just weren't selling those days. At least now I wouldn't have to imitate every other female singer in the world—that session cost about five thousand dollars.

One of the songs was a silly little ditty called "Freddy." But who was I to be choosy? I kept quiet; I was lucky to be recording. Mr. Scheck and Mr. Levy shlepped "Freddy" and the other three masters to every record company in America, large and small. And everywhere they heard the same depressing verdict; everywhere they were turned down.

I think now would be an appropriate time for me to thank personally still another giant supporter of my early career, Mr. Mitch Miller. At Columbia Records he observed: "The girl has no distinctive sound. She's like fifty thousand other girl singers. Don't throw your money away!" (Thanks a lot, Mitch!)

The last remaining company Mr. Scheck and Mr. Levy visited was MGM, and at age sixteen, I was signed by the president, Harry Meyerson, to my first record contract. Why, you ask? Because he knew for certain that I was going to become the hottest thing on wax? Nope!

There was a more down-to-earth reason for his decision. Harry Meyerson just happened to have a son named Freddy, and he thought the record would make a cute birthday present for his son. Talk about luck!

Unfortunately, "Freddy" lived only a short while; not the son, thank God—the stupid song!

Why does one performer become a star and not another? It isn't a question of whether or not you're "star material." Over the years, I've seen people who were tremendous talents, who I was sure would make it, and who never really get off the ground.

There was a gal named Tina Robin from New Jersey who started out just about the same time I did. She was a big-voiced belter in the old tradition. By every known standard, she should have become a superstar.

There was another gal who was very talented; I first heard her in '68 in the Bahamas. Her name was Misty Walker, and she sang up a storm—but nothing. It's hard to believe these gals didn't become really big stars.

I am unenvious of other performers, and I've always been enthusiastic about new talent. The first time I heard Brenda Lee's "Sweet Nothin's" on the radio, I was already a recording star, and Brenda was totally unknown to me and to the rest of America. But I flipped so for her singing that I sent her a fan letter, which read something like this: "Now I know who my competition is! You're the greatest! Good luck!" That

was one of my more accurate predictions. Brenda and
I are still friends today.

Why do so many performers fail when they seem to
have all the ingredients for stardom? Show people are
very often underestimated. Many of them are disci-
plined, bright, gutsy, creative, ambitious, and imag-
inative, and sometimes—though not often enough—
good business people. It takes an exceptional person
to become and remain a star; most important of all, it
takes incredible stamina and tenacity and the ability to
deal with rejection. Sustained success rarely happens
by accident. And, it takes a special magic, too—a certain indefinable electricity a performer generates.

Unless you're all of these things, and few of us are,
you must have your Pygmalion—a person who truly
believes in you and is willing to put up hard dollars to
prove it, someone to teach you the ropes, school you,
groom you, criticize you and plan for you. I was lucky;
I had two such people in my life—my father and
George Scheck.

George Scheck is a slim, very dapper, soft-spoken
man in his sixties. When he speaks to you, no matter
how innocuous the subject (it could be about dinner
that night), he covers his mouth conspiratorially and
whispers secrets in your ear. The whole scene takes on
the aura of a spy transmitting Top State Secrets to the
enemy.

Mr. Scheck moves and walks like the tap dancer he
was in his younger days—always gently, lightly and
secretively, just like that cat burglar on the Riviera.
He is almost totally expressionless—he has little time
to waste on humor—except, that is, when he consum-
mates an important money deal. Then, in an instant,
the man becomes Bert Parks.

Through the years, George Scheck and I have
shared many a spectacular and heady triumph and
many a defeat—both professional and personal. He
has been far more than a manager to me. He held my
hand and cried with me over a broken romance on the
most important and what should have been the hap-

piest night of my young career. And it always saddened him to see real personal happiness elude me throughout my life. We shared the loss of his only daughter, a beautiful seven-year-old, in a fire in their Long Island home, and not very long ago, the death of my brother.

Meanwhile, the Big Buzz at BHS was the Senior Prom. I bought a beautiful gown, hung it up in my closet, and waited, with great expectation, for the Night of Nights. And that was as far as it went.

It wasn't that I lacked a date for the prom—Stevie Cohen was supposed to be my date. The only thing I lacked was permission to *go*.

It seems that a few days prior to the prom, four strange kids returning from *their* prom in South Jersey were killed in a car crash. We didn't know the kids, the town, or the high school from a hole in the wall—but that wasn't enough to allay my parents' fears for my life.

They thought lightning might strike twice in another part of the universe, so Daddy said, "No prom!" I lied and told Stevie Cohen I couldn't go because I had the measles. I don't think he really believed me (there weren't any spots), but I was too embarrassed to admit the truth. (Besides, Macy's don't tell Gimbel's nothin'.)

But, there *was* one saving grace. On prom night, I got to wear my pretty new gown, though no one I knew saw me in it. I even had my hair and nails done by my girl friend, Connie. I locked myself in my room, and wore my gown all that night, played my 45s and pretended to hold Stevie Cohen as we danced the night away to "Moments to Remember" and "Pretend You're Happy When You're Blue"—the "perfect" song for the "perfect" evening.

Trying to lay a little guilt on my father today, I refreshed his memory about the terrible thing he'd done to me. Realizing the havoc he had wreaked upon my young life, he grinned broadly like the wise guy he still

is and commiserated, "Ya know, kid, my heart still
bleeds for ya. You ruined my whole goddamned day."
Then he left. I'm sure he was on his way to confession
to say an Act of Contrition. (Fat chance!)

When I graduated from BHS, I received a four-year
premed scholarship to New York University.

During the summer, MGM Records sent me on my
first major promotion tour of radio stations and DJs in
the Northeast and Midwest with a promotion lady by
the name of Janie Gibbs.

Janie Gibbs wasn't like any promotion person I'd
ever met—the rest were, you know, real show business, always "hyping." She was more like a movie star
to me. In fact, one of her closest friends was Doris
Day, and she would speak with Miss Day on the
phone for long periods of time all the way to California.

Janie was sweet, pretty, in her thirties. She was the
epitome of poise and *savoir faire*. Her self-assuredness
and *joie de vivre* only underscored how green, shy,
and ingenuous I was. At first, I found the whole thing
intimidating and depressing. But I didn't stay intimidated or depressed very long.

I decided to learn a thing or six from Janie Gibbs.
Whenever she was asleep or she'd leave the room, I'd
stand in front of the mirror and walk, talk, and use the
same sophisticated gestures she used. Sometimes I
even held an unlit cigarette.

I also imitated the way she would cordially but
firmly run the show, taking full charge of everything
on the road. I'd get on the phone and pretend I was
Janie. I'd dial nothing and lower my voice an octave.

"Hello, this is Miss Francis in room XYZ. Would
you kindly send a bellhop to room XYZ within ten
minutes? I have a train to catch. Thank you so very
much. Good-bye." Or, to room service: "Hello! How
are you this morning? This is Miss Francis in room
XYZ. For a party of two, I'd like the following: two
English muffins (crisply toasted), orange marmalade

on the side, two large glasses of orange juice, and a pot of coffee. That's room XYZ and the name again is Miss Francis. Send up a newspaper as well. It won't be too long, will it? We have a flight to catch. Thank you so much."

Janie taught me things no one in my family circle of a hundred people ever dreamed of before. Sometimes the lessons weren't all that pleasant.

In Chicago we went to Henrici's, an elegant restaurant. I was awe-struck by the splendor of it all; I'd never seen anything like it before. It had tone, all right—a real "ritzy" place, as they'd say in Newark. We were joined there by the MGM distributor, a local promotion man, and a few local DJs and program directors.

The waiters at Henrici's wore white gloves, and everything was silver and sparkling. Each man ordered a drink of liquor, and Janie ordered something exotic I couldn't even pronounce. The waiter asked me what I wanted.

I was embarrassed about my order, so I said in a bare whisper: "One Coca-Cola, please." (It was an auditory acuity test.) The waiter had to ask me three more times before he was able to hear me *shout,* "I *said,* one Coca-Cola!" Everyone turned around to stare at the boorish teenager.

I tried to plow through that evening by imitating every last move Janie Gibbs made. I even ordered the same thing she did, just so I'd be using the right utensils—and I *hate* fish!

Then the strangest thing happened. A small, heavy silver tray with a heavy lid was placed directly in front of me. As usual, I was too curious and impatient to wait for the waiter to remove the lid. So, I removed it myself to discover some peculiar kind of liquid dessert I hadn't even ordered.

A lemon floated on top of the dessert, and a cherry sat on top of the lemon.

With my heavy silver soup spoon, I dived into this new culinary adventure. Suddenly, Janie gave me one swift no-nonsense kick under the table. I looked at her, puzzled. Was she crazy?

"What did I do wrong now, Janie?" I whispered in her ear.

Janie spoke to me like a ventriloquist, smiling widely at the DJs, but speaking softly to me without moving her lips. "You don't *eat* that—and you don't *drink* it, either! What am I going to do with you, Connie? You *wash* in it! It's a finger bowl!" How was I supposed to know? I only knew from pasta bowls. Oh, boy, Belleville, Brooklyn, and Newark were never like this—thank God!

Janie knew all the ropes, all right. She knew every DJ at every station. She was warm, friendly, and radiant, but she also had a hands-off attitude toward men in the business that I gradually and instinctively developed and possess even to this day.

Taking the trans-Hudson tubes to NYU at Washington Square every day wasn't exactly like going to Wellesley. In fact, it was a big fat drag! But, because I was granted a scholarship, I was determined to get a straight A average.

That's why I was so flabbergasted when I returned home from a two-week record promotion tour and the dean informed me that my scholarship was being taken away.

"Why?" I pleaded. "I have straight A's."

"We'd prefer to grant our scholarships to persons who are more serious about their academic endeavors and goals."

Serious! All my life I'd been nothing but a boring bookworm! Serious! The nerve of the guy!

Well, maybe if my next record was a big smash, I wouldn't care so much about losing my scholarship. And, why shouldn't it be a big hit? It was aptly named wasn't it? "Goody Good-bye!"

It was Goody Good-bye, all right—to NYU, to

Washington Square, to the charming dean, to the magnificent walks in the freezing cold to the gymnasium in those short blue gym suits, to that stimulating campus life and to those sleek, scenic Hudson tubes! To all of this high living, I said farewell, good riddance, and GOODY GOOD-BYE.

7

My First Real Love

'Twas MY FIRST REAL LOVE
But my heart knew then
That I'd never find a love again
Like MY FIRST REAL LOVE*

January 1956
New York City

THE frigid winds of a New York January day had little effect on the inner glow I felt when I bounced into George Scheck's little office at 1697 Broadway. And, why not? My third record had "made a little noise, and got some air play," and insiders, especially the DJs rooting for me, were predicting that Connie Francis might "really happen." But by day's end, that warm glow would turn to ice. For I was about to meet my first real character and my first real love, Robert Walden Cassotto, a man I would love till the day he died and beyond that.

George Scheck was excited about "these two new kids," aspiring songwriters Bobby Darin and Donnie

---

* "My First Real Love" © 1956 Songsmiths, Inc. written by Bobby Darin, Don Kirshner and George Scheck.

Kirshner. On a hunch, the boyishly enthusiastic Kirshner had brought George Scheck what he called a "smash hit" for Connie Francis.

They were the "odd couple," these two, such opposites. Tall, dark, and handsome Donnie was captain of the Upsala College basketball team. He fancied himself a would-be everything—songwriter, manager, producer, publisher, whatever. He complimented me profusely and asked so many interested, ingratiating questions about my lackluster career that it became almost embarrassing.

Especially in the presence of his slight, wiry, bored partner, Bobby Darin, who obviously couldn't care less. Suddenly, Bobby interrupted Donnie: "Okay, enough of this garbage, Kirsh. Look, lady, do ya wanna listen to a hit, or not?"

"I'm *dying* for a hit!" I exclaimed, enthusiastically.

"Join the club," he responded wearily. "I dig."

"You do?" I inquired. "For what company?"

"Is this lady a gas, Kirsh?" Bobby winced, then winked. Then condescendingly he explained: "What I *meant* is, like I'm hip, lady. Like I know where you're comin' from."

"How? I've never met you before, have I?" I asked innocently. "How do you know I come from Belleville?"

"Aw, this is too much, Kirsh. Tell me she's puttin' us on, will you? Belleville, huh? Don't you mean Squaresville?"

What a truly offensive person!

"That's *gotta* be where you're from! Kirsh, is this wild?" He almost went into convulsions.

Apparently, I was in need of a good language interpreter. I wondered how the boy liked it in America.

I inched next to him on the piano bench and confidently scanned the lead sheet of the song he'd written, "My First Real Love."

"I sing this one in A," I chirped, very sure of myself. "Can you transpose?" The *nerve* of me to insinuate he couldn't!

"You want the key of A, lady, you got A," he replied, a definite edge to his voice. "You want H, you got that, too." I looked up in wonder at Donnie, the tall, more pleasant one of the two. "I don't think this is gonna work out at all," I groaned.

"Heh, heh, he's some kibbitzer, Miss Francis," Donnie chuckled nervously. "Some sense of humor, huh?"

"Yes," I observed. "He's enchanting, really."

I sang the song perfectly the first time around; all those demo dates were finally paying off. The disagreeable one on piano was impressed that I was able to read music. I fiddled with the sheet music, changing a chord or two, a few dumb notes, and some hokey lyrics here and there. When I was satisfied with the results, I said gingerly, "Now with these changes, it's not that bad. See what I mean? Let's try it again."

"This is all I wrote, lady. Take it or leave it," Bobby answered rudely, seizing the lead sheet and heading for the corridor. I tapped him lightly on his shoulder a few times with an "Are you for real?" expression written all over my face.

"Listen, and listen real careful, Mr. Whatever-your-name-is," I said coolly. "I'm not up on all the exciting new happenings in show business, but I do happen to know *you're* not one of them—unless you've made it real big out in Hollywood, California, and word just hasn't reached the East Coast yet. In New York, we're always the last to know."

"Oh, boy, I got aggravation!" Donnie wailed helplessly, explaining that Bobby was really a wonderful person deep down. I had no intention of digging that far; it would be too much work.

"Bobby, I think like maybe you should apologize to Miss Francis."

"*You* apologize to Miss Francis, Kirsh. I'm splittin'. This lady from Belleville and I don't dance to the same tune."

I knew I should be insulted, but I didn't understand what he was talking about. "Mr. Kirshner," I snapped sharply, "I don't recall inviting *this* gentleman to lunch, either."

"Ya see, Miss Francis, Bobby's in a bad mood today," Donnie stuttered, running after his friend. "He isn't usually *this* bad." For a brief moment, I sat there stunned, marveling at the chutzpah of this up-and-coming pauper.

Suddenly Donnie returned, tugged at my arm excitedly, and pleaded, "We'll make those changes, Miss Francis! You've made a big improvement in the song! You'll see—tomorrow Bobby will be in a much better mood."

I can hardly wait, I thought. Then I stomped back to Mr. Scheck's office next door to put in a complaint.

"Who sent for that character—the short one?" I asked a sorry George Scheck. "Who *is* that person? The Eighth Wonder of the Musical World? Could it be that George Gershwin has returned to us from the dead? Gee, Mr. Scheck, the guy's an egomaniac. He's *so* fresh!"

He *was* fresh. And brilliant, and multitalented—and underneath it all, scared to death.

"I don't know too much about them," George Scheck explained. "They had a combo up in the Borscht Belt where they doubled up as busboys, and they just wrote a jingle for some guy in Orange with a furniture store. And the one you don't like, he played bongos for some exotic Spanish dancer. He sings, too."

If I was expecting an apology the next day, I was in for a surprise. When Darin grudgingly played the changes I sought, I purred and said demurely, "Now *that's* more like it! See? I *told* you so!"

"Groovy," he drawled with overt sarcasm, "real groovy." Who could converse with this alien? So, I ignored him completely, and spoke to Donnie instead. "I can cut it in about three weeks."

I smiled while a delighted Donnie bounced up and down, as if Peggy Lee had just agreed to cut his song.

No one had ever gotten *that* excited before about a Connie Francis record! Donnie must have seen me as some sort of ticket to overnight success and untold millions. (Score one for Kirsh! The fella was right!)

I learned that Bobby Darin would soon be recording, too. George Scheck thought he had real potential, and so did Decca records, who signed him to a contract that very week. It would be a far different world for Bobby from that day on. It would be a far different world for me, too—a world of first real love and sweet heartaches.

I recorded "My First Real Love" (Bobby was the background "group," the Jaybirds, *all* of them), and added still another song to my ever-growing and impressive string of unknown favorites.

I quickly learned more about the "fresh" one. He was living in a Bronx tenement with his chronically ill mother, Polly, whom he worshiped, along with his older sister, Nina, her husband, Charlie Maffia, and their two children. Bobby, who had attended Bronx High School of Science, was forced to give up a scholarship to Hunter College because, he said, he didn't have the money to buy trousers and shoes for school and the phone company had just cut off their service for nonpayment.

He possessed street smarts far beyond his nineteen years, and he had definite opinions about *everything!* He hated pretense, bigotry, and dishonesty of any kind. He wasn't like anyone I'd ever met before, or anyone I'd ever meet again. Soon, we became inseparable and I looked forward to each trip to New York. During the bus ride, I counted the time until I could be with him with the second hand of my watch.

Bobby Darin was different—dynamic, versatile, chock full of an energy—a fierce determination and intensity I had never seen before; I was intrigued by his sense of urgency. He's only nineteen, I thought. What's the big hurry?

Soon he told me. "No one—nothing—can stop me

from what I have to do. My mother has always driven that home. By the time I'm twenty-five I've gotta be a legend."

"Will the world come to an end," I asked, "if you're not a legend until you're twenty-six?"

"I'm not putting you on, Connie. I'm serious. See, I've had a bad heart since I was a kid. The doctors say it'll be all over before I hit thirty. I gotta leave something behind the people will remember, and all I got are the songs in me."

I wish his words had been characteristic Darin melodrama, but they weren't. I wasn't certain yet if *I* had any special talent, but I never doubted for a single moment that it was all out there waiting for Bobby Darin. And he seemed just brash and cocky enough to give the ol' world a new kind of whirl.

Only George Scheck and I knew how terrified he was—that just before his first TV appearance on "The Tommy Dorsey Show" he tried to run out of town. And that during the show, the lyrics he had painstakingly written on his sweaty palms disappeared long before the song was over.

As far as I was concerned, his show business friends, especially the musicians, might just as well have come from outer space; most of them spoke just the way he did.

There was Dick Behrke, who would become a leading arranger and conductor; Rona Barrett, immensely successful columnist and TV personality; Steve Karmen, who'd one day write a slew of top commercials for TV, like "When You've Said Budweiser, You've Said It All" and "I Love New York." There was Dick Lord, who'd become a stand-up comic and work the "big rooms" with Bobby and me. And, of course, there was the only "normal" fellow—Kirsh.

Everything these people did either fascinated or shocked me, especially their avant-garde lingo. It was 1956, and nobody used the word "square"—except maybe in geometry class. And, their worldliness—

they used words like "broads" to mean women, and "scoring," which had nothing at all to do with NFL football.

Phrases like "Have you got a gig Friday?" and "No sweat, man," rolled off their tongues with startling ease. And, then there was the casual way they conducted their personal lives. This is hard to believe, I know, but one night Dick and Ellen Lord fell asleep watching TV *lying* on the sofa! And, they wouldn't be engaged yet for a month and a half! I wondered what my parents would say if they'd seen it all.

Bobby and I talked quite a lot about that while he saw me safely on the 33 De Camp bus for Belleville.

"You're upset about something, Connie." I nodded. He lifted my downcast chin with his finger. "I know what's wrong. You were uncomfortable about Dick and Ellen, right?" I nodded. "Okay. No sweat, honey—it'll be cool. That won't happen again. I promise you, baby."

Sure, they fascinated me—but at the same time, they made me feel so "Belleville, New Jersey," that sometimes I cringed inside.

That's why I didn't think it was such a good idea when the group came to my house—all the way from the Bronx to Belleville—for the first time unannounced. Lewis and Clark were busy that day—that's why it took five buses, three trains, and six hours for Bobby and his friends to reach the outskirts of Belleville.

So far, I'd kept my new friends under wraps. So when I saw the group, I went into shock. They should have warned me, at least! I'd have found some way to get rid of my parents! The visit was a big mistake. My parents were not pleased.

"Who the hell are they, that Darin character and his cute pals?" my father asked. "And what the hell are they doin' *here?* One of them creeps even has a beard!"

"Well, Daddy," I offered meekly, "maybe you didn't meet Donnie Kirshner yet. He's from New

Jersey. He's captain of the Upsala College basketball team." It was a pathetic attempt to lend an air of legitimacy to the whole group. Daddy wasn't buying.

"Tell 'em to scram!" he warned militantly. "Get rid of those wise guys, *now!* I *mean* it! NOW!"

When I asked Bobby and his friends to leave, Bobby said, "We're not makin' that expedition again. Call us a cab."

When I did, the dispatcher said, "*The* cab is out; you'll have to wait forty-five minutes." Everyone but me had a good laugh over that one.

Thus began the most bittersweet period of my life. My whole world revolved only around Bobby—everything he did, everything he said, every dream he dreamed for him and for me. I thought of nothing or no one else. I existed only for those new, magic moments when we could be together. It was a time of bliss, a time of real love—a sure-fire ticket to Heaven.

I felt better, I looked better, I sang better, and I tried to be a better person; Bobby just seemed to make a whole lot of things better.

Life took on all sorts of delicious new dimensions now that Bobby was in it. Ours was a world of starry-eyed romance, hand-holding over shared egg salad sandwiches in Hansen's drug store, and dreaming the most stupendous dreams of a future together.

Hansen's looked like ten thousand other neighborhood drug stores in ten thousand towns across America. But it wasn't. Minutes away from the big three—ABC, NBC, and CBS—it was the bustling mecca of the most talented, determined young songwriters and publishers in the country. They made the music that made New York "music city." Tin Pan Alley, they called it. People made things happen there. And now I felt a part of it all.

It was there that Bobby and his friends would congregate and talk of "making it big" some day. When I joined the group, I learned more about show business than I'd learned in all my seventeen years!

We eagerly discussed this *new* show business that

had emerged since the advent of Elvis. How a smash hit was the primary goal for any singer. Without one, you could work in dives till you turned gray. How that sound had to grab the kids, because *they* bought most of the 45s now. Since Elvis, the world of music belonged to them. Yes, the times they were a-changin'!

There sure as heck was no one in Belleville I could talk to about all this. The little world I grew up in was growing smaller every day.

After seeing these immensely hopeful young people, I'd take the bus home from the Port Authority to New Jersey. And late at night, after everyone went to sleep, I wrote voluminous words in my diary, especially about Bobby. Sometimes I memorized those words.

"Race music, hillbilly music, the blues. It's the music of the future, people," Bobby would predict. "Just look at Elvis and Ray Charles and Fats D! The real thing is still waitin' in the wings. You'll see, someday the blues *will* be pop music. And, you can't sound too educated—like you took voice lessons—'cause the kids don't dig that."

And to me: "Connie, I meant to tell you. From now on, when you sing 'ing' words, drop the *g* except on real legitimate stuff, okay?"

On another occasion at Hansen's I said to him, "Do you mean that if a record becomes a big hit outside the United States, Bobby, I could actually fly all the way to Europe or some place like that?"

Bobby smiled his warm, languid smile. "Yeah, you can fly all right, C.F. Let me tell you something. You can do *anything* in this world you wanna do when you're a star. There are rules in life for everybody, right? But if you're a star, they just don't apply to you. Stars make their own rules. They're the royalty of this country. Signs say: 'Do this,' or 'Don't do this,' and you know the signs were meant for the rest of the world, but not for you."

One day the bearded member of the group used a word like "hell" or "dammit" to me. Bobby quickly interjected, "Whoa! Back up, man, let's take that one from the top! And this time, mind your words when you're with my lady!"

Bobby had privately confided to his friends that he'd met a girl who was "not like any of the others," and that they must be careful what they said to her. "It's not that she's not smart, it's just that she's easily shocked." You see, I had become his girl.

Bobby saw in me an appealing innocence, and I was falling in love with this irresistibly sexy man. Bobby was unique, a one-of-a-kind kind of person. His enormous drive was contagious, and he had his own little "rat pack"—a select circle of fanatical devotees—long before Frank Sinatra ever thought of it, and long before anyone in show business ever heard of Bobby Darin.

Until Bobby, my social life in Belleville wasn't exactly "life in the fast lane." My sex life consisted of kisses in the dark with pimply-faced boys at "post office" or "spin the bottle" parties, which was okay with my folks—"but make sure the parents are home." Bobby soon realized how painfully naive and uninformed I was about every aspect of life and love.

I know it sounds like the tired old joke, but the one and only time I asked the question, "Ma, what's sex?" my mother quickly answered, "Never mind. Just shut up and eat your macaroni before they get cold!"

Bobby always protected me. He would delicately explain how beautiful sex could be, but "not now." He talked to me as if I'd break if he chose the wrong words.

I learned to adore him for all the reasons I always would—his respect for the little guy, his sense of fairness, his phenomenal sense of humor, his intellect, candor, and self-confidence, his brashness, toughness, and sweet tenderness—all the contrasts that made him so fascinating.

But the thing I loved most about him was how he venerated his mother, Polly—good, gentle, strong-

willed Polly—who had encouraged him to be in-
quisitive and instilled in him a love of poetry, politics,
philosophy, and good books.

She had raised him alone, along with her older
daughter Nina. Her husband, who had been a part-
time gambler and hoodlum, died in prison, from the
side effects of morphine withdrawal, before Bobby
was born.

Before his death, Bobby's entire world would col-
lapse when Nina revealed to him that Polly was really
his *grandmother*. She, his "sister" Nina, was his *real*
mother; she'd borne Bobby out of wedlock. To a man
of truth, the discovery that the very foundation of his
life was a lie must have been devastating.

Every day I learned something new and wonderful
about Bobby. And never had I been so excited about
show business. Everything till now seemed like kid
stuff. We constantly analyzed, compared, mimicked,
learned from each other, and encouraged each other;
and we were both hopeless workaholics.

Before the mirrored walls of the big rehearsal studio
next to Mr. Scheck's office, we'd practice hand and
body motions for hours. Bobby would do comedy, impersonations, and little dance routines like Donald
O'Connor. *I* tried doing dance routines too, but I've
always been the world's premiere *klutz*. (Bobby
thought I was Cyd Charisse.) He'd dance like Bill
Robinson and say, "Don't tell *me* I'm not part Negro
down deep somewhere. Man, I really feel for those
people and their music." And I fell deeper in love.

My world glistened and I glowed. All my senses
seemed keener. It was magic—*we* were magic—just
super together! But there was one fellow, by the name
of George Franconero, who did not share these rave
reviews about us.

"He's in show business," he said accusingly. "He's a
wise guy, he's a bum, and he's goin' nowhere. Why do
you hang out with garbage people?"

(Tell someone at *The National Enquirer* that if

Jeanne Dixon ever decides to retire, my father doesn't need the job.)

Our first real date in New Jersey should have been an indication of what the next period of my life would be like. My mother and I were at home in the kitchen when, from a block away, we heard the put-put-put of the decrepit Chevy Bobby had borrowed for that special night.

"What the hell is *that*—a motorboat?" my mother asked encouragingly. She knew very well it was Bobby's car. The old Italian-Jewish guilt trip again.

"It's Bobby's car," I replied on cue.

My father wasn't home and I was real glad. From him a civil "Hello, Bobby," or "You kids have a nice time," would have been impossible. Or from my mother, for that matter, whom I had learned long ago was simply an appendage of my father.

We headed for a party at the home of Donnie's girl, Linda. It was snowing heavily that night, and while the blizzard raged outside all the kids laughed and chattered, told jokes and danced to the Platters' "The Great Pretender" and "My Prayer." Except for me—I was too busy concentrating on my own prayer and that was to get home by my usual liberal 11:00 P.M. curfew. Tonight, the fifteen-minute trip home would take at least a half-hour.

Linda, a sensible girl only a year or so older than I, but with normal parents, warned, "You guys are kidding, aren't you? Connie, call your folks. Look what's going on out there. It's too dangerous. C'mon, we'll play charades, my parents will make us some breakfast, and before sunup they'll probably have the streets cleaned up."

In Linda's mind there was no way Bobby and I could leave. In mine, there was no way we could stay. The idea was preposterous, that's all! Call or no call, if I stayed out the entire night with anyone, let alone Bobby, only a major atomic attack would have been vindication. You could forget about your average tornado or earthquake.

The blizzard continued to rage on. I'll never forget the curious sight that greeted us when finally, about 2:00 A.M., we crept laboriously up the hill toward my home in Bobby's Chevy. Clad only in a robe and nightgown and standing knee-deep in snow with a flashlight in her hand—like the Italian Statue of Liberty—was my mother, waiting to yank me out of the car by my hair.

Bobby, being of sound mind and spirit, was horrified. He pleaded with me for a chance to talk "man to man" with Daddy, the real culprit of the scenario, and "end all this jazz."

But I knew that with George Franconero, no ordinary man when it came to preserving his daughter's precious virginity, the encounter would surely have ended in an exchange of blows. Bobby had always been a gentleman toward my parents, but when he realized the utter futility of any attempt to make peace with them, he reverted to the surly side of his nature.

One night, believing only my brother, Georgie, was home, Bobby stepped into the living room. He was greeted by the icy, implacable stares of my parents and by our barking dog, Mambo.

"Oh," he observed off-handedly, "it's only Mambo," and he went home.

One February night Bobby sat quietly at the piano, his hands resting on the keys, playing nothing.

"What is it, Bobby?"

"I was just thinking, baby, it's almost Valentine's Day. And, I'm so happy, I'm kinda scared of the feeling."

I sat down next to him on the piano bench. "Bobby, do other people in the world feel about each other the way we do?"

"No. No, Connie. They don't, really."

"Then what are you afraid of, Bobby?" I smiled contentedly. "Didn't anybody ever tell you that love conquers all?"

"No, it doesn't, baby," he said tenderly, wrapping me closely in his arms. "You're such a little girl. The truth of the matter is that everything conquers love—or tries to."

And then suddenly, brightly, he said: "Guess what? I have a Valentine present for you. It's all I can afford right now, but it's the best thing I have to give you, 'cause it's my favorite." And then he played and softly sang "My Funny Valentine."

8

Among My Souvenirs

AMONG my souvenirs I have some letters—I guess about a hundred of them—that might tell the world what Bobby Darin was all about. I wonder why no one close to him ever really has?

It's true that he became a polished performer and that his record of "Mack the Knife" was one of the greatest successes in recording history. It's true that he was one of Las Vegas' biggest draws and a consummate actor, nominated for an Academy Award for his role in *Captain Newman, M.D.* And it's also true that he was a composer who wrote and published several dozen hits. But, before and beneath all of that, he was a sweet and loving person.

From Buffalo he wrote: "There's a little stream in back of the club, so I kicked off my shoes, rolled up my pants, and gosh honey, I must sound silly, but it's wonderful here. I felt just like Huck Finn."

And from Indianapolis: "All I gotta say is that I'm M-I-S-E-R-A-B-L-E, so damned unhappy and miserable without you, that I feel the lump inside my throat like the one you get when you're going to cry."

And from God knows where: "Each time you pop into my mind's eye, I want to sit at the piano and write for you the most beautiful symphony the world's ever heard."

Each letter was interspersed with ILU for "I Love You" and IMU for "I Miss You," and each one meant we were apart, but not really. We had both begun that long, hard climb, Bobby soon learning what I'd learned long ago—that it was hard work to travel the road from city to city, dive to dive, radio station to radio station, DJ to DJ, record hop to record hop, from one little three- or four-dollar-a-day hotel room to the next. Bobby traveled with his best friend, Steve Karmen, who had joined the act, because at first, Bobby was afraid to do a solo act. I was with Mom, and we hit all the hot spots like the Purple Onion in Indianapolis, the Erie Social Club in Pennsylvania, and the Gay Haven Supper Club in Detroit.

After his very first show as a headliner, Bobby wrote me of his triumph from the Wolverine Hotel in Detroit (three dollars a night). "We're being held over (beginner's luck). I'm so happy, I'm flipping (ILU), but I must keep a level head (I hope) (IMU). When you said you knew I was going to make you proud of me, I felt better and greater than anyone else in this world."

And of his disasters, too: "Last night was a lulu. I just knew they weren't with me, so I tried even harder. That's what hurt most. But I don't care, really, if I know you love me."

Mr. Scheck would tell us, up front, how each new spot would be; he was always a little too enthusiastic, to say the least. "Wait till you see *this* room! Hottest spot in town!" (They were all "toilets.")

Bobby was well aware of this. He wrote: "When Mr. S. said: 'You'll love it. You're right in with the people,' he was right. The steam from the lady's soup fogged up my eyes. Oh, the club! Let me tell you about this room—and that's what it is, a room. It's about the size of your basement (so hit me for five or six feet). The stage is as big as a john. As a matter of fact, during intermission it doubles as a john."

Meanwhile, I was having my own troubles on the road. Mom and I had just checked out of a Boston hotel with healthy roaches and even healthier hookers. We took the bus to the club where I was booked to sing. The club was owned by two scary-looking, burly Italian brothers. When we entered the closet they called a dressing room, Mom took one look at the clothes rack, grabbed something from it, and with fire in her eyes, stalked in search of the two brothers.

"What the hell's this supposed to be?" she gasped to the extra-mean-looking one. "I hope it isn't what I *think* it is!"

It was a G-string—the little patch of material that belonged to the belly dancer the club had hired to appear with me on the first show. I'd never seen a G-string before.

"So?" the man sneered. "So what's the big deal, lady? There's some men's group here tonight and they want a little 'special' entertainment. What do ya think—your kid's a star or somethin'?"

"A star?" Ida roared. "I'll make you and your fat brother *see* stars! My kid and I are goin' to the movies! By the time we come back, I'd better not see your 'special entertainment' *or* her G-string. Got it?" And to the movies we went!

My mother, who is ordinarily a very shy woman, especially in show business circles, was a wall of stone, a true street fighter, when anyone ever did anything to hurt her kids.

Then there was the White Elephant—not exactly a Vegas showroom either. Oh, boy, do I ever remember the White Elephant! It was aptly named. One Saturday night I did my 2:30 A.M. third show—I kid you not—for one polluted drunk, a brother-in-law of the owner. I mean, how many times and ways could I sing "My Melancholy Baby"?

After the show, Mom and I were talking with some of the chorus girls in the community dressing room. The boorish owner entered the room and ordered, "Okay, ladies, off your butts! Time to mix with those customers! C'mon, little girls! Mix! Mix! Mix!"

I thought Ida was going to land him one of her left hooks. "Mix! Mix *who*? Mix *what*? Mix! I'll mix your head in a blender!"

When Bobby learned of these brawls I kept getting myself into, he wrote: "Honey, you're a panic. You know better than to fight with club owners. That ain't healthy! Even though he was wrong, you must be sweet, apologetic Connie, so he doesn't have anything to say. You know darned well that these guys get together and discuss acts, and they can make it miserable for you. Enough preachin' 'cause you know you can't do anything wrong in my eyes."

Some hotels didn't have a housekeeping department. At a place like the Avery in Boston (four dollars a night) one could hardly expect hot and cold running handmaidens. To my mother, it didn't matter either way; she always made the beds *before* the maid arrived. God forbid someone should think she didn't keep a clean room—someone like General George Patton, who just might happen to stop by.

Each morning she'd get up very early and, sometimes in ice and snow, find the nearest place to buy me bagels and orange juice for my breakfast. This was Ida's version of room service. Even if we hit the rare hotel that *did* have room service, who could afford it? Not this kid! Everywhere I worked it would *cost* my father money he couldn't afford, but the experience was invaluable.

The last thing either Bobby or I could afford was Western Union. But, on opening nights, I was always sure of at least one telegram—and that was the only one I really cared about.

In his letters, Bobby would often refer obliquely to his amatory adventures. From New Orleans he wrote: "Whatever you hear about New Orleans is true. (And this is from one day and two nights' experience.) But, I couldn't concentrate on what I was doing at all, and so it was a complete dud."

Bobby's encounters with other women didn't faze

me at all. After all, he didn't want pimples, and we intended to maintain my virginal status until we married.

And so he wrote: "Honey, the things you want so badly to know about life are not the things you can understand by reading 'recommended' literature. Of course, that can help you to see things from a healthier angle, but it can never make you appreciate the real beauties of life." It's hard to believe now that he was only nineteen.

Once in a rare while he even threw in a good word about George Franconero, Sr. "I'm glad to hear your dad's better, 'cause with all the trouble, if it weren't for him, there wouldn't be you."

Bobby believed that all the grueling work would turn out to be worth it. The quest for that elusive smash hit recording—the one that would make you an "overnight" star—was the gold ring.

But the kids at the record hops were, at best, lukewarm to the bomb records we kept turning out with frightening consistency. About these "winners" he wrote: "You told me about not being satisfied with 'Forgetting.' Well, move over, 'cause I just heard 'Silly Willy.' What garbage! But have faith. If Cathy Carr and Elvis Presley can make it, so can we!"

Bobby's words encouraged and inspired me. He was so positive we'd make it that he made me believe it, too. Sometimes, we'd *really* splurge and telephone each other long distance. Getting to know Bobby was a continuous learning process. He wasn't a person— he was an experience.

"Make mental notes of every move you make on that stage," he advised long distance. "Remember on stage you learn from every single show you do. You either learn something to do or something *not* to do. If a piece of business works for you, grab it— make it yours. If it doesn't, lose it! Try somethin' else!"

*   *   *

For Bobby and me our first love was performing for people on the stage. There never has been any high like it in the world.

"Last night's show was the best," Bobby wrote. "We tore the room down. I felt it as soon as I walked out. You know, honey, what I mean. Sometimes it's just there." And, "Last night's show was a gas. What a feeling it is when you have to beg off. (Enough bragging, right?)"

Neither Bobby nor I smoked, drank, or did drugs, but we were fast succumbing to the applause of the crowds—for sure, the most addictive drug of them all.

Meanwhile for me, life on the road moved merrily along. In Cleveland, Mom and I went to visit a doctor for a bladder problem I was having. The doctor must have thought he was being real cute when he chided, "Don't fool around so much with your boyfriend, and your bladder problem will straighten right out."

Mortified, I burst into tears, dashing from his office door before he had time to write the prescription. Imagine this man of medicine even *suggesting* I was "that kind of girl"!

My mother was outside looking at the bus schedule. When I sobbed to her about what the doctor had said, she stampeded back into his busy waiting room, and stormed past the startled nurse toward the doctor's consultation room.

"Just a second there, madam!" said the alarmed nurse. "The doctor is in *conference!*"

"In conference, huh? *I'll* give him a conference!"

"Madam! You'll simply have to wait with the rest!"

"Oh, no, I won't! I'm gonna *put* him to rest—real fast!"

I never really wanted to know exactly what went on between Ida and that unfortunate doctor, so I never asked.

The antipathy and overt antagonism between Bobby Darin and my father lasted a lifetime. It was sad for me when I recently heard my father tell someone about Bobby: "I always knew that kid would make it. He had too much guts, determination, and talent not to! I always admired him. He was a natural."

"Why," I ask myself, "didn't my father want a relationship for me with someone he knew was going to be a winner?" (Interesting question.)

Until the time I met Bobby, my family life had been relatively tranquil. Why not? I had always been a "very good girl," and never made waves. Not once had I ever rebelled against the rigidity of my father. Now, I wonder why.

One evening, upon arriving home from still another frowned-upon date with Bobby, I discovered my unmatched luggage (all two pieces of it) packed outside my front door. I was distraught. You might wonder why I just didn't open the door with my key and walk right in. *What* key? Italian daughters never get keys. During the day it's unnecessary, because Italian mothers are always home—in the kitchen, cooking. And if they gave you the key at night, they just might fall asleep and miss the opportunity of greeting you at the door themselves and "flooding your life with sunshine."

We both stared in disbelief at the bags. "M-m-m-m," Bobby reflected, "I always knew these Calabrese were hardheads." He was still for what seemed like an eternity. Then he dropped onto bended knees, gently took my hand in his, and ceremoniously said in a clipped British accent, "Well, m'lady, it was very good of the Franconeros, don't you think, to pack your luggage for our trip."

"Trip?" I asked, nonplused. "What trip?"

Picking up one bag in each hand, he motioned with his head for me to get into the car and said, beaming, "C'mon, Concetta, let's get ourselves married."

For a moment I hoped he might be joking, adding a little levity to this desperate and very scary situation. But he wasn't.

"Married!" I blurted. "You wanna get married *now*, Bobby? But we're so *young!*"

Bobby put the bags down, kissed me gently and held me for a long while. "I would like you to be my wife, my friend, my partner for life, and the mother of my children. Don't you see? I cherish you because you are every single thing I've ever considered right, important, and beautiful in my life. Get in the car, C.F."

Bobby was animated and optimistic about our future together as we headed for God-knows-where. "We can work like an Italian Nelson Eddy and Jeanette MacDonald, right, baby?" Then his voice softened. "No, we won't. We'll just be two good, happy people. When we wake up together each morning and I see my little girl with her happy face hangin' out, then I'll be happy, too—'cause you're such a part of me."

My heart was breaking. While Bobby dreamed of a white house with a picket fence, I foresaw something else—a funeral! Ours! "My father will kill the both of us, Bobby!"

"No one is going to kill anyone. I'm a big, strong guy, and *you*—you're my little baby, and I'll never let anyone hurt you, not ever."

"Bobby, where will we live?" I cried. "How will we *eat?*" Food was such an important thing to me, and I was remembering how, since our very first time at Hansen's Drug Store, not *once* could we ever afford one whole egg salad sandwich each. I was always running around starved.

"Please, Bobby! In six months you won't be able to stand me. You'll hate our life if it stands in the way of your career, and it *will!*" The thought of Bobby going out to look for a job somewhere, like a civilian, sent shivers up my spine. I never really believed we could actually make a living in show business. It always *cost* my father money!

"I'll make it all turn out right," he said, undaunted. "You'll see, baby."

"I'm so scared, Bobby," I wailed in a Niagara of tears. "I'm really not as grown-up as you think I am!"

"That's exactly what I love most about you. You're

not all grown-up yet, but you're also my woman . . . an unbeatable combination. Don't knock it, Concetta."

He pulled the car over to the side of the road and, wiping my tears away with his hanky, said, "Are you my baby?" I nodded. He kissed me gently—a hundred baby-feathered kisses on my face, neck, and fingers.

"If you love me, then have some faith in my judgment. I can't take your father any more. I won't! I've gotta end all this noise once and for all. Don't you realize that if you go home now, the man will definitely be the world's number one undisputed champion tyrant of all times?"

I wasn't listening very hard. I was too busy concentrating on what was going to happen to my life when I got home.

"Bobby, don't be angry with me," I sniffled. "I love you so much, but please—*please* take me home! I've gotta go home *now. Please!*"

I was quite desperate; Bobby was quite serious. I knew that, because he called me "Connie."

"In that case, Connie, we can't be with each other any more."

"Ever?" I said with trepidation.

"Not till I assess this whole thing, and my head's on straight." I was afraid to ask what that meant, so I said nothing.

"Someday, Connie—someday very soon—I'm never going to have to say 'sir' again. Not to anybody."

We stood there shivering in the cold night air. He cupped my face in his hands and said sadly, "You know, I'm a dreamer—a real Pollyanna. I actually believed no one could ever come into our world."

9

Breakin' in a Brand-New Broken Heart

If my friends should ask for me
Here at home is where I'll be
There's no one else I care to see
I'm BREAKIN' IN A BRAND-NEW BROKEN HEART

Let me take the count of ten
Then I'll bounce right back again
Let me be alone till then
I'm BREAKIN' IN A BRAND-NEW BROKEN HEART*

In the several months since I'd seen Bobby, life had become a Greek tragedy. Everything that could possibly go wrong, did. The world was a colorless, joyless, hostile place. It was a time of mourning for me. And I mourned *everything*.

I mourned Bobby, as if he had died; I mourned the loss of my youth; I mourned the ugly house we were living in; I mourned my career which was crumbling down all around me; I mourned the day my parents met; but most especially, I mourned the night I was conceived.

The thought of living another day without the bright prospect of seeing Bobby was almost unbearable. My heart hurt. Now I knew what the words to all those love-gone-wrong songs really meant. And I was convinced I'd never sing another love song that wouldn't be my own private tribute to Bobby—the only man I thought I'd ever love.

Even today, I never dismiss a teenage romance as "just puppy love," because I remember Bobby and me and the depth of our feelings. When we're young we feel all kinds of emotions more strongly than we ever will again. We've yet to become inured to pain and disappointment. We're more fragile, uninitiated, and very often, not taken seriously. If just one more grown-up had said to my parents, "Don't worry. She'll get over it," I would have had an apoplectic fit.

Here we were! Right back in scenic Newark, in our ugly "new" house. I was helping my father put up the bedroom wallpaper I had chosen; it was black with white stripes. I chose black just in case my parents were curious about what kind of mood I was in. Yup! Black paper with teeny white stripes reminded me of jail. Why not? It was a fitting touch, wasn't it, for my dismal new bedroom in my dismal new house?

We had to sell our pretty little middle-class house in Belleville, because my father, who has a Depression mentality, who eagerly predicts the imminent end of the world on a daily basis and who *never* takes chances—took a chance.

He'd invested all the money he'd saved during his twenty-three-year marriage—a $15,000 fortune—in some kind of bleach they used to sell to Italian housewives in Newark; he'd lost the $15,000 *and* the house.

The wallpaper ($1.75 a double roll) was the only luxury item my mother had allowed in our rented three-family "estate," with its exposed radiators (like in the olden days) and its uncarpeted wooden floors that put splinters in my feet whenever I was stupid enough to walk barefoot.

The house was rented because even *we* weren't

dumb enough to buy it. To add to my joy, we'd left suburbia only to land in this tacky neighborhood. It was the worst place we'd ever lived in.

And my heart ached so for Bobby. I confided my misery to the only sympathetic ear around—my diary. It would have been futile to talk with my parents.

For me to express even the slightest interest or admiration for a boy was a true act of valor. It really bugged my parents, especially my father, who was happy only when I was talking music.

On the rare occasions when I did manage to say something flattering about a boy in school, I was invariably greeted by the same healthy response—icy silence. After a while, I gave up.

The day after my abortive "elopement" with Bobby, my father stormed into George Scheck's office like a one-man Panzer division; he was livid. In his usual conciliatory voice, he demanded: "Get ridda that bum! Make up your mind, Scheck! Dump Bobby or I'm takin' my daughter away from you. You can't manage them both! I don't want Connie runnin' into that wise guy in this office any more."

George Scheck had developed a very special relationship with Bobby; he was the closest thing to a father Bobby had ever known. And now he was in a real quandary over this latest and most unreasonable ultimatum.

Reluctantly, he summoned Bobby to his office. "Bobby, you've got more talent than anyone else out there," he said sympathetically, "and you're gonna make it to the top. But I can't manage you any more."

For a long time Bobby just stared at the floor, visibly shaken as Mr. Scheck continued. "Try to understand, Bobby. Connie's been with me since she was a little girl, and my loyalty belongs to her."

I *had* been with Mr. Scheck before Bobby ever appeared on the scene—four years and a $17,000 investment before. When Bobby finally looked up at him, George Scheck found it hard to meet his gaze. There was no further need for words as Bobby, his eyes brimming with tears, left the office—a broken human being and out on the streets again.

My father returned from his successful mission and announced, "Well at least now I won't have to lay eyes on that son-of-a-b——— again."

I was speechless with rage. To be even more precise, I became Helen Keller. I said nothing. I saw nothing. And, I heard nothing. I just grunted a lot— but only when a response was absolutely necessary to my survival.

What had happened to our happy home? The battle lines were now clearly drawn; for the first time ever, it was open warfare—the two wardens against the little Italian kid—and they were leading 20–0.

From that day on, if such a thing was possible, it was downhill all the way. Well, at least MGM hadn't given up on me—yet. Poor MGM. I felt guilty. The bombs just kept a-comin'. They were becoming my trademark, a foregone conclusion.

I wondered what it must feel like to be somebody really important like Joni James, who had become MGM's darling in the early fifties, with a long string of hits. A little bird told me that whenever she did a promotional tour, MGM put her up in a $35-a-day suite— inconceivable to me.

When George Scheck was sick one day, I had to go alone to MGM to keep a 12:30 appointment with none other than the president of MGM himself. I badly wanted to make a favorable impression, so I made a valiant effort to appear perky—no mean feat these days. In recent months, I'd been looking as if I'd died three years before, and no one had had the heart to tell me about it.

I waited and waited. The president was in a very important meeting with none other than Miss Joni James and some of the MGM attorneys. The receptionist said they were "not to be disturbed."

After five hours of perkiness—while Miss James,

the president, and all of his men were still in conference, and all the secretaries and other employees had gone for the day—I left, too, dejected and rejected. Bobby had hit the nail on the head, all right: "Stars are the royalty of America."

Well, coping with being a star was one thing I wouldn't have to worry about any more. Some time during that day, MGM told George Scheck how "terribly sorry" they were, but my next record would be my swan song—the last for the label. Who could blame them? They'd spent enough money on sessions that had produced nothing but bombs.

The only *guaranteed* sale of a Connie Francis record was to a steady customer named George Franconero, Sr. He always bought at least two boxes (fifty) of each new record "to give to George the butcher, that guy Tony who owns the Gulf station, and Phil, who's got the fish store Down Neck." (That's what some people still call our old Italian neighborhood.)

The Great White Way wasn't exactly knocking down my door either. But, after thirty-five unsuccessful auditions for Broadway or off-Broadway shows, I had the feeling that *this* audition was gonna be the Big One.

The audition was for *West Side Story*, and they wanted young, talented people. Going in, I had one big advantage—I could easily look Spanish.

I was in especially good voice that day, so I selected a song you really had to belt out, Jerome Kern's "Can't Help Lovin' That Man" with one of those Big Paramount Picture endings I always love to sing; I call them my "money notes."

When I arrived at the rehearsal hall, I couldn't believe what I saw. Every girl singer in America, Puerto Rico, and Italy was there. And seated behind a long, skinny table was a panel of long, skinny people who looked constipated. And these good folk would be deciding the futures of this roomful of wall-to-wall girl singers!

But I wasn't the least bit intimidated. Why should I be? After all, how many kids my age had had over five years of experience on TV? And, what about that recording contract that was *not* about to be renewed? What was *I* worried about, anyway?

I studied each girl with great interest as she performed. One girl was singing a song with a long special arrangement—six whole piano pages worth. Suddenly, toward the end of the fifth page, the female member of the panel, who looked like the boss, interrupted the singer. Stiffly, she told her good-bye and said they'd "be in touch."

She'd better not hold her breath, I thought. These people are outrageous—especially that barracuda making all the decisions, the one with the personality like a lox! The nerve to interrupt that poor girl before she had a chance to get to the sixth page. How dehumanizing! How rude and unprofessional!

Then it was my turn. Pulling myself up to my full five-foot-one, I placed my biography and 8x10s on the skinny table and strutted over to a very bored-looking piano player. Confidently, I handed him my blockbuster ballad, the one that was sure to win me at least the lead and put me in clover.

And, even more confidently, I said: "Okay, folks, I'll begin whenever you're ready."

The lox nodded.

Singing in my very best Mario Lanza voice, just a split second after the first two bars of the song: "Fish gotta swim, birds gotta fly," I heard: "Okay! That's it! Trained voice! Next!"

I picked up my music, and walked out the door, startled and embarrassed, but so happy for Ethel Merman and Mary Martin, whose careers were no longer in immediate danger.

Things just had to pick up. And, for a change, I was correct. I was going to do something I'd never even dreamed of—a screen test for the lead in a real motion picture, the forgettable *Rock, Rock, Rock.*

I wanted to look really spiffy that day, so it took

only forty-eight hours to get in shape. I had my ponytail restyled into the latest Gina Lollobrigida Italian-boy haircut with the spit curls; I really blew the budget on a sixteen-dollar dress at Klein's Department Store in Newark; and I treated myself to my first legitimate manicure at Bamberger's beauty salon.

During the screen test, I was halfway through the first page when something pertinent occurred to me I hadn't even considered before: I had to be able to *act* to play the lead in this movie. And, as an actress, I was always a good daughter.

When Mr. Scheck failed to mention the results of the audition for nearly two months, I surmised that someone else landed the lead. I was right again! It was some kid named Tuesday Weld, who was pretty.

If I had any doubts about whether *I* was pretty or not, they were quickly dispelled. It was the rare audition when at least one critic failed to say to Mr. Scheck or my father: "She's too short." "Her nose is too big." "She's too fat." "Don't waste your time." "She's not show business material." And, finally, the unkindest cut of all: "That girl's got nothing."

"Well," I reflected sadly, "it's a good thing that for the first time in recorded history, the whole world is in accord."

And, it was most considerate of these people never to talk about me behind my back. They always made sure I was within earshot of these accolades.

But, all wasn't lost—not by a long shot! Hollywood *was* beckoning; they *did* want me for the film! I was handed my first triumph in a long time—a real plum. I got to be Tuesday Weld's singing voice in the picture!

"*This* straw," I wailed, "just broke the camel's back!"

There were going to be a few changes now; I had to have some direction in my life. If only Bobby were around. He'd know what to do. He always did; Bobby always made everything right.

But, Bobby wasn't around, so, against my religion,

I was forced to have a discussion with my parents. I'd decided that the world of show business was just going to have to make it without me. I was going to go back to college, to study premed at Rutgers University. I was certain I could get another scholarship.

I knew my father would be tempted to take the gas pipe when he found out. How could I *do* this to him? How could I dream of abandoning my illustrious career? It was like committing patricide. After all, I'd only been struggling fourteen years now! What did I expect—a miracle?

My mother couldn't care less about show business; she was upset about something else. My brother Georgie's dream was to be a lawyer, and he had been accepted to Alabama University. My parents really needed some extra money.

I realized we might be forced to wait a few months before we bought that summer home down the Jersey shore, the Swiss chalet, the speedboat, and the condo in Miami Beach. Finances were tight, all right, but what the heck! We had all the money we'd ever need, unless we wanted to buy something—like food.

After some guilt-producing soul-searching, I abandoned my college plans with a heavy heart. Italian girls didn't have to go to college, anyway. What for? To go find themselves a husband there? They could accomplish the same thing in an office or a factory. Grow up, Italian girls!

Well, if nothing else, there was consistency in my life. My bad luck continued uninterrupted by any bright spots.

Aunt Marie always said I had the ability to do anything in life I made up my mind to do. So, I decided to take her up on her word. I visited her at her office at the Fireman's Fund Insurance Company in Newark and applied for a job.

After demonstrating my filing, typing, and stenographic skills, I waited at her office for some response. And, as I waited I reviewed, just like Clive Barnes, the performances of all these people who were making my life miserable.

I really shouldn't be too harsh on Mom, I thought; I had her to thank for one thing. Just think, if she hadn't been such a snoop—forget the CIA folks—and peeked in my diary every day, I wouldn't have been compelled to send for the *Gregg Book of Shorthand* and learn it out of self-defense and every human being's need for some privacy.

Without *her* input, where would I be now? Not *here*, waiting hopefully for some word about this potentially unspectacular job. It suddenly occurred to me that winning the New Jersey State Championship at age fifteen wasn't such a big deal after all; the whole thing was *goishe nachas!* (Jewish people use this expression to mean: "Only non-Jews could get excited or be proud of achievements such as these.")

When I got home, I could hardly wait to inform my parents that there was going to be an additional breadwinner in the house. "I'm gonna be a file clerk, a typist, and a stenographer at Aunt Marie's office," I said with a measure of satisfaction. Daddy, as usual, did his utmost to encourage me.

"Don't feel too bad. You're not the first failure that ever was!" It was always so kind of him to try to cheer me on. Besides, how could I type and be the world's biggest recording star at the same time?

The next day George Scheck told me he had a spot for me on CBS's "Jackie Gleason Show." In view of the fact that I wasn't even a semi-legend yet, this was an impressive thing. But not impressive enough to change my retirement plans. My brother's dream was law school; *my* dream would have to take second money for now.

I dreaded telling Mr. Scheck that as soon as I cut my last record, I was going to quit the business and leave all this glitter and glamour behind.

Earlier that day, I'd gone to the bank to withdraw all the funds I had amassed since I'd started my show business career fourteen years before—a fat five hundred dollars! I calculated that this came to thirty-five dollars a year or sixty-seven cents a week. It was obvious to me that from singing, I'd never make a living.

Poor George Scheck! He had invested over $17,000 in me. And now I was acting like Benedict Arnold's illegitimate daughter.

I handed him the five hundred dollars, vowing that if I had to type until I was a hundred and twelve, I'd repay all the rest to make up for the misplaced faith he'd shown in me.

Within a year of the day I gave Mr. Scheck the five hundred dollars, I was well on my way toward earning my first million dollars. I didn't think about it much at the time. And even now, it doesn't seem all that important.

How many times have we heard people say: "Things always seem darkest before the dawn"? I was always dumb enough to believe that Communist lie. What the great muses neglect to tell us is that soon after a *very* short dawn, things go right back to where they were— but even bleaker and darker than before the dawn showed up.

Thus, I wasn't at all prepared for what happened that fateful day of "The Jackie Gleason Show." After all, what or who could *possibly* spoil this day? This wonderful day in the life of suddenly the happiest girl in the U.S. of A.? "Happy" is not the word, because just the night before, somebody had handed me my life back.

The phone rang and it was my Bobby. He decided we just shouldn't face another grim, empty day apart. Bobby said he would come to my camera rehearsal the next day.

"We have so much to talk about, C.F. This time we're gonna deal a little differently with some of those good folk. This time we're gonna make it all work out. I promise you that, honey. You're *my* little girl now."

The conversation was romantic and wonderful. The

world and every human being in it was romantic and wonderful. Bobby, of course, was Mister Wonderful incarnate. And I? Well, that day absolutely nothing or no one could rain on this gal's parade!

Wanna bet? If I live to be three hundred, I shall never forget that day of the Gleason show at CBS on Broadway and Fifty-third. Forget Pearl Harbor, guys! It's this day, in *my* mind, that will live in infamy.

I was afraid my heart was going to burst at the seams. It wasn't used to this much happiness anymore, especially the soaring kind I felt as Bobby and I cuddled together at the studio during the camera run-through, clutching each other's hands tightly.

Although so much had happened in the months since we'd seen each other, it was as if we'd never been apart.

We spoke few words; they weren't necessary. We didn't care to talk small talk or even to dream big dreams. We just wanted to revel in our togetherness or, as Bobby put it, in "coming home again."

When it came time to block my song on camera, I sang "When You're Smiling" as if smiling and being happily in love were about the only two things anyone sane in the whole wide world should be doing. But by air time that night, the whole world turned upside down.

The startling event that followed is like *Rashomon*—you know, the Japanese movie in which three different persons give an eye-witness account of a horrendous crime, each account significantly different.

First, there's *my* account of what happened that day, which shouldn't be taken all that seriously, in view of the fact that I was in total shock at the time.

Then there's the George Scheck version, which is probably closest to the truth. He remembers well Daddy's quaint entrance, as he barged through the stage door, brandishing a firearm like some kind of hit man from out of town and hotly announcing his intention to obliterate Bobby once and for all.

A terrified George Scheck, his young assistant Joey

Kahn, Bobby's good friend Dick Lord, and another fellow restrained my father while George Scheck excitedly shouted, "Run, Bobby, run!"

Then we have George Franconero's updated version. Just recently, he said in disgust: "Did you read the Darin biography?"

"Yes. As a matter-of-fact, I read it only a few days ago."

"It says in the book that I had a gun."

"Yes, I know that. Did you?"

"I went there to knock his goddamned block off! I could-a done it with both hands tied behind my back. What the hell did I need a gun for?" Then after a moment's contemplation: "I'm suin' all of them."

"That's heavy duty," I said. "Who? Just whom are you suing? And on what grounds?"

"Don't worry about that—I have grounds. The bastards!"

"I'm not sure about that, Daddy. I don't think you can sue a writer or publisher for telling the truth."

"Oh, yeah? Who's gonna prove it?"

"Well, *there* you may have a point, Daddy," I conceded. "Bobby won't contradict you, because he's dead. *I* won't, because I didn't *see* whether you had a gun or not." (Besides, Italian girls are enjoined from testifying against their fathers.)

"And George Scheck," I continued, "he's your friend, so he won't testify against you, either. Come to think of it, you just might have a strong case. The only stumbling block *I* can foresee is the testimony of the three men it took to restrain you from murdering Bobby . . . or maybe that of the other seventy-two witnesses at CBS that day."

Wisely, he abandoned any immediate plans for litigation.

All I can say for certain is that the dress rehearsal went swimmingly until I neared the end of the song's tag:

> So, if you're smiling
> I said, smiling

> I do mean smiling
> Then this great big world will smile at . . .*

I heard a cacophony of sound before I could reach the word "you" like World War III had begun in earnest. I heard a voice shout, "Run, Bobby, run!" I saw Bobby, who'd been watching me on the TV monitor, leap from his seat and dart through the rows of empty seats up the aisle toward the men's room (from where, I learned later, he escaped through a window).

I've often thought that if the studio, the men's room, and the window had been on the thirty-second floor of a skyscraper and not on the ground floor, the world of music would surely have suffered a major loss.

My memory's not bad, but if one were to press me about exactly what I did after that harrowing episode, I'd have to invent something. I was so unnerved by the entire explosive incident that the only thing I can recall is what happened that night on the actual live broadcast.

How I wish my memory would fail me for a change. But unfortunately I've replayed that scene in my mind a thousand times, as if on some kind of videotape.

I was wearing one of those fitted, voguish hourglass gowns, I hadn't worn at rehearsal, the kind with the fishnet bottom that flared out like Esther Williams as a mermaid. It was so tight at my calves and ankles that I was able to take only teeny-weeny Geisha girl steps to reach center stage and the overhead microphone.

The usual four-bar introduction to "Smiling" just didn't give me enough time to reach my mark and begin singing the song. I knew I had to start somewhere, but it wasn't going to be at the beginning. It was too late for that, because the orchestra had already *played* the beginning without me.

---

* "When You're Smiling" by Mark Fisher, Joe Goodwin, and Larry Shay. © 1928 by Mills Music, Inc. Copyright renewed. Used by permission. All rights reserved.

Still shocked from the earlier incident between my father and Bobby, I did not have both oars in the water, which largely contributed to the most pathetic and embarrassing live TV show I've ever done.

I simply forgot the words—*all* of the words! I think I managed a *few* words, but they happened to belong to another song, a minor goof I'm sure no one even noticed—unless they happened to be watching me on TV that night.

"Why me, God?" I asked. When I finished "Smiling" I left the stage looking as if I'd died. Backstage, not a single member of the normally friendly, encouraging crew could muster up a single word of consolation.

But if it was words I yearned for, I didn't have to wait too long for that. In a pinch, I could always depend on George Franconero.

"When that son-of-a-b——— is around you, you forget your own name!" he alleged, with stunning disregard for the role *he'd* played that day.

On the telephone to Bobby from the theater that night, I was in torrents of tears. And, I knew that if he said just one wrong word I'd make a total fool of myself.

"Did you see it?" I asked in a little-girl-lost voice.

"Take it easy, baby. It's okay," he said soothingly. "Listen to me, honey. Tonight was just one little step backward; tomorrow it'll be twenty-one steps forward. The world's yours, sweetheart. I've always told you that. You're gonna be the number one lady singer of all time. And I'll do some good ol' tunes, too.

"It's all gonna happen, C.F. Years from now, when you're a big star and no one can ever touch you or hurt you again, you'll laugh about everything that happened today. Someday when we're both very, very old, we'll laugh about it together—you'll see. In this vast world, sweetheart, who loves you?"

"You do, Bobby."

And he never called again.

Lincoln Tunnel, Jersey Side
December 1, 1960
Opening night of my first
    Copacabana appearance,
New York City

It sounds corny now, I know, but even years later hope always sprang eternal in my heart. The hope—no, the full expectation, really—that somehow, sometime, somewhere, some way, Bobby and I would be able to be together, this time forever.

And so it was, on that day, December 1, 1960, as my father and I were driving to New York, approaching that great big curve which leads to the Lincoln Tunnel. That moment for me is frozen in time. It's like another moment three years later, on November 22, 1963, when just about all of us remember exactly where we were and what we were doing when we heard of the assassination of our president; one doesn't ever forget.

The big clock above the tunnel entrance said 9:55 A.M.; the radio said something else.

"Entertainer Bobby Darin and motion picture actress Sandra Dee were married earlier this morning by a Newark magistrate. The popular couple will spend their honeymoon in Los Angeles."

While I held my stomach with both my hands to keep from vomiting, my father, without batting an eyelash, said: "Well, it looks like that bastard is finally outta my hair!"

I knew I was going to become very ill, but at this moment, I had no desire, time, nor room in my life for illness. I wanted something far more dramatic to befall both me and my father. (I definitely didn't want to leave my father out of what I wished for us.)

I wished that somehow God would cause the Hudson River to come gushing in and entrap us in that tunnel; that one gigantic tidal wave from Hawaii would swallow up the car, me, and last—but certainly not least—my father. Anything would be better—anything at all—than reaching the other side of the tunnel and the cruel world that waited just outside it.

For my father, it was VE day. For me, well, I was an old Parisian lady sobbing openly on the Champs Élysées because the Nazis had just occupied my world.

PART TWO

10

Who's Sorry Now?

WHO'S SORRY NOW, WHO'S SORRY NOW
Whose heart is aching for breakin' each vow
Who's sad and blue, who's cryin' too
Just like I cried over you *

ONE November day in 1957, I wrote in my diary:

Dear Diary:
Mr. Scheck called today and said GAC would like
to set up a publicity date for me with a young fellow
they also have under contract—a date for the pre-
miere of Pat Boone's new film, April Love.

"C'mon, Mr. Scheck, give me a break! You know
I've been dating that boy Pete from Long Island and
I've *never* gone on one of those fake publicity dates
yet. I hate that phony stuff! Who *is* he, this fella, anyway?"

"I dunno, but I think you should go. You might get
to meet Pat Boone. But look, if you don't wanna go,
then don't go—it's up to you. All I know is that he's
recording on some label in Philly."

"Well, I'm not sure about this whole thing, Mr. Scheck. He could turn out to be a real stiff."

"Look, Connele, if you're so uncomfortable about it, I'll come with you, or else, his manager said he'd be glad to take the two of you."

"Well, what else did they say about him?" I asked warily. "Is he a nice fella?"

"Call up GAC. They'll tell you about him. Just let me know what you wanna do."

"Look, Mr. Scheck, I've never even been introduced to the boy. Okay, okay. I'll call."

"Is he a nice person?" I asked the GAC agent.

"How the heck do *I* know? He's from Philly—that's all I know," the impatient agent replied.

"Well," I asked tentatively, "is he dating anybody?"

"Look, Connie, for all I know, he could have eleven kids and a bride in a tree in Tahiti somewhere." It was a real fishing expedition.

"How old is he? Is he younger than eighteen? 'Cause if he is, I won't date any—"

"Look, Connie, whadda you want us to do—hire a private investigator?"

"Well, just tell me how old he is, at least."

"I think he's seventeen."

"You mean he's a year *younger* than I am?" I exclaimed, terribly distressed.

"Yeah. So what's wrong with that?"

"What's *wrong*? What's wrong is that at the age of eighteen, I don't have to start robbing the cradle!"

"I don't believe this," said the jaded agent. "Look, Connie, you're not doing me any favors. Don't go! I just thought maybe you'd like to see a first-class movie premiere."

Agents are smart; he knew he had me there. I'd never been to a big-time premiere before. I was so upset about the age difference between the boy and me that when I hung up I forgot to ask his name. When I called the agent back, he told me: "Frankie Avalon."

When the night of the premiere arrived, I took the bus to the Port Authority in New York alone. I wore my most special outfit; a black velvet top with a scoop neckline, a wide cinch belt, and a white organza skirt with a horsehair crinoline beneath it. My mother thought it was far too sophisticated.

"It's too low in front," she observed.

"Where? You can't see a thing."

"Go ahead. You always do what you wanna do, anyway. Who the hell can talk to you?"

"No, you're right this time, Ma. I'll wear something *you* like instead! Why don't you go downstairs to the basement and dig out one of my old 'Startime Kids' jumpers?" I wore what I wanted for a change.

At the bus terminal, a stranger approached me.

"You Connie Francis? Frankie's waiting for you." On a long wooden bench sat my date, Frankie Avalon. As soon as he saw me, he jumped up and introduced himself.

I took one look at him and he was so gorgeous, I was afraid I'd swoon right on the spot, which wouldn't have been cool at all. The fellow was a living doll; he wore a tomato-red blazer, gray flannels, and white bucks.

The stranger, who turned out to be Frankie's manager, Bob Marcucci, said we had about an hour to kill. "Why don't we take a ride through Central Park," he suggested.

As we rode in the horse-drawn hansom cab, Frankie spoke: "Hey, Con," he said animatedly, "do you like Frank Sinatra?"

"Do I like Frank Sinatra!" I shouted, as if I'd just discovered plutonium. "Are you kidding? I'm crazy about him! For my birthday, I buy myself nothing but Sinatra albums."

"Wow! That's the end, Con!"

Well, that was the real icebreaker! From that moment on, all we did was talk Frank Sinatra. Frank Sinatra was Frankie Avalon's whole life. He went into rhapsodies about Sinatra's latest album, the way he dressed (Frankie said he liked the way his shirt cuffs peeked out from under his jacket), the way he used words like "broad" and "pally," and so on and so on. Before long we felt like lifelong friends.

At premiere time a light snow began to fall. We got into a taxi at Fifty-ninth Street and Central Park and as we approached the Roxy Theater with its large "klieg" lights, we saw a master of ceremonies with a microphone standing outside, and television cameras and photographers all over the place.

As each limousine arrived, the fans excitedly peered inside to see who was in it. When they took a look inside our taxi cab and saw only Frankie and me, they couldn't contain their disappointment. We heard a unanimous and depressing: "Nah, forget about it. It's nobody."

Frankie and I looked at each other pathetically. Then we heard a big commotion behind us and turned to see Joan Collins, Robert Wagner, and Tab Hunter. The fans practically trampled us just to get a glimpse of them.

Frankie looked so downcast, he made me forget how miserable I felt.

"Hey, Con," he lamented, "you'd think somebody would've noticed my white bucks, thought I was Pat Boone, and asked for my autograph."

Seeing the movie made Frankie and me even more despondent. "Con, *now* I'm really disgusted! I've been in this business my whole life, and I'm still nowhere."

"Let's face it, Frankie," I offered consolingly, "not everybody can be in the movies."

"Yeah, I know, Con, but it all started out so great. I even had a teenage nightclub, and I danced once on 'The Jackie Gleason Show'. Everybody said, Frankie, you're in! But nothin'. I haven't had one record that's even made a little noise. Let's face it, Con, I'm just a big flop."

"Believe me, Frankie," I commiserated, "you're not alone. If my new record, 'Who's Sorry Now?' doesn't take off like yesterday, I'm giving up myself. It's too

Connie with Dick Clark. Dick, always one of Connie's biggest fans, introduced "Who's Sorry Now?" on national television.

Above: The Startime Kids. Connie (at thirteen) is at far left, producer (soon to become her manager) George Scheck at right, and the legendary Milton Berle center rear. *Left:* Connie's grandmother's house in Newark, where she lived from age three to five.

Right: Connie with Neil Sedaka in 1959. Neil helped write some of her biggest hits, before his own career took off.
Below: Connie sings to a packed Carnegie Hall.

Above: Connie preparing for her NBC-TV special in 1961. That's an intent George Scheck in the background. *Below:* One of Connie's proudest moments was starring on the top-rated "Ed Sullivan Show."

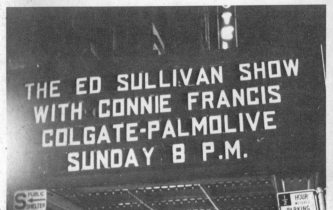

THE ED SULLIVAN SHOW
WITH CONNIE FRANCIS
COLGATE-PALMOLIVE
SUNDAY 8 P.M.

Connie often appeared on national TV. Above, with Tab Hunter on her own special; below, in a skit with Jack Benny on his TV show.

Left: Connie and Danny Thomas in a scene from one of her movies. *Below:* Connie meets Queen Elizabeth and Prince Philip after a Command Performance in Glasgow.

Connie was given the "This Is Your Life" treatment by Ralph Edwards. Above, surrounded by family and friends, she holds her brother Georgie's hand; below, a touching reunion with Bobby Darin.

KING AND QUEEN OF HEARTS

Bobby Darin and Connie Francis, elected King and Queen of Hearts in a nationwide poll of disc jockeys, are asking deejays and juke box operators to "turn the tables on heart disease" in behalf of the 1960 Heart Fund Campaign. They will appear on the Ed Sullivan show Feb. 28 and made special appearances on NBC's "Monitor" last weekend.

HEART-TO-HEART

Above: Former sweethearts Connie and Bobby Darin were named King and Queen of Hearts in a nationwide disc jockey poll in 1960. Right: Connie and Bobby Darin sing a duet on "The Ed Sullivan Show."

tough a business. My record's been out two months now, and nothing. And you know what they say. If it doesn't break through in a few markets in three or four weeks—it's all over."

"Me, too. My new record, 'Dee Dee Dinah,' is as big a flop as I am. Con, we don't have a shot at all, do we?"

"I don't know about *your* chances, Frankie, but with *my* luck, if I *do* get a hit, the next morning the universe will run out of phonograph needles."

"I'll tell you the truth, Con. Tonight did it for me— I've turned the corner. *I'm* givin' up, too."

"Okay, then! Let's shake on it!" I said, resolutely. "Let's look at it this way—at least we've made a firm decision."

"It's a deal!" We shook on our mutual failure and our less-than-rosy future.

Outside the theater, newspaper photographers were taking hundreds of flash pictures of all the big stars; the brass band from Columbia University was playing lively marching songs, and all the fans were squealing. But not of course, for Frankie and me. Frankie looked so dejected that I had to say, "Frankie, forget about these kids. Who needs 'em? To *me*, you're America's number one teenage idol."

"Con," he smiled warmly, "to me, you're Number One with a *Billboard* bullet. Incidentally, I've wanted to tell you all night I love you in that dress."

I flipped! I absolutely flipped, that's all! Sorry, Mom, you were wrong, as usual. He loves my dress! I made a silent vow to wear it if ever I saw him again. See him again? What a joke! Where? Behind my typewriter in Aunt Marie's office? Dream on, Italian kid from Newark.

> Right to the end, just like a friend
> I tried to warn you somehow
> You had your way, now you must pay
> I'm glad that you're sorry now.*

January 1, 1958
Newark, New Jersey
4:00 P.M.

One day, with the flick of a switch, I became a star.
Deep inside I've never really felt like one.

The day started off like every other New Year's Day
I could remember, with festivity in the air, a ton of
relatives, and enough of Ida's food to feed Ecuador.

But, it would prove to be unlike all the rest for this
January first marked the beginning of a totally new life
for me—one that would never be the same because of
it.

Precisely at 4:00 P.M., I excused myself from the
dinner table. Like 8.5 million other loyal teenagers, I
tuned our black and white 16-inch Motorola to ABC's
"American Bandstand" and its host and my idol, Dick
Clark.

"American Bandstand" had become a way of life for
most of us. I'll bet there wasn't a lonely teenager in all
of America because of that show; it united us. It was
as if we were all together at a giant rock 'n' roll party.

How could a teenage girl feel lonely when she knew
for certain that just about every other girl in the country was doing exactly what she was doing? We were
comrades, with a tacit, national esprit de corps. And,
we were never alone, not with 8.5 million of us united
by a strong common bond.

Besides, it was always happier in the house when
"Bandstand" was on. With its 40 percent lion's share
rating, it was daytime TV's number one show ever. It
literally changed the face of the American pop music
scene, and it was the one sure-fire vehicle that cata-
pulted unknowns to superstardom overnight.

Mr. Clark's young Philadelphians, the kids who
danced on the show, set the trends in everything—
clothes, fads, slang, dance, and music. If Carol de-

cided to change the color of her hair, a lot of us thought maybe we should try it, too.

To me, Dick Clark was something of a deity. He was Americana personified—like the Lincoln Memorial or Philly's Liberty Bell. In vicarious rapture, I gazed as Justine and Bob slow-danced while Sam Cooke expressed their sentiments with "You Send Me." I danced along with little Peggy, trying to learn her newest steps as she tore it up "At the Hop." I watched that attractive pair, Fran and Mike, do a mean lindy to Jerry Lee's "Great Balls of Fire," and Arlene and Kenny lead "The Stroll."

I heard Dick Clark mention something about a new girl singer. So, what else is new? I thought. Ninety-five million females in the country, and I'll bet ninety-five percent of them sing songs.

"There's no doubt about it," predicted Mr. Clark. "She's headed straight for the number one spot."

I began feeling sorry for myself and a bit envious, too. Good luck to her, I thought. And then Mr. Clark just happened to play a song called "Who's Sorry Now?"—MY "Who's Sorry Now?"

Well, the feeling was cosmic—just cosmic! Right there in my own living room, it became Mardi Gras time, the kickoff at the Super Bowl, and New Year's Eve at the turn of a century.

The ruckus I raised was startling enough to tear thirty-odd ravenous Italians away from their mountainous portions of manicotti, and everybody knows that's no mean feat!

"Daddy! Mom! Hurry up!" I squealed. "Georgie! Aunt Marie! Quick! Dick Clark is playing 'Who's Sorry Now?'"

"Oh, yeah? Someone else cut the thing, too, huh?" Daddy said with customary optimism.

"No, no, Daddy! Listen! It's *my* 'Who's Sorry Now?'"

"Nah. Can't be. It's been out too long. The thing's dead."

"Daddy, for godssake, will ya listen already! Sssh! Quiet, everybody!"

My father's initial reaction was not unwarranted. We had both thought "Who's Sorry Now?" had begun gathering dust just like my nine previous duds or, more likely, been discarded with last month's *Billboard* and *Cashbox* in every radio station across the land.

We all have milestones in our lives, but more often than not, we recognize them only in retrospect.

This milestone wasn't like that at all because I recognized it in five seconds flat. What I didn't know was that I would forever be able to pinpoint the precise moment that turned my life around—a sharp 180-degree turnaround.

Dick Clark and his "American Bandstand" were a large slice of Americana, to be sure. The tremendous power that a single man wielded in such a huge billion-dollar industry was truly astonishing. He was a starmaker and everyone in the music world knew it. "Dick Clark? He can make or break anything."

Nineteen fifty-eight was a sweeter time, a more innocent time—not only for me, but for the rest of the country, as well. Our teenage world was a world of pajama parties, diaries with keys, charm bracelets, friendship rings, and girls who got pinned. A writhing Elvis begged, "Wear My Ring Around Your Neck," and we yearned to oblige the boy. When he was drafted into the army and his famous locks were shorn military-style, we mourned the passing of those locks. Each hair was probably worth a hundred dollars on the open market.

Our pin curls were replaced by rollers, our bobby socks by colored tights. We wore pedal pushers, the sack, strapless prom dresses, teased hairdos, and the pageboy cut. Fifty-eight was a year of significant firsts: we saw our first transistor radio, our first jet plane, and our first stereo.

The country went fad-crazy that year. We swiveled

our hoola hoops and made stars of every male group smart enough to sing a lot of "Doo-wah, doo-wahs." College students swallowed their goldfish and crammed themselves into phone booths.

Even the records we bought had a gimmick. Alvin and his Chipmunks sounded like an LP played at 45 rpm; the sounds of "The Witch Doctor" pounded at our senses; and Sheb Wooley warned us of those horrific "Purple People Eaters." And, we bought 'em all—from "Alley Oop" and "Yakety Yak" to "Short Shorts" and "Itsy-Bitsy Teeny-Weeny Yellow Polka Dot Bikini."

The bikinis were teeny-weeny, all right, but not nearly as teeny-weeny as a girl singer's chances for success these days. For several years now, no major female recording artist had surfaced; it was a totally male-dominated market. Small wonder I was so flabbergasted that day.

"Will somebody pinch me, please!" I shouted to a captive but enthusiastic audience. "Okay, family members! All those seeking my autograph line up to the right! I may not wanna hang out with you guys anymore!"

"Well, what did I tell ya?" Daddy said, reveling in sublime and supreme satisfaction. And so he should have. "You don't wanna listen to your old man, right?"

Five months earlier, in September, just after I'd given George Scheck that last five hundred dollars, I began to plan my farewell session. After Daddy listened intently to the new songs I'd chosen for the date, I asked, "Well, what do you think, Dad? Super, aren't they?"

He shook his head in disgust and shuffled over to the piano, a lead sheet in his hand.

"They stink," he replied congenially. "Here's your hit, dummy!"

"What bright idea have you come up with now? C'mon, let's get it over with already!"

"Here's the standard I've been tellin' you about for a year, 'Who's Sorry Now?'"

"Oh no! Not *that* lousy old song again! Spare me! When was that thing written anyway?"

"Nineteen twenty-three," Daddy said.

"Nineteen twenty-three! You mean people were actually writing *songs* back in 1923! I betcha people didn't know how to write their own *names* in 1923!"

"For somebody who's supposed to be so smart, you're really stupid!"

"Leave it up to you, Daddy. You never cease to amaze me. I can just picture those hip kids on 'Bandstand.' How did they *or* Dick Clark survive so long without that song?"

Our encounters were always like the Korean War.

"C'mon, Daddy. Give me a break! It's so square, it's pitiful! I'd have to be so embarrassed, I'd have to ask MGM to put Kay Starr's name on the label!"

Every time Daddy brought up that jerky song, I reacted violently, but he just kept looking at me contemptuously and grunting. So, as usual when I'm in a corner, I took the offensive.

"That's it!" I shouted. "I won't talk about it any more! I go through this same torture with every new session!"

"You don't know a goddamned thing!"

"But *you* know everything, right, Daddy? Well, I happen to know that the kids at the hops will boo me right off the stage—but not without throwing a hook around my neck first, like on the 'Amateur Hour'!"

"You've got a head like a rock. You said you're quittin' the business anyway, didn't you? You picked nine bombs—that's eighteen sides! How many more stiff records do you wanna add to your list? Now, for a change, let *me* pick one song and you can pick your usual two or three duds, okay?"

I was adamant. "Forget about it!"

Then my father came up with a truly revolutionary idea, something that hadn't been done quite that way before.

"Why don't you sing it just like any regular ballad, but add rock 'n' roll triplets behind it? It'll be a new song to the kids—they'll wanna dance to it. And the grown-ups—they've already made the song a standard."

I agreed just to humor the man; I had it all figured out, anyway. Rarely could we fit four songs into a four-hour session, so I planned to save Daddy's song till last. I *did* have the arrangement written, though, just in case there *was* time; anything to get him off my back.

In October, at my final MGM session, my diabolical plot worked like a charm. I gazed at the big clock with the second hand in the control room—1:40 P.M. I'd already cut the three songs I liked. There wasn't nearly enough time to record and mix a complete other side in the remaining twenty minutes.

"I'm scratching the last number, guys, okay?" I said casually over the control room monitor. "There's not enough time left. Thanks anyway, fellas."

"You got twenty minutes left?" Daddy barked sweetly. "Then do the goddamned song, for chrissakes!" The man has a quaint, but elusive charm.

"Okay, Mr. Lipman. Let's give 'Who's Sorry Now?' a try," I said wearily over the speaker to the arranger. Then I sauntered over to where Mr. Lipman stood at his conductor's stand.

"Listen, Mr. Lipman," I whispered. "This song is the pits. But, I'm up the creek. If I don't do it, my father will walk around the house with a long face for the next two years."

"You're not gonna cut it in sixteen minutes, Connie," he warned with good reason.

"Please, Mr. Lipman! *You* don't have to go home with the man tonight! Let's give it a shot."

He winked knowingly at me, and as he handed out the parts to the musicians he said half-heartedly, "Okay, boys, let's wrap up this turkey."

I hadn't even glanced at the song since the first time

Daddy had shown it to me. First of all, I never thought we'd get to it, and secondly, I couldn't stomach it. Not the lyrics! Not the melody! Nothin'! Even *with* Daddy's rock 'n' roll triplets, it was the worst!

So, that session I did something I'd never done before—I completely forgot about a "style" of singing; I forgot to imitate every other girl singer in America—that old throwback from my demo days—and I sang it like myself. No gimmicks, no style, no imitations. It was different for me.

The record business itself is far different today than it was in '58—more compartmentalized, transistorized, synthesized, and just plain antiseptic. Back then, everything was recorded before you ever left the studio. If you didn't have a finished master mixed perfectly when you left, there was little even a spectacular engineer could do about it. There were no second chances.

Everything and everyone was recorded all at once, because there were no multiple tracks yet—no stereo, not until the middle of the following year. It was togetherness, all right—the rhythm section, the strings (or sweetening, as it's called), the brass, the reed instruments, the background singers and the lead vocalist—all mixed together in one room simultaneously by a great engineer who had to be a certified rocket scientist. (Thanks, Don Rickles.)

Record people have it much easier today. With sixty-four distinct and separate tracks and so many other miracles of modern technology, I'm convinced they can make an orangutan sound great. (Thanks again, Don Rickles.)

When you record nowadays, everybody shows up on a different day of the week. The violinists never meet the rhythm section; the rhythm section never meets the background singers; and God forbid anyone should meet the singer whose record it is.

The singer comes in whenever it's convenient for him, and naturally, on a day when he's in good voice—like maybe the first Monday in October after all the work is over and done with, all the work and all the creativity. It's all very sterile and dull, dull, dull!

True, there's a great deal more clarity and separation of sound for stereo aficionados; true, it makes insecure egos more secure (artists vie with one another to see who can spend the most money on the production of a record, and the royalties they are paid are at a far higher rate); and true, it allows a few less-than-professional, unprepared, and/or gifted folks to eke out lousy fortunes.

But, it's also driven session costs clear through the ceiling. The record business has made a lot of people richer, to be sure, but not the record companies and/or the artists who pay for these sessions. And predictably, it's driven many of *them* right out of the business.

What's almost as sad is the fact that the fun's all gone—the spontaneity, the challenge, the surge of excitement you experience when you know you've come up with a great new sound, a smash hit right on the spot. You just can't beat that feeling when you leave a session knowing that with a little bit of luck, you've got it made.

But, I suppose this holds true in almost every area of the entertainment industry today. Today an album is sometimes made over a period of a year—in six different cities, in twelve different studios, with twelve different engineers. C'mon you guys, grow up! Why record company executives allow themselves to be so buffaloed is beyond me.

October 2, 1957
Olmstead Studios, New York
1:45 P.M.

Nope! No way we can do it, thank *God*! Not in twelve minutes. But, who wanted to hear Daddy if I didn't pretend to give it a shot? After getting a mix, the engineer said: "Let's lay one down, okay, Connie? You got time for one take that's about it."

About halfway through the take, I stopped to ask Mr. Lipman and the orchestra to improvise more and to ask that great guitarist, Tony Matolla, and the rest of the rhythm section to give me a stronger triplet beat.

"Connie, you *may* get through one take, but it's chancy," the engineer cautioned. "You got four minutes, kid."

Record sessions, especially in New York or Los Angeles, are timed to the split second. If I'd sung the last note and exhaled at 2:02 P.M., MGM would've been forced to pay for another entire four-hour session. Anyway, we did manage one take of "Who's Sorry Now?" with no seconds to spare.

"Who's Sorry Now?" wouldn't be the only hit my father would pick for me—he went on to select a whole bunch of them. His musical tastes were plebeian—down-to-earth, unsophisticated, middle America. For hours each day, he'd listen to Newark DJ Walter Brenner play country and western music, but real Ozark stuff. Each week he watched Mitch Miller, Ed Sullivan, and Lawrence Welk with religious fervor—but so did the rest of America. He had the uncanny knack of knowing just what the public would or would not accept from me.

He taught me never to try to appeal to esoteric tastes or to the critics—only to the people. "Those other jerks, they don't buy your records, anyhow. The hell with 'em!" He also taught me to appeal to both the kids and the grown-ups and especially to all the Italian and Jewish grandmas. It was like wearing five different hats, but each of them felt comfortable.

After "Who's Sorry Now?" whenever I needed material for an up-and-coming recording session, I never looked to the charts in order to determine what kind of songs I ought to record. Daddy taught me not to follow, but to set trends, and to do only those songs that were "just right" for me and the people who enjoyed me. The following exchange was typical:

"That song ain't for you. Forget about it."

"But Daddy, it's a hit!"

"Yeah, I know it's a hit, but not for you. Let somebody else do it. You sound phony when you try to sing that kinda song!"

"It's not being done now" was, in Daddy's thinking, the very best reason to do something. "Don't be like everybody else and forget what made you a hit in the first place."

And, I quickly learned the first rule of a business like show business that there *are* no rules, not about anything. Even today, after having been out of the business for almost a decade, whenever someone says to me: "That's not the way it's done anymore," my first question is: "Not done by whom? And why not?" I'm not an iconoclast—sometimes there *is* a good reason, but more often, there isn't. I ask, "who's the genius who made up this rule?"

I say, in anything creative, *you* are.

October 2, 1957
Olmstead Studios, New York
2:00 P.M.

After the one and only take of "Who's Sorry Now?" Daddy beamed: "Now, *that's* a different sound! That damned song is a hit!" I let him revel in his pipe dreams.

The only other person who felt as Daddy did about that atrocious record was my MGM Philadelphia distributor Ed Barsky.

"You've gotta come to Philadelphia and promote this record," he urged. "You've done promotional tours with every other release! This record can do it for you, Connie!"

"Please, not you too, Mr. Barsky! My father's been bugging you again, right?"

"No, Connie. I really believe you're missing the boat."

"I'm awfully sorry, Mr. Barsky, but I'm not gonna promote this doggy record in Philadelphia or in Rangoon, either! It's a stiff! Anyway, I told you, I'm quitting the business. I've gotta do something useful with my life."

"Well, I'm going to bring it over to the Clark office, anyway." But that had been so many weeks before, that I'd forgotten all about it.

At any rate, it seems that one day Mr. Clark picked up a record that was lying on his desk—the record Mr. Barsky had been prodding him about; he played it, and he liked it. So, that January day, after the song stopped playing, I rushed to telephone Mr. Barsky at his home in Philadelphia.

"Mr. Barsky!" I shouted gleefully. "Will Mr. Clark play 'Who's Sorry Now?' again?"

"Who knows? He told me he likes it. I'll check on it first thing in the morning."

Well, Mr. Clark *did* play it again. And again. And again. Every day until the last week in March when over a million records had been sold.

Dick Clark heard in me a new and commercial sound that seemed to have gone unnoticed by the record industry before. Or, if anyone did notice, they weren't in a position to do anything much about it.

I shall always consider Dick Clark my creator, my mentor, and certainly the single most important influence on my career, and therefore on my life. If my friend Dick Clark hadn't happened along, there simply would have been no career. And, I hadn't even met the gentleman yet.

But I did get to meet my idol Dick Clark, and, eventually, to develop a most special friendship that has endured a lifetime. That year I would meet many exciting people I'd seen only in fan magazines or newspapers, visit faraway places that had existed only in geography class, and experience the kinds of dizzying experiences we all know "just happen in the movies."

It wasn't like real life at all—not any of it. For better or worse, life would never be the same again, not for me, my family, nor for any of those lives that touched mine.

In writing this book I discovered that I could recall so many events, big and small, of my childhood and teenage years with a great degree of accuracy and clarity, and I was able to do the same with the last decade of my life.

But when it came to the vertiginous years of my budding career, the facts—dates, places, professional events, all the many things that happened to me— seemed to blur, with one Las Vegas engagement, one foreign tour, one command performance, one TV special or appearance blending into another. The only thing that remained vivid in my mind were people and my relationships with them. And all the mementos and scrapbooks that chronicled, seemingly on a daily basis, the frenetic events, the triumphs and the defeats, of those days were destroyed in two separate floods in the basement of my home.

Were it not for fans like Pat Niglio, Barbara Clarke, Gunther Worshack, Karen Martylewski, Ron Roberts, Hank Weiland, Wilfred Weiler, Mike Motta, Carol Adams, (I could go on and on), it would've been virtually impossible to write with any degree of accuracy of those years. These fans eventually became friends, and they gave me their own collections of memorabilia, which were put together so painstakingly, and were far more extensive, accurate, and detailed than my own.

Reading the accounts of all these frantic and exhilarating events refreshed my memory greatly. But still I felt as if I were reading about another person. I said to myself, "Wow! Did I actually do all those things?"

*   *   *

By December of 1958—in the astoundingly short span of twelve months—there would be cocktail parties held in my honor on the roof of New York's St. Regis Hotel and a press conference for me on London's River Thames. I would appear in leading nightclubs across the country and guest star on the "Ed Sullivan," "Perry Como," "Pat Boone," and "Mantovani" TV shows, *and* on Dick Clark's first ABC-TV Saturday night just a month after the day Clark first played "Who's Sorry Now?"

I hired my first secretary, my first conductor, my first public relations man, and a team of accountants and attorneys. Three gold million-seller records would hang on the wall of my humble home, and I would become an even bigger personality across the Atlantic, visiting London twice to star at the Palace and the Palladium and to tour England and Scotland. I also toured Newfoundland, Hawaii, and Canada.

Fan magazines and trade papers began calling me "America's Sweetheart of Song," and that year, as the fan mail rolled in at the rate of five thousand letters per week, I earned slightly under a million dollars.

I was voted the Number One Female Vocalist in all the trade papers and by the Juke Box Operators of America; and in London's prestigious *New Musical Express* poll I was named the World's Number One Female Vocalist.

During that first whirlwind year, I spent only three or four weeks in Newark, New Jersey. There was no time to tune in to "Bandstand" anymore, but on the first "Bandstand" poll, by a write-in vote of over half a million people, I was named America's Top Female Vocalist—a title I was lucky enough to retain for each of the five years of the poll's existence.

It was the first of the golden years, and it was filled with those delicious absurdities of which fantasies are made—very heady fare, indeed, for a youngster from Newark, or anywhere else. *It was heady.* And it was— well, just plain wonderful. Thanks for it all, Mr. Clark.

11

If My Friends Could
See Me Now

Tonight at eight, you shoulda seen
A chauffeur pull up in a rented limousine
My neighbors burned! They'd like to die!
When I tell 'em who is gettin' in and goin' out is I!

All I can say is "wow—wait till the riff and raff
See just exactly how I sign my autograph"
What a step up! Holy cow! They'd never believe it
IF MY FRIENDS COULD SEE ME NOW*

January 25, 1958
Newark, New Jersey
11:00 P.M.

Dear Diary:
I got some fabulous news today! Just in case I'm
dreaming, nobody wake me up, okay? Dick Clark

*has invited me to be a guest on his first Saturday
night ABC-TV show from New York on February
fifteenth. Imagine his picking me! And I'll be in some
fancy company, too, diary. Dick Clark's other guests
will be Pat Boone, Johnny Ray, Jerry Lee Lewis,
The Royal Teens, and Chuck Willis.*

February 15, 1958
The Dick Clark Show
The Little Theater
New York City

"EXCUSE me, please," I said, inching my body side-
ways between the two lines of kids who stood
immobilized in the narrow alley, as they patiently
waited in a blizzard to see the dress rehearsal of Dick
Clark's first Saturday night show at the Little Theater
on Seventh Avenue.

It took me half an hour to struggle through the mob
scene on the sidewalk. There were policemen all over
the place, and at least a thousand kids-turned-snow-
men were milling around and drinking the hot chocolate Dick Clark had sent out. Finally, I reached the
head of the line and the security officer at the stage
door.

"I've gotta get inside for the show," I explained,
pointing toward the heavy door and blinking the frost
from my lashes.

"So do the rest of the kids," he grumbled humor-
lessly.

I was reluctant to inject my less-than-immense personal prestige at this point; I'd only been a hit for a
few weeks. So I skipped the name-dropping.

"I'm a singer, sir," I whispered meekly, "and I'm
doin' 'The Dick Clark Show.'"

"Yeah, I know, kid. Me, too. Only, I'm a ballerina."

Where the heck were Mr. Scheck and Daddy?

"No, honest-to-goodness, mister," I whined plaintively. "I really *am* a singer. My name is Connie Francis."

My voice was barely audible; I was too embarrassed to let the kids hear me.

"No kiddin'?" the guard answered. "Well, my name is Geronimo, and ya see my partner over there? He's one of my braves. Hey, Pete, come 'ere. Listen to this one."

"What's the problem, Joe?" Pete inquired.

"This little runt says she's singin' on the show. What does she think I am, stupid, or what? Everybody knows the music's canned that they only use records. She's lookin' to be a wise guy, Pete."

I thought it would be smarter to deal with the more reasonable-looking one, Pete, but I wasn't about to be humiliated again, so I decided to test him first on some of the other guests who were appearing. I began with calm, precise logic that would have delighted a military strategist.

"Excuse me, sir. Would you happen to know who Johnny Ray is?"

"Yeah. 'Cry,'" he growled, glancing at me suspiciously from the corner of his eye. This guy was as bad as Joe, the first one.

"That's right," I said encouragingly as a few of the kids started to snicker.

"And, Pat Boone, sir, do you know who Pat Boone is?"

"Who the hell doesn't know Pat Boone?" (He forgot to add the word "dummy.")

"Right again!" I said with lots of spirit. (What was I gonna do on camera *now* with my lousy wet hair?) "Now, how about Jerry Lee Lewis?"

"Ain't he that crazy hillbilly?"

This was no time for nitpicking. "Hey, you're doin' really great so far, mister. Okay. Let's see! The Royal Teens—you know who they are, doncha? 'Short Shorts'?"

"You tryin' to get smart with me, kid? I never heard of 'em."

I was in trouble, but I was in so deep already that I decided to keep going.

"That's okay, mister. Don't worry about it. What about 'Who's Sorry Now?' You know, the one by Connie Francis."

"Get to the back of that line, kid—NOW!" he sputtered.

The red kerchief covering my pin-curled hair looked like a white mantle. Even my jeans and car coat were wet with melted snow.

Just then, the show's producer and my knight in shining armor, Tony Mammarella, noticed me at the end of the line of frostbitten kids.

"Hey, Connie! Why are you standing out here in this blizzard? Go inside the studio."

"The guards won't let me in, Tony."

"This is one for the books," he said, laughing cheerfully as he took my hand and headed for the front of the line.

"You guys been givin' my friend here a rough time?" Mr. Mammarella asked the guards.

"Hey, Tony, we didn't know she was your friend," Joe apologized profusely. "She didn't say nothin' like that. She just made believe she was a singer."

In retrospect, I often think that it might have been better if Tony Mammarella hadn't rescued me that day. My performance that evening was not what one would call moving. In fact, my body and my face looked as if rigor mortis had set in. I tried to blame it on the cold weather.

Whenever I see those early films from the Dick Clark archives—and to this day, they pop up on TV with disheartening regularity—I pray that one blazing inferno will some day destroy them all. (Just the films of *me*, of course.)

The mortifying episode with the Dick Clark guards was a far cry from the royal treatment I was accorded just the week before at the big bash MGM threw for me on the roof of New York's St. Regis Hotel.

"Who's Sorry Now?" had firmly established itself as a hit, and all the New York DJs and press were invited to the first big cocktail party in my honor.

After Dick Clark began playing the record, the rest of the DJs around the country jumped on it. They were really rooting for me. Or perhaps they were just tired of seeing me pop up at their stations with each new release.

The St. Regis roof was a symphony of crystal chandeliers, and pink moiré wallcovering. The champagne flowed like a river. My escort was Stanley Mills; we were friends. Stanley's family owned Mills Music, one of the major music publishing companies in New York and the publisher of "Who's Sorry Now?"

"I know you don't drink, Connie, but this is a very special occasion," Stanley said graciously. "How about a cocktail to celebrate?"

"No thanks, Stanley," I smiled disarmingly.

"A little Scotch on the rocks then?"

"Stanley, I'd get drunk on Scotch tape. Forget about it."

"Well, what *would* you like to drink then?"

"Buttermilk."

"How can you order buttermilk at a cocktail party like this?"

What did I know from cocktail parties like this? The only parties I knew were spin-the-bottle parties. We settled on a seltzer with a wedge of lime; it looked like a cocktail at least.

It was an occasion, all right. I was awash in a sea of people all asking me questions. Photographers were taking my picture with each of the DJs, the trade paper people, and some VIPs from MGM. The whole setting reminded me of something from the movie *Sunset Boulevard;* I felt just like Gloria Swanson without the sunglasses.

I was basking in all this unprecedented attention when suddenly Stanley Mills made an astounding proposal.

"You look tired, Connie. I think all of this tumult is getting to you."

"It's okay, Stanley, really. I'm fine."

"You're just saying that," Stanley said, most concerned. "C'mon, C.F.! Let's go. Let me take you away from all of this."

I looked at him as if he had a screw loose somewhere.

"You do that, Stanley, and I'll wring your neck like a chicken's!"

After all the years of blood, sweat, and toil—not to mention the depressing anonymity I'd suffered—the man was insane enough to suggest that I leave all this glory behind, this fantabulous party!

I'd better make it in show business—I was ill-prepared for anything else in life. Domestically I was a washout. At the beginning I tried to conceal this gap in my development, especially from older Italian women—like the mothers of boys I dated. But more often than not, I got caught just the way I did at Pete Aiello's house that Sunday.

Pete was a boy from Corona, Long Island. We began dating in '57, just a few months after I saw Bobby for the last time on that never-to-be-forgotten day of "The Jackie Gleason Show." Pete was in the audience at the Safari, a nightclub on the Island where I appeared.

After the show Pete came backstage and invited me out. That was gutsy; nobody had ever done that before. Pete was Italian (which didn't hurt), handsome, fun, and personable, and he had a lovely family to boot.

My mother liked Pete a lot. She even said he was "her type," but I didn't tell Daddy. As far as Daddy was concerned, Pete had one fatal flaw—he was male, and that was always cause enough.

There *were* two men in my life Daddy actually *encouraged* me to date. Everyone suspected that one was homosexual (in fact, it was obvious). The other one was studying for the priesthood. Talk about playing it safe, Daddy!

Pete wanted to marry me, but marriage just wasn't in the cards for me—not for a long while. Anyway, that particular Sunday at his house should have changed his mind about houses and picket fences with me.

We were all relaxing in the finished basement of Pete's home when Mrs. Aiello casually mentioned that she was going upstairs to the kitchen to make us coffee. "Oh, please, Mrs. Aiello! I'll take care of it," I volunteered. (All good Italian girls are supposed to do that.)

I went upstairs to the kitchen, placed the delicious-smelling Colombian coffee on the gas burner, and returned to the basement. After a few minutes, everyone started sniffing; a distinct and most offensive odor was permeating the room.

"My God!" Mrs. Aiello shrieked. "There's a fire in the house!"

We all raced to the place where the foul smell and the smoke were strongest. Of course it was the kitchen.

"Oh, no!" Mrs. Aiello shouted. "Connie, that's my electric coffee pot you put on the burner!"

The smell of burning plastic is the worst! In a kitchen or a laundry room, I feel like an illegal alien, or at any rate, a trespasser.

After some hard dollars started rolling in, I made my first major expenditure. I had always had my heart set on a first-rate supper club act like Lisa Kirk's, always dreamed about a planned, professional act with patter (dialogue) and material written for me.

I was told of two fellows about town who seemed to be creating more acts for more performers than the Ringling Brothers. They had a most impressive list of credits to their names.

When my father discovered that I'd commissioned an act and spent nearly ten thousand dollars on it, *excluding* the arrangements and copying fees, he nearly had a stroke. He was being petty, as usual.

"You know, Daddy," I said judiciously, "you have to *spend* money in order to make it." (I'd heard that somewhere a few days before.) "Don't think so small."

I introduced my new and very sophisticated act at the Casino Royale in Washington, D.C. In my heart, I knew that nothing these two fellows had come up with was really "me," but I thought that perhaps "me" should become somebody else.

After the less-than-enthusiastic reaction of the audience to the "new me," I reluctantly asked:

"How was the new act, Daddy? Very New York, huh?"

"You mean you gotta ask?" he replied with his usual flair.

"It wasn't the act, Daddy!" I told him defensively. "It was that stiff audience! The minute I walked on that stage, I knew there was an audience out there, but only because I could hear them breathing."

"Cut the comedy, honey," he said, "and stop blamin' the audience."

"It just wasn't my kind of crowd," I insisted.

"Look, they paid to come 'n' see you, didn't they? It was a full house, so they liked you goin' in. Only you helped them change their mind with that jerky act of yours."

I cringed inside as I thought of the enormous sum of money I'd blown on my first and only "act."

"Well, Daddy, for the rest of the engagement, what am I supposed to do with my new act?"

"Give it to the Salvation Army along with the two idiots who wrote it. Now get out your old arrangements and do the twelve best standards you got. *That's* your act! You keep doin' the kind of stupid stuff you did tonight and you'll win yourself three new fans a show and lose yourself nine hundred and three!"

*   *   *

Daddy was oh-so-right. I've given the same advice to many performers when they feel they have to do something dazzling on stage. Except in a review, people don't want to be startled or dazzled by a performer—they just want to be plain ol' entertained. Case in point: Wayne Newton, who in my opinion is the best entertainer in the business.

Even today, whenever I try to do songs that are just a little too artsy, subtle, or sophisticated, for *me*, anyway, they are colossal disasters.

One classic example was a medley of more obscure tunes written by that wonderful Brazilian composer, Antonio Carlos Jobim. I spent a small fortune on the intricate and subtle Ralph Burns arrangement that I'd prepared for a Las Vegas opening.

During rehearsals for that Sahara Hotel opening, after the Louis Basil orchestra and I had run through the tasty arrangement smoothly the first time around, every musician rose from his seat, whistling and applauding enthusiastically.

Immediately, I knew what I had to do. "Joe," I whispered to my conductor, Joe Mazzu, "put this turkey in the back of the book. We're not doing it."

"Are you crazy? You saw the band's reaction, Connie! The routine's great!"

"Uh-huh. You musicians are hip people. If *you* guys are so wild about it, my audience will hate it."

Joe convinced me to try it for at least one show. I did it for two shows and both times it laid a big egg.

The first internationally known nightclub I appeared in with a big name act was the Chez Paree in Chicago. I performed there with top popular comic Joe E. Lewis. Naturally, I opened the show, and it went fairly well.

Then Mom and I stood in the wings in order to watch Mr. Lewis's act. The man was so hilarious that I was convulsed in laughter—that is, until he got to one particular off-color joke, the joke about me.

"By the way, ladies and gentlemen," slurred Mr.

Lewis, "I hope you liked our girl singer tonight, Connie Francis. She's gonna be a big star some day. And, I'd like her to know," Mr. Lewis continued, "that she's in for a very exciting evening—if only she'll listen to reason!"

Were my ears deceiving me? Was the man actually making off-color remarks about me, tarnishing my reputation, in front of a packed house? Of course he was! This was a first for me!

An eery, shrill *geschrei* emanated from my throat, which brought the GAC agent and everyone else backstage running.

When the agent saw me sobbing hysterically, he handed me a hankie and exclaimed, "What the hell happened back here?"

"I dunno," answered Ida, nonplused. Naturally, *she* didn't know. How could she be insulted, when she didn't even understand the salacious story to begin with?

"Mr. Lewis told a dirty joke about me right on stage," I yowled, wiping my tears away.

When I regained my composure enough to tell him exactly what Joe E. Lewis had said, the agent tried to explain: "For godssake, Connie, don't take it so personally! Joe E. Lewis does that joke every time he works with a girl singer!"

"Please," I said, sniffling, "please ask him to leave it out for the rest of the engagement—or I'm goin' home!"

When Mr. Lewis learned about the big to-do, he came to see me in my dressing room.

"Are you feelin' better, little girl?" he asked kindly. I nodded. "From now on, the joke's out, okay?"

Joe E. and I would work rooms together for years afterwards. I grew to love that man. And every time we saw each other, we would laugh about that memorable night at the Chez Paree.

For me, 1958 would be a year of "all of a suddens." All of a sudden, in every town I worked there was a young, handsome, charming agent that GAC would send to escort me; they wanted to make me happy, I guess.

I have never to this day mixed business with pleasure. I won't date anyone who works with me. When I work, I work.

In 1958, this was a typical scenario:

"Do you always work eighteen hours a day, Connie?" an agent would invariably ask. "Doncha have any fun?"

"My work is my fun," I'd respond demurely without a second thought.

"Before we leave for the show," he'd propose, "suppose I meet you in the lobby, and we'll have a drink?"

"Thanks, but I don't drink."

"Okay, so we'll have a malted. What time shall I pick you up?"

"What time do I have to be at the show?"

"Eight-thirty."

"How long does it take to get there?"

"About thirty minutes."

"Super! I'll see you in the lobby at eight!"

After the show, on the way home, an agent would often say: "I know a very quiet place where we can still have some dinner."

"I'm going to order up room service," I'd reply. "It's five hours later in Europe now—a perfect time to make my overseas business calls!"

One day I complained to Mr. Scheck about how I felt, and soon after we had a meeting with the vice president of GAC.

"What's the problem, Connie?" Buddy Howe asked, genuinely concerned.

"Well, Mr. Howe, you know these fellas you keep sending on the road for me? They're all very nice, Mr. Howe, but next time, don't send me Tyrone Power, okay? I don't feature hangin' out with boys who are prettier than I am." (I wasn't about to tell him that I'd dated only two boys in my whole life.)

"Who do you want us to send—Boris Karloff?"

"Just send me someone who's eighty-two with some *sachel* [smarts]. If I want something pretty to drape over my arm, I'll bring my stole."

My father had done a good job on me, and his reputation and mine preceded us wherever we went. Often I'd overhear two fellows speaking.

One would say: "Hey, she's a cute little kid, isn't she?" The other would caution: "Leave 'er alone. Her old man's a nut!"

That's exactly what one of the "Ms" should've done if he was smart—leave me alone. But he wasn't. Or else, news of my father hadn't hit his hometown yet.

The "Ms" are a rock 'n' roll group of note. In defense of my father I'd like to state here and now that he takes most of life with a grain of salt, does everything in moderation (obviously a screw-up in genes) and has flown off the handle only a few thousand times or so in my lifetime. But when he did, it was a beaut!

At any rate, shortly after "Who's Sorry Now?" made the charts, I was appearing at a theater in New England in a rock 'n' roll show.

After my performance I changed into my jeans and went backstage to watch the other acts from the wings. I was munching on a large apple; I thought I was alone.

"Hi, lady love. Can I have a bit of your little apple?" asked one of the "Ms," a lascivious grin on his face. (The other four "Ms" weren't around.)

"Here. You can have the whole thing," I offered naively. "I've got a whole bag of them in my dressing room."

"That's not what I asked you, little love. What I *said* was, Can I have a bite of that great big beautiful apple of yours?"

Just from his tone of voice, I knew he was trying to convey something suggestive, but I didn't know or care what. My father, however, knew. And all the while he'd been standing right behind me and the "M."

In a flash, Daddy pounced on the "M" like a frenzied panther leaping from a tree, took hold of the "M," who was at least a head taller than he, by the collar of his tuxedo shirt and pushed him hard up against the concrete wall of the theater.

"Gimme that goddamned apple!" Daddy yelled to me as a horrified group of onlookers gathered. (I wanted to throw myself under a truck.)

"Here's your apple, you *!x#o x#o!*" (I couldn't possibly repeat it.) Then Daddy proceeded to take the apple and grind it into the man's startled face until it looked something like mashed potatoes.

"You want another apple? I'll be in my daughter's dressing room—I'll be glad to give it to ya. But make sure when you come back you bring all your pals, so I can take care of all of ya at once!"

I told Mr. Scheck I didn't think I wanted to do rock 'n' roll shows anymore. Anyway, I'd always enjoyed working for grown-ups in nightclubs better. In order to win over an adult audience, you had to put on a top-notch performance; with a teenage audience, you were presold by your records, your movies, whatever. I always remember receiving much more applause from teenagers when I was introduced than at any other time during the show—especially after my closing number. After my name was announced and the squeals of delight subsided, it was downhill all the way.

March 31, 1958
Newark, New Jersey
12:00 noon

Dear Diary:
Today I received the grooviest news yet! I'm going to be singing a duet on "The Perry Como Show"

with—would you believe this one, diary?—Charlton Heston! Remember I saw Naked Jungle *twelve times just 'cause he was in it? Everything's happening so quickly, my head is spinning all the time.*

                                                    May 7, 1958
                                                    The Perry Como Show
                                                    New York City

"Mr. Heston, I . . . uh . . . I . . . well, uh . . . I saw *Naked Jungle* twelve times, . . . uh . . . just 'cause you were in it," I stammered looking all the way up at the movie idol of my teenage years. It took me fifteen minutes to muster up enough courage to utter a word to him. It was an awesome experience.

Mr. Heston was looking down—all the way down—at my half-eaten plate of cottage cheese and fruit salad with a curious expression on his face.

"Mr. Heston," I continued awkwardly, "you're my very favorite movie star in the whole wide world!"

"Well, thank you, Connie," Mr. Heston replied graciously, "but any hope of a torrid romance between the two of us is out."

I didn't understand. How could he possibly know I had dreamed rapturously of the two of us together every night since the day I got news of the duet?

"Gee, Mr. Heston," I managed, "did I do or say something wrong?"

"Well, not intentionally. It's just that my father always warned me never to get involved with girls who eat cottage cheese and fruit salad."

There was a split second's pause before we both broke into peals of laughter. When he smiled that wide, congenial Pepsodent smile of his, I melted. I could hardly wait to see what dreamy, romantic ballads we'd sing to each other. I brought at least twenty of them with me, and any one of them would fit the bill!

In my dreams I had envisioned the two of us stand-ing side by side, alone on top of Mt. Sinai, a soft breeze blowing through my white chiffon gown and my long, black, flowing hair.

Instead of holding his scroll, Mr. Heston was hold-ing me, just as he'd held Eleanor Parker in *Naked Jungle*, and all the while we romatically sang "Love Is a Many Splendored Thing" to each other. (I would've settled for "When the Moon Comes over the Moun-tain.")

When the show's producer, Nick Vanoff, handed me the lead sheet for the duet, I knew that what I'd settle for and what I was going to get were two totally different things.

Did I say Mt. Sinai? On the show we stood side by side, all right, but not on top of Mt. Sinai. They wanted a close-up shot of us together, and we looked like Mutt and Jeff. So they had me stand on top of a box! It would be the first of many boxes I would stand on for just that purpose.

Did I also mention a white chiffon gown and long, flowing hair? Well, I struck out there, too, guys! Our heads were covered entirely by a cat's costume—with whiskers, yet!

Did I boldly announce the song, "Love Is a Many Splendored Thing"? Wrong again, Concetta! That night Mr. Heston and I dueted to "Come Meow, Come Meow, Come Meow, My Purty Kitten."

Who wrote the material for that show, anyway—Daddy? Talk about chasing rainbows!

Well, at least "The Perry Como Show" ran smoothly—which I can't say for my first appearance on "Ed Sullivan" just a week later. I found myself back at the same theater on Fifty-third and Broadway where that apocryphal episode with Bobby and Daddy had occurred.

It was one more day that I prefer *not* to press into my book of memories. It was the first time I ever heard that *f* word—that word I'd seen only on black-boards and sidewalks. Where else would I have heard

it? From Ida or George? At the movies? From Eleanor or George Scheck? No way!

Halfway through my opening number, I asked the
orchestra leader, Ray Bloch, to stop the music. Apparently I'd given the arranger the wrong key for the
song, so I asked Mr. Bloch to have the band play the
arrangement a whole tone higher. (That's when I first
learned how much musicians hate to transpose.)

"S———! Did you hear that, Mel?" said one disgruntled band member. "We've gotta play the f———
in' thing a whole tone higher!"

At first I was stunned! Then I became so mortified
that I screeched at the top of my range: "Oh, my *God!*
Did I hear right?" Then I became plain old furious—
just fit to be tied!

I stormed off in a huff across the wide stage and
toward the dimly lit stage door exit on Fifty-third
Street, where I came face to face with the show's producer, Marlo Lewis.

"Connie, where are you going in such a big hurry?"
Mr. Lewis asked. "Are you finished with the orchestra
runthrough already?"

"There isn't going to be any orchestra runthrough,
Mr. Lewis," I informed him.

"Why not?"

"Well, you won't believe this one, Mr. Lewis! But
one of those lechers in Mr. Bloch's band said that
word . . . you know . . ."

"What word?"

"You know . . . the one that starts with an *f.* I can't
even say it, Mr. Lewis. I can't even bring myself to
spell it. . . . What an insulting thing!"

"He said that word to *you?*"

"No, not to *me,* Mr. Lewis! He just said it!"

Mr. Lewis put his arm around my shoulder, patting
it, and said, "Okay, Connie, okay. C'mon, let's go
back. He'll apologize. You know, Connie, you're in
the grown-up world of show business now."

"I may be in show business, Mr. Lewis," I blurted,
"but I can still smell a rose!"

Fortunately for me, I'd be seeing a lot more of those talented gentlemen of the Ray Bloch orchestra and a lot more of Ed Sullivan, too, which would prove to be one of the most significant factors of my career. After a Sullivan show, every time I had a Las Vegas opening—or any opening, for that matter—the club or hotel would always do SRO business. That's how important "The Ed Sullivan Show" was to a performer.

It even helped to fill Blinstrub's in Boston when I appeared there a week later. Blinstrub's was a twenty-five-hundred-seat barn of a nightclub in South Boston. It was owned by a gray-haired, cherubic gentleman named Stanley Blinstrub, one of the finest and kindest people in the world and one of the top five people I have ever met in show business.

Stanley Blinstrub was an influential, successful, and well-respected figure in Boston. But he was never too full of self-importance to cook the fried potatoes himself to feed those twenty-five hundred people, or to sweep the floors of the spotless kitchen of his nightclub.

I began working at Blinstrub's before I ever had a hit record. I don't know why, but I was always a hit with Bostonians before I ever had a hit anywhere in the rest of the country. Each time I played there, on opening night in the dressing room, I would find two dozen pink or yellow roses, my favorites, and a card from Mr. Blinstrub that read: "To my little sweetheart." He was another man it was impossible not to love an awful lot.

At any rate, on this particular night, even with all those nice Bostonians in the audience, I could easily have blown my whole career. As usual, it was Daddy's bright idea.

"You sound like you're hoarse," he observed.

"I know I'm hoarse, but not when I sing, just when I talk. I can sing over a cold."

"Well, just don't take any chances, sister," he said sweetly. "There's a full house out there. You'd better take something for it. Last week an opera singer at the Sullivan show told me that for hoarseness, she takes hot wine."

"You know, Daddy, you listen to everybody! That's one of your big problems."

"Go ahead," he urged. "Do what you want. Go sound like your throat's been cut. Who the hell cares?"

Who wanted to hear Daddy if the show was no good? So ten minutes before showtime, holding my nose with my thumb and index finger, I gulped down a distasteful glass of hot wine.

When I was introduced I barely managed to teeter down one of the long flights of steps on the side of the stage and to safely reach my only visible means of support, the piano. For the remainder of that fifty-minute show, I was so inebriated, that if I hadn't clung tenaciously to that good piano, my reputation would've been tainted forever. Lillian Roth had nothing on me!

Actually, there was nothing wrong with me—*I* was leaning perfectly still. It was the audience and the nightclub that kept spinning all night!

After the show, Daddy griped, "Who were you tryin' to impersonate up there? Helen Morgan, Joe E. Lewis—or both of 'em?"

My words were slurred as I retorted, "It's all *your* fault, Daddy! You and your old hot wine trick! What did you expect? You *know* I can't drink!"

"You *drank* it?" he asked in amazement. "You were supposed to gargle it, dummy!"

After that night, I stuck to lozenges and steam vaporizers.

Blinstrub's was one of those clubs with which I never had a contract. In years to come, whenever I'd finish an engagement there, I'd ask: "How did you do, Mr. Blinstrub?" He'd tell me what he thought I should earn that week, and it was always okay with me. Whatever Stanley Blinstrub said was okay with me.

There were other club owners like that. I never had contracts with South Jersey's Latin Casino owner,

Dave Dushoff, or with Dom Bruno and his Three Rivers Inn just outside Syracuse, New York.

I learned a great deal in those first few cyclonic months. I learned that a contract is merely a piece of paper, that there are lots of things you simply cannot write into a contract. Like enthusiasm, trust, goodwill, faith, and true concern.

But this was only the tip of the iceberg. There still awaited a myriad of wondrous things to learn, places to see and, most of all, new and fascinating people to meet and know—people who became not only a part of my life, but shapers of my destiny.

12

Stupid Cupid

STUPID CUPID, you're a real mean guy
I'd like to clip your wings so you can't fly
I'm in love and it's a cryin' shame
And I know that you're the one to blame
Hey! Hey! Set me free!
STUPID CUPID, quit pickin' on me*

A day in late May, 1958
Newark, New Jersey

"Okay, Donnie, I'll listen to their songs," I told Donnie Kirshner impatiently. "Who are these kids, anyway?"

"Well, the kid who plays piano and writes the music is Neil—he's attending Juilliard on a scholarship. And the one who writes lyrics was a 'go-fer' at Famous Music. Now he's workin' for National Cash Register."

"Look, Donnie, I'm on such a merry-go-round that I don't have time to breathe. Are they any good?"

"Are they any *good?* They're sensational! They've

got real potential, Con! And, they've written a whole bunch of stuff! When have you got a couple of hours?"

"I haven't got a couple of minutes, Kirsh, but I'll tell you what. I'm going to the hairdresser's at Bamberger's in Newark. Suppose you and the boys meet me on the corner of Halsey and Broad. My appointment's at three. It usually takes a couple of hours or so."

The day was an unseasonal scorcher. Donnie thought I said I'd *meet* him and the boys at three. So for two and a half hours they drove around and around the block in that oppressive heat. All the while Neil asked optimistically: "Donnie, are you *sure* you know her?"

The heat wasn't the only thing that had me hot under the collar that day. At the beauty salon I got a call telling me that a publisher had broken a promise he made to me. He'd given me his word that I'd have an exclusive on a song, and then he gave it to another artist. I had my *heart* set on that great ballad—it was a smash, and I knew it.

When I finally appeared all teased and lacquered, I spotted the car limping around the corner for the four hundred and first time.

"Hi, Con," Donnie said, looking very wilted.

"Have you been waiting, Donnie?" I asked absent-mindedly as I got into the car.

"Only ten minutes or so, Connie," he fibbed.

"Today I'm really ticked off, Donnie! I hate liars!"

Donnie paid no attention to me; he was used to my temper and the rest of my *shtick*. He knew it would blow over in five minutes.

"Con," he said eagerly, "this is Howie Greenfield and this is Neil Sed—"

"I will never again trust another publisher as long as I live!" I pouted, clearly steamed and distracted.

"But you trust *me*, don't you, Con?" Donnie ventured.

"I said, *all* publishers!"

Now, Donnie *and* the two young songwriters looked wilted. They glanced at each other with pitiful expressions on their faces.

As a publisher, Donnie wasn't exactly sitting on top of the world, *or* the Brill Building, for that matter. He did have an office on the third floor there—if you could call it that. One small room with a dilapidated desk and a broken chair.

We drove to my dreadful house on Brookdale Avenue, with its bare floors and exposed radiators. I hadn't given the house a second thought until I saw that "this-place-should-be-condemned" look on Howie's and Neil's faces. A few months ago I was a pauper. What were they expecting—Tara?

When Mom took a look at Howie, the tall, lanky one, she said, "Who is *he*? Bring him in the kitchen. He looks like he's starvin'."

Neil Sedaka, the student, began singing and playing on the piano a well-written but uncommercial ballad. It was difficult to tell at first that it was uncommercial because, as I would later learn, whenever Neil demonstrated a song he played it as if it were already a hit.

Then Neil played another ballad and another and another, until it seemed as if he had played me a medley of every ballad ever written. It was really good music, but I knew the kids wouldn't dig it. Too educated.

At one point, Mom popped into the room and said to me: "Why are you makin' these poor kids play so many songs? Just pick a song and sing it! You make a big ceremony out of everything you do, anyway!"

After the umpteenth ballad I stretched out on the sofa and began to scribble secret thoughts into my diary. This was going to be a long siege. Neil continued to play on into the future.

Howie, the tall "go-fer," said to me:

"Hey, Connie, What are you writin' there?"

"I don't mean to be rude, Howie. Believe me, I can do three or four things at the same time. I'm listening

to every note and every word you wrote. Go ahead—
I'm just writing in my diary."

"Ooooh," squealed Neil, "can I peek at it?"

"There's nothing in it, believe me, Neil. It tears me
up to admit it, but I mean *nothing!* Regardless, nobody sees my diary."

"Just a little peek," wheedled Howie.

"Uh-uh. You wouldn't be able to read it, anyway,
guys! There are only a few words—like names and
places, stuff like that—that aren't in shorthand. Forget the diary, Howie. You're both very good. Keep
playing more songs."

And they did. Donnie was smart—he'd left two
hours earlier. The whole thing became sleep-inducing.

"Don't you guys have anything a little more lively?"
I asked, looking up from my diary. "You're putting
me to sleep."

"But we thought you only sing ballads," Neil said
defensively.

"I *have* been known to sing other songs, too, you
know!" I responded just a little indignantly. Then I
thought about that. "Nope! I guess you're right, Neil!
I *haven't* been known for anything else, have I?"

"Pssst," buzzed Howie to Neil, "play 'er the one we
gave to the Shepherd Sisters."

"No, Howie, not that song!" Neil whispered back.
"She's a classy singer. She'll be insulted."

"Go ahead, already, Neil! Play it!"

Neil refused again.

"Look, she hates everything we wrote, doesn't she?
What have we got to lose? Play it already, Neil!"

"Play the song," I said wearily as I continued to
scribble. "At this point, I don't care what you play.
I've been falling asleep for the past eighteen hours."

Then Neil, with great prodding, played and sang:

"STUPID CUPID, you're a real mean guy
I'd like to clip your wings so you can't fly
I'm . . ."

I leapt to my feet.

"Stop! Stop it!" I screeched, jumping up and down enthusiastically.

"What! What!" cried an alarmed Howie and Neil. "What happened?"

"That's *it!*" I shouted.

"*What's* it?"

"That song! *That's* it!" I screamed, dancing about the room. "That's my next record! 'Stupid Cupid'! What a smash!"

"I can't believe it!" howled a joyous Howie. "Wait'll they hear this in Brighton Beach!" Soon afterward, Howie said, "I'm so excited, but we gotta go now, Connie. I gotta get up early to go to work."

"No, you don't, Howie—not anymore. You won't ever have to go to work again." (And I was right!)

During the long ride home to Brooklyn, Howie couldn't contain his joy. "We're gonna have the next Connie Francis record!"

Neil, characteristically, was having thoughts of his own. "Howie, don't get yourself all worked up over nothing."

"Nothing!"

"Look, she said she's on her way to Florida, didn't she? Anything could happen to her . . . she could lose her voice . . . the plane could crash . . . anything!" (Thanks, Neil.)

"Stupid Cupid" wouldn't be the only big smash that emerged from that fortuitous meeting in May. Howie and Neil had been trying to write a top commercial song for Neil to record for over a year, and they kept coming up dry. But when they got home that night Howie sat down and wrote himself a song:

> "Oh, how I'd like to look
> into that little book,
> the one that has the lock and key . . ."

And with "The Diary," Neil, too, would soon have his first smash record.

As Neil and Howie were leaving my house that day, I overheard Mom say:

"Listen, I wanna wish you kids a lot of luck. I hope my Connie makes a big hit for you."

"Connie said she's recording our song, Mrs. Franconero," reported an elated Howie and Neil.

"Look, who knows? My daughter's nuts," Mom said encouragingly. "Here—you poor kids didn't eat a thing. Take this mozzarella cheese and fruit—you'll eat it on the way home."

Nothing changes. Five years later, I was in Beverly Hills, California, doing a movie. It was the last week of a four-month stay in the outrageously luxurious suite MGM arranged for me at the Beverly Hilton Hotel.

There were no kitchen facilities in the suite, but that didn't bother Mom. With an electric frying pan, one electric burner, and a pot, the woman could wipe out world hunger.

Another "up-and-coming" songwriter came to the suite that day to play me some new tunes of his. After telling him he looked puny, Mom asked if he wanted some homemade pasta. He did. When it was time for him to leave, I heard her speak to him.

"Listen, what's your name again?" (She's the worst with names.) "Listen, I can't tell my Connie a lot of things anymore. She thinks she's a big shot now . . . but I *am* gonna tell her to sing your song, okay? And then you spend that money on some good food, hear me?" He agreed to do that.

"Oh, yeah, I forgot. Here—take some gravy home. Don't put it in the freezer. Tomorrow you'll heat it with some pasta. Good luck on your songwritin'."

He really needed it, Ma. That songwriter was none other than Johnny Mercer, who had already attempted a few things like "Autumn Leaves," "Blues in the Night," "Moon River," "Days of Wine and Roses," "Come Rain or Come Shine" (there simply isn't room for them all).

When I told Mom who the man was, she said, "I

don't care what he wrote—*everybody* needs good luck. And, besides, the man doesn't eat. Do his song."

April 1958
The Ted Mack Show
New York City

Dear Diary:
Today I spent the entire day in front of mirrors. I even took a magnifying mirror into the car with me. I was practicing how to look surprised. It all happened because of that MGM messenger boy. He told me by mistake that Ted Mack was going to surprise me and present me with my first gold record (for "Who's Sorry Now?") on his show tonight. I don't think I pulled it off well at all. (You know what a lousy actress I am.) Well, anyway, on the air, when Ted Mack told America that I was a "Ted Mack Amateur Hour" alumnus, I didn't have the heart to tell him that I flunked the TV audition for his show. Once I heard something, diary, and each day, it's beginning to make more and more sense to me. I heard that success has many fathers, but failure is an orphan. I guess that may be true, after all.

July 7, 1958
Floyd Bennett Field
Brooklyn, New York
6:00 P.M.

Dear Diary:
Mom, Georgie, and I are having dinner in an immense hangar the navy has converted into a dining room. I'm lying on my tummy in the lounge in the ladies' room. Mom spotted this comfortable place and told me to try to catch some sleep if I could. We've been waiting over twenty hours now. We're

*flying in the admiral's plane to Newfoundland, where
I'll entertain the navy. But it seems there's been some
delay due to a malfunctioning of the plane. Anyway,
this morning, when we first heard of the delay, I
called Howie and Neil and Georgie and I went with
them to Coney Island. We enjoyed all the rides. I had
six rides on the Cyclone alone—my favorite. I sure
hope that the old plane will be ready soon.* . . .

July 7, 1958
Floyd Bennett Field
Brooklyn, New York
7:30 P.M.

I must have dozed off while writing in my diary. All
I know for certain is that I was in a deep, deep sleep
when something weird enough occurred to put me into
deep, deep shock and another person into a deep,
deep freeze.

I was awakened from my sleep by the touch of a
hand sliding up my leg underneath my cotton shirtwaist dress. The anonymous hand belonged to none
other than the wife of one of the navy brass.

When Mom heard my bloodcurdling screams, she
raced into the ladies' room.

I have to say this for that "lady"—she was per-
sistent. Despite my screams, she didn't remove her
hand. That's why it was necessary for Ida to remove it
for her in such a gentle fashion.

"What the hell are ya—CRAZY?" Mom howled.
When Ida pulled the lady's hair back, it gave her just
the right opening to land a left hook to the lady's jaw
that would've made Jake La Motta green with envy.

But the lady wasn't getting off that easily. For her
closing number, Mom dragged her—jaw, hair, body,
and all—from the ladies room, clear across the dining
room floor, where she dumped her in front of her husband. A study in shiny brass medals, he was dining at
the table with the other VIPs. I never found out what

his rank was. This was no time to ask questions. Anyway, Ida wasn't interested.

She stalked over to that navy officer, looked him straight in the eye, and offered what I believe was some prudent advance notice.

"The next time, mister, send your wife to the *men's* room instead! Tell 'er this ain't my kid's week for girls! If anything like this happens again on this trip, tell them up in Newfoundland *now* to make sure they know how to play 'Taps.' Got me?"

I love fan mail! I love my fans! So sue me! What normal, well-adjusted person wouldn't love to receive concrete and unconditional evidence each day that they've won the approval of the people they've worked so hard to please? Over the years I've established some close friendships with people all over the country who started out as fans. And, they remained fans—until they got to know me better, that is.

I began receiving fan mail when I was thirteen years old and a "Startime Kids" regular. (Hi, Lynn, in Scarsdale, New York—remember me?) And, ever since that first letter from Lynn, fan mail is something I take very seriously.

My mother and father felt the same way. In 1958, before I could afford "all the trappings," I remember walking into that tiny, poor living room on Brookdale Avenue. Invariably, I would see Mom and Dad along with several of Mom's friends sorting huge mountains of fan mail.

On the kitchen table, I'd always find mail in several assorted baskets, letters my parents felt required my personal attention.

There was a basket of mail from people who were ill, disabled, or handicapped, a basket from servicemen, a basket from clergymen, a basket of special, worthy requests for benefits or personal appearances, a basket of just, well, very special mail (I probably still have most of those), and so on and so forth.

I remember once meeting a famous politician while

on the road singing. He told me he'd sent a letter to my home that he thought I would be interested in.

When I returned from a trip, I walked into our living room on Brookdale Avenue. In order to reach the kitchen, I had to dodge in and out of mountainous bales of mail. I knew that this system couldn't go on much longer.

My father was at the stove frying sausage. (What else?)

"What are you lookin' for?" he asked pleasantly.

"There's a certain letter I want to find."

"Well, just tell me what kind of letter you're lookin' for, and I'll tell you where you can find it. All those baskets over there are marked. Just read 'em."

I looked at the label on each and every basket at least three times, but I couldn't find my letter.

"Where's the mail from people in government?" I asked Daddy.

"What government?"

"The U.S. government! The government of the country you were born in! Where's the mail from governmental—you know, political figures?"

"Ya mean politicians?" he asked in amazement. "We don't have one."

"Why not?"

"'Cause they're all a bunch of phonies, that's why. The hell with 'em."

"Daddy! That's awful!" I protested idealistically. "It's unpatriotic!"

"Look, whatever they gotta say, you're not interested. You can't take it to the bank. Forget 'em."

There was one thing I had a great deal of difficulty forgetting, and that was George Scheck's last name. Since I was thirteen, I'd never called him anything but "Mr. Scheck."

One day Mr. Scheck's wife Eleanor told me that it was time that I called Mr. Scheck "George." I used to practice it at home and on my way into the city, but each time I actually tried to say it, the word got stuck in my throat.

One day Eleanor, George Scheck, and I had lunch at Lindy's. Lunch was something I just didn't have time for anymore. But Mrs. Scheck made such a point of my being there that I should have guessed the whole thing was a set-up. She began casually, as if it were off the cuff.

"By the way, Connie, I almost forgot. I've been meaning to speak with you about something. From now on you *cannot* wear those tacky, clear plastic shoes."

"Why not?" I asked, puzzled. "They go with everything. I don't have to worry about anything matching."

"That's the point. You can't *do* that anymore. You're a star now. From now on you'll have to have your shoes dyed to match each outfit."

I dismissed the whole idea as unconscionable and profligate, but I didn't have the nerve to say so to Mrs. Scheck. Then Mr. Scheck took over.

"Look, Connie, between us girls," he said conspiratorially, "you look like a *shlump*. You have to go out with Eleanor and buy some gowns. It's embarrassing. People are talkin'. Eleanor will take you tomorrow morning."

"Why? Why do I *have* to?" I objected, stamping my foot beneath the table. "Just because I've been a hit now for six and a half months? Let's not rush into anything, Mr. Scheck!"

"Connele . . ." Mr. Scheck purred meekly, "you're going to star in England."

"I know that, Mr. Scheck, but I've got the feeling that you're talkin' about an awful lot of money here."

"Connele," he began again softly, "you're a bigger star on the other side of the Atlantic than you are here. 'Who's Sorry Now?' has been number one for six weeks there."

"That doesn't mean a thing, Mr. Scheck," I said, being practical. "I've had only two and a half hits, you know. Even with 'Stupid Cupid,' it's still only two and a half hits! You hear those grim words every day, Mr. Scheck. You know 'em—flash-in-the-pan. I didn't make up those words. Let's face it, Mr. Scheck, it could be all over in two months. Look, we'll just wait and see, okay?"

"No, it's not okay!" Mrs. Scheck insisted. "You're going to be seen on TV all over the British Isles from the stage of the London Palladium. You realize, don't you, that the people who buy your records in England are people our age and your parents' age? The kids haven't come into power yet as they have over here. You'll be taken more seriously over there. You won't be thought of as just another rock 'n' roll artist. Now what exactly are you going to wear at the Palladium?"

"My little red dress?" I asked tentatively.

"Which one?"

"You weren't with me, Mrs. Scheck. I got it at Ohrbach's in Newark."

"Oh, no! I think I know the one you're referring to. Don't tell me you mean *that* red one?" Then her voice became very firm. "Connie, I've made an appointment for us to see two very nice ladies tomorrow morning to look at gowns."

"What are they," I asked, "dressmakers?"

"Well, let's say they're more like designers."

"Same thing. That's just a fancy name for dressmaker! If they call themselves designers, they just charge you more, that's all. Look, Mr. Scheck . . . I just spent all that money on that ridiculous Marlene Dietrich act, and now you want me to buy gowns, too! Where is all this money going to come from?" I hate to be put in a corner. I felt like escaping to Turkey.

"From royalties, Connele," Mr. Scheck said matter-of-factly.

So far, I hadn't seen a dime. Maybe they sent royalties by way of Sydney. Then Mr. Scheck began doing "shame, shame" with his two index fingers. "*Tsatskele*," he began again, "Eleanor will meet you tomor-

row at eleven. You'll have a good time. Stop eating
the cheesecake."

The whole thing was a veritable tug-o-war. Suppose
all this money everybody was talking about got mailed
to the wrong address by mistake? But what could I
do? I was up the creek. I didn't want Eleanor Scheck
to think I was small like Daddy.

The next day we met at an establishment on Fifty-
seventh Street. It was decadently opulent. The whole
scene looked exactly the way I imagined a bordello
would look. Everything was a dusty lavender. And
that Victorian furniture I hate even worse than Early
American.

We were greeted at the door by two very tall, posh,
and sophisticated ladies. They both had that skinny
wartime look. They also had strange foreign accents
even *I* couldn't identify. They didn't fool me,
though—they were from Brooklyn, too.

One of them began looking me up and down.
"Mmmm, let me see," she said studying my figure
clinically, making me feel self-conscious about those
seven pounds I'd gained. "Oh, yes! Oh, yes!" she
squealed, as if she'd discovered the cure for the common cold. "I think we have something pair-fect for
Mees Frahncees! We have a smashing little red
number that will be divine for the frame, stature, and
weight of Mees Frahncees!" (I don't know why, but I
got the feeling the whole thing was a put-down.)

The dress showed everything I wanted to hide and
hid everything I wanted to show.

"Oooh, Mees Frahncees!" observed one of the
ladies (they looked identical), "You look like a vision!"

"*I* think I look like a fireplug," I said.

But I was outvoted. They *all* thought I looked like a
vision! Just smashing! (I hate that word.)

I tried on another gown that was passable. Not
great—just passable. It didn't look any different than
the stuff I got at Ohrbach's. Everyone agreed on the
black and white number, too. It was just the end!

Pair-fect! Edith Head would die of envy! (I couldn't see it for dust.)

When the ladies walked away for a moment, I hissed,

"Pssst! Mrs. Scheck! See what the price tag says on those two dresses!"

"Please, Connie!" whispered an annoyed Eleanor Scheck. She was beginning to grit her teeth now, which is always a bad sign with Mrs. Scheck. When she got crazy, she was as bad as I was. "They don't put price tags on garments in a place like this!"

"Then get an estimate, for godssake, Mrs. Scheck! I can't take these gowns just like that!" I was beginning to get panicky, and Mrs. Scheck was no help at all. Was it against the law if I asked these two ladies from Brooklyn the price?

"Oh, Mees Frahncees—for you, my little dahling? You may have it for a song."

I took a shot. "How about a chorus-and-a-half of 'Who's Sorry Now?'"

They pretended they didn't even hear my offer. They tallied up the price of those two dresses as if they were preparing their income tax returns. Finally, one of the ladies named the dreaded sum.

"The first one is—let me see again—five hundred dollars." (She didn't even bother with 499.) I was thunderstruck!

"Mrs. Scheck! For godsakes!" I gasped. "That's extortion! People go to jail every day for less!" But, it was no use; Eleanor Scheck just told me to lower my voice. And it got worse yet.

"That other number—that was so completely ravishing on Mees Frahncees—practically made for her. That one is only five hundred seventy-five!"

"Let's get outta here right *now*, Mrs. Scheck," I pleaded in vain. "The minute I walked into this place I knew it spelled money—MINE!"

They wrapped the two dresses in a box that was far more spectacular than the gowns. Unfortunately, that

first shopping excursion with Mrs. Scheck was the first
and the last time, when it came to buying clothes and
a thousand other good things in life, that I hesitated,
even for a split second, to throw dollars—or caution—
to the wind. And it was all part and parcel of "the
good life."

13

Once in a Lifetime

ONCE IN A LIFETIME,
A man knows a moment
One wonderful moment when fate takes his hand
And this is my moment,
My ONCE IN A LIFETIME
When I can explore a new and exciting land*

> August 12, 1958
> International Arrivals and Departures
> Idlewild Airport
> New York City

"WHERE the hell is your daughter?" Daddy griped to Mom with customary élan. "The older she gets, the worse she gets! I hope the goddamned plane leaves without her!"

"You're right, Mr. Francis," George Scheck chimed in. (They always agreed on everything. It was disgusting!) "Her first international trip . . . a major press conference scheduled for her arrival at Heathrow Airport . . . this is terrible!"

Now he had Mom pacing the floor, too. And she was talking to herself, as usual.

"That kid always makes me so nervous! She's gonna give me a migraine! You know, George, your sister Tessie was right. We should've made her go work in a factory!" (Fat chance, Ida.)

"I'll fix her wagon!" Daddy threatened. "The hell with 'er! You people get on that goddamned plane and go to London *without* her!" (At last a voice of reason and sanity shone through.)

"That's a wonderful idea, Mr. Francis," Eleanor Scheck concurred. "But if she's not *with* us, what are we going to do when we get there?" Even Daddy had to think about *that* one a while. Did they expect me to kill myself working like this and not *eat*?

"Connie, hurry up! Leave the corned beef sandwich, already!" urged George Scheck's young assistant Joey Kahn. "Mr. Scheck said you have to get there earlier for an international flight. There's passports and all of that. . . ."

I wasn't worried; I knew it was cool. They always told me to arrive at least an hour earlier so I'd be on time.

"Let me ask the man behind the counter over there to wrap up my sandwich, Joey. I'll eat it on the plane."

"Connie! There's no time! This airport food stinks, anyway! And they're gonna feed you dinner on the plane in an hour."

"Joey, did you ever see the food they serve you on planes? I used to feed my brother's guppies better stuff! They don't serve normal Italian portions. You're Jewish—you should know that! Same thing! Excuse me, mister, could you please wrap up this corned b—"

"Connie! For godssake, there's your father! He's goin' nuts!" Joey yelled. "And Mrs. Scheck, too! Hurry up, already! Everybody's lookin' for you!"

"Hi, Daddy," I said casually. "Am I late? Is everybody about ready to leave?"

"Don't be cute, sister. Wise up, will ya? Now get out your goddamned passport and *run* to that agent over there, or *you* ain't goin' nowhere!"

What did I know from agents at airports? The only agents *I* ever saw were at GAC.

I ran a mile-a-minute, with Mom, Joey, and the rest of the world in tow.

"Here, Ma," I gasped, still running. "Here, take this money. I just cashed a hundred-dollar check for tips. But you'd better give it to Mrs. Scheck. You'll tip too small and embarrass me, as usual. Bye, Daddy! Ah, shoot, I forgot my *Seventeen*, my *Glamour*, and my *Mademoiselle!* Shoot!"

"You keep makin' out these big checks, lady, and you'll wind up on some breadline!"

"That's yesterday's show business, Ma. I'm sorry to destroy your day, but there *are* no more breadlines!" Both my parents are real crepehangers.

On the plane my mother came to tell her little girl a bedtime story and to tuck her in.

"Did you eat?" she inquired. (What else?)

"I can't eat this kinda junk, you know that. The British must put jelly on everything—and butter, too! Yuk!"

"I know. It's a sin, isn't it? Everything's so skimpy. How do these poor people live? Look at this. You can hold up this piece of bread to the light, and the light shines right through it." Then she added: "You never rest your brain, do ya? What are you doin' now?"

"I'm writing in my diary, what else?"

"Forget your diary, will ya? What have *you* got to write about? You sound like your life's important, or somethin'. Here, put these little slippers on. And, help me pull this divider out so I can make you a nice bed. Now sleep—you don't get enough sleep any more."

"You know I can't sleep on planes, Ma. I'm so

scared, I jump every time the plane jumps. I wish I
drank, or took Miltown or something like that."

"You don't need that garbage! Just close your eyes.
And stop thinkin' all the time—that's your trouble.
You know, you're gettin' to be a real pain in the ass to
be with. Everybody says it. Now, just relax; I'll get
you some hot milk. And say your prayers for a
change. You'll feel better."

I'm so glad a British man saved this clip from my airport press conference, because it was so typically me:

A WASP SCARES CONNIE

Flowers to greet a smiling star, America's Connie Francis,
arriving at London airport today. Connie flew in on a
Boeing 707. "We had a fine flight," she said, "but I'm
scared of these new jets. In fact, I'm scared of flying of
any kind."

Then she saw a wasp, jumped about four feet back and
said: "I'm scared of them, too."

> August 25, 1958
> The Savoy Hotel
> London, England
> 2:00 A.M.

Dear Diary:

*Everybody here is getting a big kick out of my
New Jersey accent. Isn't that funny? I love the British
people, and I love the way they speak, too. With that
wonderful British accent, even if you aren't brilliant
you sound like an Oxford graduate! It's super over
here! I can't believe they have fan clubs for me in a
place so far from Newark. The only thing I don't
like, diary, is the food. It's the worst! Remember
how I used to hate butter? Well, now butter has become my whole life. All I do is eat butter and rolls,
butter and rolls. I've gained five pounds. I wish that*

customs inspector hadn't confiscated Mom's suitcase. That Genoa salami—the provolone—all those goodies Mom had to leave at the airport. It's a cryin' shame! One other thing, diary—the toilet tissue's exactly like wax paper. The next time we come, I'm going to bring a whole bunch of toilet tissue. I don't think customs will take *that* away. The press is very direct here, much different than at home. It's comical how they ask such personal questions. At the River Thames press conference the other day, a reporter asked Mom if I pay her for traveling with me. Mom said to him: "Once in a while she gives me a hundred dollars for tips and stuff like that." In this morning's paper the reporter related what Mom said, and then added, "How's that for keeping Mum?" That's cute.

> August 25, 1958
> The Savoy Hotel
> London, England
> 11:30 A.M.

"Order your lunch," prodded Mom. "Call room service."

"I just ate an hour ago, Ma."

"So, you'll eat again. Go ahead, call room service."

"I just ate breakfast, Ma! You *know* I've gained five pounds since we got here. I just had six of those little rolls with butter and jelly. Yuk! And, that coffee—it's the worst!"

"We'll be drivin' around all day again with that snooty chauffeur. Order somethin' now, I'm tellin' you."

"Are you afraid I'll fall away to a ton, or what, Ma? Why are you so anxious for me to call room service?" I asked, squinting my eyes in suspicion. I knew for sure there was a method to her madness. I was right again.

"Well . . ." she hesitated, "we're gonna leave this fancy hotel soon."

"So?"

"Well . . . I've only got eleven of those tall glasses—you know the ones I mean—and I need one more to make a set."

I should've known. I should've been used to it already. The woman stole everything.

"I just hope the customs inspector finds those Savoy glasses, Ma."

"He won't find 'em. I have them hidden underneath your wigs."

August 25, 1958
The Savoy Hotel
London, England
12:30 P.M.

"Ma, here's your glass. Go ahead, hide it. Take a look at these vegetables, Ma. They're always shriveled up over here. What's the matter with them? They look like they died!"

"They're just sick, that's all. If you never got any sun, you'd look sick, too. Eat them. Don't waste good food. The poor kids in Europe are starvin'."

"We're *in* Europe now, Ma. And, they're not starving here anymore. Pick another place, okay?"

August 25, 1958
London, England
1:30 P.M.

"This, madam," boasted our driver, Derek, "is our internationally known Piccadilly Circus, the very hub of the theatrical dist—"

"If you think *this* is so great, Derek, you should take a look at Times Square," Mom interrupted for the third time. "You know, every New Year's Eve, they have Guy Lombardo . . ."

"Indeed," said Derek.

"Sssh . . . . Keep quiet, Mother . . . you're embarrassing me," I whispered reprovingly; then I leaned forward. "It's truly fascinating, Derek, I must say. Thank you so much."

Mom was really bugging Derek, the verrry, verrry proper British chauffeur that EMI (MGM in London) assigned us. This was our one and only chance to view the many wondrous landmarks of London Town. Derek persevered, trying valiantly once again to impress Mom.

"And, tell me, madam, what do you think of this glorious automobile—our Rolls-Royce," Derek inquired with great pride. "I say there, Mrs. Francis? . . ."

"I'll tell ya the truth, Derek, we've always had Chevys. . . . My husband says he's never had a minute's trouble with a Chevy. This thing's like ridin' in a hearse!"

"Mother! For godssakes! You just can't say whatever pops into your head!" I whispered desperately. "You're a guest in this man's country!" I leaned forward once more.

"It's a rare privilege for us, Derek. We're indebted to you. Be sure to thank Mr. Newell at EMI, too, won't you, for the use of the car *and* your services." Then my mother had a few well chosen words for *me*, too; I knew that from the curious expression on her face.

"What the hell's the matter with you, anyway?" she murmured in a whisper. "You're in the country three-and-a-half minutes, and you're talkin' like the Queen, already. If you knew how phony it sounds, you wouldn't talk like that." Meanwhile, Derek forged ahead, seemingly undaunted.

"And here, madam," he swaggered, "here is our famous Hyde Park! I'll stop so you can catch a picture of it. Grand, isn't it? The scene of many a—"

"Derek," Mom interrupted rudely. "Let me tell ya somethin' . . . you don't know what a park *is*, until ya see Central Park! It's right in the middle of—"

"Give me a break, will you, Ma?" I rasped. "What are you trying to do—wipe out my career in Europe overnight all by yourself?" I leaned forward still another time. "It's quite lovely, Derek, really. Thank you so much."

"How many times do I have to tell ya—you sound like a real phony!" Then, Derek passed on a bit of cultural information to me about the park.

"Last week, Miss Francis . . ."

"Please, Derek, call me 'Connie' okay? Everybody in London keeps calling me 'Miss Francis,' and it's making me very uncomfortable."

"Whatever . . . I was about to relate a rather humorous incident, Miss Francis—quite silly, really. . . . Last Sunday over the loudspeaker, a gentleman in the Park called the Queen a COW!"

"What the hell was he," Mom shouted, "some kind of nut!"

"Ssssh—Ma!" Why me, God, I sighed.

"And, now for the piece de resistance . . . the pride of London Town. We are about to approach it. . . . There it 'tis . . . London's most famous landmark . . . our Big Ben . . . the internationally known symbol. . . ."

"Do yourself a favor, will ya, Derek? You take a trip to New York with your family. You'll come to the house for dinner, and then my husband, George, will take all of ya to see the Statue of Liberty. He won't mind . . . when the kids were small, we used to . . ."

There's a limit to everything; the whole scene was just too much for Derek to bear any longer. He stopped the car abruptly, turned around, and with undisguised contempt said: "Madam! Let me say just one thing, and I vow that you shall never hear from me again. Trust me, madam—I *shall* remain speechless—forever!"

"Look, it's a free country, isn't it? Say whatever you wanna say—I don't mind."

"In that case, madam, I should merely like to say: BULLY FOR YOU!"

I was grateful they never made it to Buckingham Palace versus the White House.

September 27, 1958
Newark, New Jersey
2:00 A.M.

Dear Diary:
Today I hired a secretary. She's only eighteen, but she's worked for fan clubs since the age of eleven. She was Bobby's old fan club president. She's cute as a button. Her name is Joyce Becker (Pigeon). Diary, you won't believe this, but she's shorter than I am. (Why do you think she got the job?) She doesn't know how to type or take shorthand, but that's okay. If we need it, I can always do that kind of stuff.

Pigeon and I were like two giddy teenagers—more friends than employer/employee. Shorthand and typing weren't the only secretarial skills Pigeon lacked—organization was not her forte, either.

I must say she *did* make a note of every last detail. The question, however, was always "Where?" She'd write notes on the back of a stamp, lick it, and mail it somewhere. And if there weren't any stamps handy, she would jot down notes on the most minuscule pieces of paper and stick them in her shoes, in her pockets—anywhere. She probably had some notes stenciled inside her bra, too, or on the back of one of Frankie Avalon's 8 x 10 glossies.

Frankie Avalon was Pigeon Becker's whole life. She lived only for those moments when she could be in the same room as Frankie.

October 1958
Newark, New Jersey
3:00 A.M.

Dear Diary:
I'm going to be seeing Frankie today. We're going

*to do that benefit show at the big arena in Albany.
I'm so happy that Frankie is such a big success. I
think I'll wear the dress he loved me in!*

October 1958
Albany, New York

Dear Diary:
   *When Frankie and I saw each other today, just like
that* first time *we'd seen each other after the* April
Love *premiere, we asked for each other's autograph.
Even now we always have a big laugh over that one.
It's fun to recall how we shook hands on the death of
our careers at that horrendous premiere.*
   *A limousine that didn't end, with a chauffeur
wearing a shiny black hat, drove us up to Albany.
When we arrived, a priest met us; he took Frankie
and me to meet the bishop and we knelt before him
reverently. With proper decorum, we kissed his ring,
and he blessed us. As soon as we did, he asked us for
our autographs for his nephew. We couldn't believe
it! A bishop!*
   *After the show, in freezing weather, we drove back
to New York City in the limousine, which now had a
broken window. The fans broke it when they jumped
on our car. Frankie smiled at me impishly and said,
"Hey, Con! Not for nothin', but did you think it was
gonna be easy bein' a teenage idol?" We laughed our
heads off. We stopped at a diner and ate the world's
worst veal parmigiana (Frankie's favorite). Mom always said, "Don't eat Italian food in American res-
taurants." Then Frankie curled up on the back seat.
He had a cold and he was trying to sleep, but he kept
shivering. So Pigeon, Mom and I took off our coats
and covered him, and we all huddled together to
keep warm. (Pigeon swooned.) We couldn't sleep, so
we just talked about what an angel Frankie is. What
can I tell you, diary. He looked dreamy, that's all.*

(The last time we laughed about that premiere was January 31, 1982. We talked about Pigeon, too. See how I keep your name alive in Hollywood, P.B.?)

November 30, 1958

Well, dear diary, it's official! I've been voted the Number One Female Vocalist in the country by the Jukebox Operators of America. I know I keep repeating myself, but will somebody pinch me! It's funny, diary. Not long ago I said, "Someday I want a dozen babies." Now, I say, "Someday I want a dozen gold records." Who knows? Maybe someday, if I'm really lucky, I can have both.

December 27, 1958

. . . as this year comes to a close, I believe I have a much more assured approach to my work on the outside, and toward meeting new people, too. But, there's no calmness inside my head, where it really counts.

December 31, 1958

Dear Diary:
This is the end of the most successful and happiest year of my life. I don't want it to end. I'm so reluctant to close you, diary, and put you away in my memory drawer along with all those other diaries. You sure are a far cry from sad 1956 and 1957! I love life! You bet I do!

Yes, life was very good to us back then. Before
year's end, I bought Georgie a shiny yellow T-Bird. I
bought myself a Fleetwood Cadillac ($6,100). George
Scheck and I moved to brand-new offices, which we
would share for many years to come. I bought Mom
her first fur coat.

And, Daddy, at age forty-six, retired from the roof-
ing business and began to manage my four music publishing companies. That year I also began a practice
that would prove to be a total exercise in futility each
and every time I did it—but I never learned. I bought
Daddy his first designer wardrobe.

No matter what you do to him, he still looks like a
derelict. Daddy always put up a gallant fight. He
didn't want to retire from his roofs, and he didn't want
the wardrobe, either.

To Daddy, burgundy pants and a red shirt are coor-
dinates. He'd wear the same pants all day and all evening—to rake the leaves, clean the pool, paint the
house, and go to a formal wedding. I'd buy him Yves
St. Laurent, and he still looked like an unmade bed.

A few years later, when we moved into the palace
of a house I built in Essex Fells, one of the neighbors
complained bitterly to my housekeeper: "Would you
kindly have Miss Francis ask her gardener not to tend
the lawn in his T-shirt?" (Betcha can't guess who the
gardener was.)

For me, it was a time of 180-degree turnarounds—
and flip-flops, too. We moved from our "dismal"
good-luck-charm-of-a-house on *Brookdale* in Newark
to a modest, seven-room ranch house on *Dalebrook* in
Bloomfield. I left the black-and-white-striped wallpaper for someone else to inherit, and hoped it would
bring her good luck, too.

On moving day, I realized that we'd failed to notify
the post office of our new address. So, the usual bales
of mail arrived.

One was addressed to Georgie. It was obviously an
error—an application form for him to become a
charter president of a Connie Francis Fan Club. After

reading it, Georgie said some unkind things about me that I don't care to mention right now. He thought the whole business was silly. My brother had a real belly laugh that day, the dope!

Defensively, I grabbed the stack of mail from Georgie's hands—mail sent directly from point of origin to that poor little house on Brookdale Avenue.

I glanced casually at the envelope on top. There were ten weird stamps on it. It was from Holland and all it said was: "Conny—*My Happiness*, America." The envelope just beneath it was postmarked Kyoto, Japan. That one read: "To America's Sweetheart of Song, U.S.A."

14

Frankie

FRANKIE, wherever you are, I love you
Though you've found a new love
I still miss you so-o-o
I just can't forget you
Though you'll never know-o-o
FRANKIE, my darlin'
I'll never let you see me cry*

February 26, 1959
Savoy Hotel
London, England

MERRILY, I spread out the newspaper reviews of my formal variety act debut at London's Palace Theatre. "Okay, adoring fans! Let's read 'em and weep!" I said confidently to an eager Pigeon and George Scheck.

"I don't wanna let these reviews start going to my head, Pidge. If two thousand people a day tell you how great you are, you can start believing it yourself." There was a disconcerting lack of comment on Pidge's

---

* Used by permission of Big Seven Music Corp.

part. Finally, she said ruefully, "I don't know how I'm gonna tell you this, C.F., but *you* don't have that problem—not today, anyway. Here, you'd better take a peek at what this obvious newcomer, Milton Schulman, says."

"Go ahead, Pidge. Read it to me."

"Are you real sure?"

"Is it *that* lusterless or do you think I'm insecure, Pidge?"

"It's okay by me—whatever makes you happy, Queenie. But it's not that fabulous. . . . Here goes, anyway. 'Vaudeville may not be dead yet, but the bill at the Palace last night looked suspiciously like the onset of rigor mortis. The acts were bundled on to the stage as if someone in the wings was trying to get rid of them.'"

"Look, Pidge, the man just wasn't bowled over with the production in general. I'm not taking the whole rap for that one!"

"Well, thank *God*, he's not the only reviewer in town. Hey, *now* we're cookin' with gas! Here's another one in *Showpiece*. Ooops! You sure you want me to read it? Okay, you wear the gown, C.F. 'Twenty-year-old Connie Francis slams over her numbers in a voice which ranges between a roar and a shout. I preferred Italian tenor Tony Dalli. He's going to become a big name. . . .'"

"Wanna spread more cheer, Pidge, or is that about it?" I said, crestfallen.

"No, it isn't, I'm sad to report," Pigeon said. "I'd better read just the best part of this turkey, okay? 'It's all very well for Connie Francis to fly in sixteen hours before her stage entrance, all calm and collected, but the lack of preparation was painful. The only act that succeeded was the Hedley Ward Trio.'"

"That was the *best* part?" I said, now joyless. "Good luck to the Hedley Ward Trio, whoever they are."

"Don't let these blokes throw ya, C.F. It means nothin'! Do these guys think you're just another shootin' star? Hey, hey, hey! Lookie, lookie . . . I knew there'd be one guy with some smarts!"

"Spare me, will you, Pidge? Your job's hanging on a thread as it is."

"Good! I wanna quit, anyway, but my brain would go into shock—it couldn't handle sanity again. This one sounds like one of your fan club presidents wrote it."

"That good, huh?"

"Better. 'No experienced veteran could have displayed as much confidence as twenty-year-old Connie Francis. . . . We commend Connie for a shock premiere show. . . . Seatholders were not fans, but show business people. . . .'"

"Obviously, at no time did any of these three fellows attend the same show!"

"There's more, Queenie. Listen. 'The rare gift of performing any class of song with equal authority . . . few could impartially name any present-day singer who could have won greater acceptance, let alone equal the magnetic spell Connie cast on a sea of human faces. Congratulations, Connie, on such an impressive stage bow. . . . You're a Crown Jewel.' *I* know! Aunt Marie's the one who wrote *that* one!"

"Without you to spur me on, my career would go right down the tubes! Pidge, bring me my letter from Scott, please. It's on the bed."

"You've only read his letter fifty times today. There's the phone, anyway. It must be the one o'clock interview with that journalist."

"It'll take her an hour just to get through that lobby. Bring me my letter, will you, Pidge? And, order up some ham sandwiches, but tell them to hold the jelly and butter. The stuff's bad enough without it. We must have constitutions like iron not to get ptomaine poisoning from this chow. It's gotta be worse than KP rations."

"Con, get Mr. Scheck off the phone, so he can order somethin', too. He's got this demented thing for phones! He breaks out in a cold rash when a phone isn't within four inches of his earlobe!"

"Here's Scott's letter, C.F. Enjoy. But, you'd better get that love-sick look off your *punim*. If that reporter takes one look at you with that letter, she'll make a big deal out of it, and Scott'll read about it in *Modern Screen.*"

As I read my letter, an attractive older woman in her forties walked into the suite. She had a gentle winsomeness about her, a lovely delicate quality found so often in British women.

"Hello, Connie. May I ask what it 'tis you're reading?"

"It's a love letter from her boyfriend—he's a DJ," George revealed spontaneously.

"George, why don't you fly home to Dodgers Stadium and announce the status of my lovelife over the loudspeaker there! Sarah, meet my manager, Mr. Scheck. He's the kinda fella you don't take on a holdup with you—likes to talk a lot. I ordered up some lunch for us, but Sarah, you know how beastly English food is. So we'll hope for the best. What else can you do?"

"Well, actually I have little else with which to compare our food."

"Well, I do, Sarah. Trust me. So far, it's the worst in the world!"

"Incidentally, Connie, I was deeply impressed by your performance the other evening . . . very impressed, indeed. Congratulations! But back to that letter again . . . are you serious about the disc jockey who wrote it? Is there the prospect of marriage in the offing?"

"Married? *Me?* Oh, no, Sarah, I think of marriage only in terms of other people."

"Why do you suppose that 'tis?"

"Guess it's the way I was brought up—I don't know—the concept of wedded bliss wasn't exactly forced down my throat. Besides, no man could ever make me as happy as when I'm on that stage feelin' so relaxed and free. Someday when I'm a lot older—like in my forties—when I have no spunk left—and when the kicks are gone . . . maybe, then . . . someday . . . but this business never runs out of challenges. There's always something new and exciting you can make happen . . . I just don't see that day ever happening!"

"But what if Mr. Right came and swept you off your feet?"

I casually shrugged my shoulders.

"Plainly an academic question, true?"

I nodded in the affirmative and explained.

"It's true that every girl dreams dreams like that. I do almost always . . . but . . . my God . . . incidentally, thank you God, for giving me all this energy, 'cause there's a zillion things I've gotta do with my life yet! I want to be popular all over the world, Sarah—then maybe I can be like a good-will ambassador for my country through music. I mean, America wrote the book on popular music, Sarah.

"And my manager, Mr. Scheck, here—he wants me to be a movie star . . . it's a joke . . . he's convinced himself I'm an actress." I winked as I made an O with my thumb and index finger. "But we both know better, don't we, George?" George scowled at me as if I'd just leaked out secret information to the enemy.

"I mean, there's the rest of Europe—especially those living behind the Iron Curtain . . . People in the record business laugh at me. They tell me you can't collect any royalties from Communist countries. But the idea that you can really make an unhappy person so far away happy . . . just by singing . . . Wow! . . . And then there's Australia, Japan, and South America—the whole world must love American music! And I want to meet my fans so that we become real to each other."

"What do you mean by that?" asked Miss Stoddart.

"Well . . . one day a lady introduced me to her four-year-old little boy and told him 'Say "hi" to Connie Francis.' And the little boy answered, 'No,

Mommy! That's not Connie Francis! Connie Francis is a record!' That's cute, isn't it, Sarah. But then again, I'm a person, too, and I don't want to be just a name on a label to the people."

"Where do you find all this indefatigable energy? Have you always been so intense about your work?"

"I *am* my work! What—*who* would I be without it? It's the very best part of me—or anyone else for that matter. It's a reflection of everything you are. And besides, your work is the only thing in life that truly belongs to you. Not a person in the world can ever take it away from you.

"Besides, no matter what project I undertake—I always do it with commitment and I guess, passion—it isn't just show business."

"Well, why is show business, in particular, so special to you, Connie?"

"Well, for two reasons, I suppose! The people—to me, that's the most important thing—to know you've touched millions of people's lives, even in some small way—the knowledge that you've made a little difference."

"I understand your father had a great deal to do with your success."

"He sure did! But my father's original dream was for me to have my own accordion school. My family knew from nothing about show business."

"What constitutes winning to you, Connie?"

"Winning means getting what you want—not even what you think you can *realistically* get—but your *dream*—you go out, and you just make it happen, that's all. Besides, I have no choice," I chuckled, "I'm the world's worst loser."

Then I said effusively, "Sarah, you're a winner when you have something you love to do, when you wake up excited about all the day might hold in store. Sure, sometimes you're nervous or you're hyper or even scared, but so what?"

"What if you were to fail, Connie—has that thought ever occurred to you?" Sarah asked intently.

"Oh, Sarah? Who thinks like that! I mean, if you fail, sure you're allowed to be a little disappointed, but *defeated*—never! You give anything you really care about your all. And if you doubt yourself, even a little, then you're doomed to failure! Period!"

"What about your role as a woman?" she asked.

"What role as a woman? That's always been secondary in my life. And the fact that it is, gets me down sometimes. I guess 'cause I'm such a hopeless romantic," I confided, a little broodingly. "There's always a conflict raging within me. I'm really very feminine inside—all fluff and powder. I love a man who's a strong, but benign dictator—that is, if I have total respect for him—which isn't very often. But who's got time to think of stuff like that *now*?"

"You said show business is important to you for two reasons. What's the other reason?"

"Well, I'll try to explain it . . . Let me see . . . Okay! . . . In America we have a TV show called 'Queen for a Day.' On each show a worthy woman is honored as the Queen for that day. They roll out the red carpet for that lady—she's given the royal treatment—anything her heart desires. Nothing's too good for her, and she may even get a write-up in her hometown newspaper about it.

"For that one special day in her life, Sarah, she's made to feel like a very special 'someone'—everything revolves around her—people curry her favor. Sarah, it's got to be the very best day of that lady's life!

"Imagine—to be the center of attention, to get all dressed up in some outrageous creation, to have someone fix her hair and nails and toes and makeup, to have people take beautiful photographs of her—and to have the public rooting for her—adoring her just 'cause she's 'Queen for a Day.' How many times do you think that happens to a woman in a lifetime, Sarah?"

"A few rare times, indeed."

"That's right. Like when you graduate, or you go to

your school prom, or on your wedding day—maybe two or three times in a woman's entire lifetime."

"Well, Sarah," I said, my eyes dancing, "that's the way it is almost *every* day of my life! What a wonderful existence! It's like playing house—like being Cinderella every day! *All* those things actually happen! It makes me all aglow inside, that's all! It's like I'm always expecting some marvelous little secret to be hiding around every corner.

"Do you see what I mean, Sarah? Singing and performing—making people happy is my *raison d'être*— my reason to *be* (that's the only French I know)." I smiled contentedly, so in tune with the sweet strains of success.

"Don't you find this kind of life all-consuming?"

"Yes, of course, it's all-consuming! That's why it's so stupendous!" I enthused. "It's like living six lifetimes!"

"Connie, how does it feel to have broken the male monopoly in the recording industry?"

"I don't even think about things like that, Sarah. There's room at the top for lots of good singers—male and female. I just do the best songs for *me,* that's all. I don't like to sing songs I know other people can sing better than I. I'm not envious of other performers— except that I *do* religiously analyze the charts every week—because it's such an ever-changing business. And if my record isn't doing so great that week, it doesn't bother me at all. I just throw myself under the nearest truck, that's all." Sarah Stoddart giggled.

"This wellspring of ambition of yours, Connie—do you sometimes feel it's somewhat excessive?"

"Oh, no, Sarah, because all of us have the potential to be so much more than we are? Here—try one of these yukky sandwiches the waiter brought. . . . Wait! I know! Forget that junk! What if I heat up some tomato sauce and make us a plate of pasta? I made some last night on this little electric burner.

"But Italian food isn't exactly bland, Sarah. That

fabulous aroma must filter right down to the con-
cierge's desk in the lobby, because they keep sending
all kinds of hotel employees in and out of here on
false pretexts. You'll see, I always get caught red-
handed whenever I try to cook at this uppity hotel.
Food-wise, you've gotta fend for yourself in England.
Believe me, *I'll* never write a cookbook, but this is
survival time!"

"I'd enjoy a bit of your pasta, thank you, Connie.
It'll be quite a treat for me. Tell me, these eighteen-
hour workdays I've heard you put in—what about the
danger to your health that goes along with this kind of
pressure?"

"Only boredom is dangerous to your health,
Sarah," I explained, carefully stirring the savory
tomato sauce. "Pidge, put the water on this burner
now—I'll take the sauce off—it's tough with one
burner. Where's the rigatoni, Pidge?"

"Over there in that fancy Louis the Something rel-
ic . . . You're bad, C.F. . . . you turn every hotel
room into Mamma Leone's or the Stage Deli. I'm
warnin' you—I'm gonna quit this job!"

"Pidge always says that, Sarah—everybody who
works with me does."

"How much longer will you remain in the British
Isles, Connie?" Sarah asked.

"Just till I finish my tour and do a few albums—an
Italian one, a Christmas album—like that. . . ."

"Very well then, I'll send you a copy of the story
before you leave town. Thank you so much, Connie,
for your candor!"

I toured the British Isles, cut a whole slew of songs,
(including the Italian album Daddy shoved down my
throat), and made my second appearance at Glasgow's
Empire Theatre. I remember so well the best of
Scotland and the worst.

The worst was that horrendous Central Hotel built
directly over the subway station. Nightly I fell into a
fitful, uneasy sleep with almost certain expectation of

being awakened by the roar of an oncoming train at full throttle headed straight toward me and my bed.

The best part of Scotland is its people. Two of my life's luckiest friendships are with my two favorite "Scotties." They're people who became associated with me first as employees, and now, most certainly, as friends—my hairdresser, Libby, and the girl Libby introduced me to, her friend, Mary Minto—we call her Mac. She's taken such good care of my home and my son since he was an infant.

The sweetness and congeniality of the Scots, their refreshing pluckiness, that quickness to laugh at life's vicissitudes—all these qualities probably make them among my favorite people in the world.

I did box office business at the Empire Theatre that week. I still have the picture on my wall at home of the hundreds of people waiting outside the theater in a torrential downpour, trapped beneath a blanket of umbrellas.

One of those people waiting outside the theater that evening was Mary (Mac), who would become like a member of our family some fifteen years later. Just the other day, in a huff over something or other I'd done, she told me in no uncertain terms, "Connie, I'm taking a maddie! If I'd've known what a brat you are, I wouldn't have stood in the rain to see you like the idiot I am!"

On the day we left England, Pigeon handed me the article. Looking back now, the words seem all the more ironic.

THE GIRL IN THE SHADOW OF GARLAND

By Sarah Stoddart

Connie Francis is the girl in line for the Garland mantle, but it could be a heartbreak road. On stage, the girl with the million-dollar heartbreak in her voice belts out "Who's Sorry Now?" . . . But offstage, Connie told me

what it costs to be a top pop star as she carefully folded
away a fourteen-page letter. . . .

How does the other half of Connie Francis live? This
twenty-year-old ex–college girl is one of the few disc sen-
sations who are better on stage than on their recordings.
She mops up every teardrop of emotion in a song with the
volume and assurance of a young Judy Garland. Like
Garland, she's faintly desperate about her career. . . .
"And it isn't the money I care about!"

Like Garland, her energy is super-charged. . . . During
her twice-nightly British Variety tour she worked all
through the night at a London record studio cutting three
LPs. If anyone is ready to wear the Garland mantle, this
restless, eager, talented girl is well in line. . . . But remembering that well-thumbed love letter. . . the struggle
to stay slim . . . I sincerely hope she doesn't also inherit
the heartbreak and bitterness that surely comes with
being a legend.

March 30, 1959
Bloomfield, New Jersey

"Got any ideas, Concetta?" asked Howie Greenfield as we sprawled lazily on the wall-to-wall
carpeting of my new $27,000 seven-room home.

"Yup, I sure do. A name, Howie—I need a name."

"I think you've already *made* a name for yourself,"
Neil Sedaka said, naively.

"No, Neil, not *my* name—somebody else's! Names
are always big hits! Names of towns or states or people. Think about it—the list is endless. I just checked
the charts yesterday. Lately, there's been 'The Battle
of New Orleans' and 'Canadian Sunset.' And then
there's 'Maybelline,' 'Eddie My Love,' Paul's 'Diana,'
'Wake Up Little Suzie'—"

"I'm reading you loud and clear, Concetta!" said an
inspired Howie.

"Wait, Howie, I got a zillion of 'em! 'Good Golly,
Miss Molly,' 'Mr. Lee'—"

"All right, already! A name! You want a ballad or an up-tempo?" asked Howie.

"A ballad, Howie—a real dreamy ballad the kids can slow-dance to. I love to dance like that at parties, don't you? It's always groovy if you've got the right 45s."

"Happy or sad?" Howie asked. "You want a dreamy, happy song?"

"Howie, how can you even ask such dumb questions? Sad! You should know that by now—*always* sad. Women love to cry, especially teenage women. You feel pain more when you're young. Make it a simple name like Johnny, Okay?"

"What's the matter with Moishe or Seymour? You anti-Semitic, or somethin'? Okay, let's see . . . the lady wants a simple name like Johnny."

"She's just saying Johnny, Howie," Neil teased. "I know who she *really* wants to sing about!"

"Do me a real big favor, will ya, Neil? Make sure you tell *Confidential* all about it. Anyway, you're completely off base!" I said a little too vehemently. "Thank God I got over Bobby a long, long time ago. It was just puppy love. Actually, we weren't mature enough. And how could two egos like ours co-exist, anyway? It's yesterday's show business!" I went on unconvincingly.

"I don't know why those fan magazines don't give up, I can't pass a newsstand without reading some heart-rending story that says I'm home alone slitting my wrists while Bobby's having a party with half the females in the world. And, I mean sophisticated, sexy, female-type females like Peggy Lee!"

"Oh, well, I really couldn't care less," I lied. "You know, those folks in Hollywood are really a different breed! Do they ever print the truth out there?" Obviously Neil had hit a sore spot.

"Look at this one, Howie. Just *look* at this jazz in *Photoplay*. It says I'm dying of despair over a lost love. 'Our lives read like a storybook, but it's a bygone romance, and now I'm afraid, completely dead!'

They make me sound like a lovesick beagle! It's disgusting!

"And, just get a load of this one, Howie. Even *you* haven't come up with a lyric *this* tragic for me. 'Connie and Bobby are the reigning King and Queen of the pop music world, but they do not share the same throne . . . so Connie has nothing but her music now. Her One Reason to Live.' What a drag!"

"It's downright humiliating! Because, as far as I'm concerned, if he married his heart throb Lana Turner tomorrow, I think I'd manage to live to vote for the first time."

"Gets ya right where ya live and breathe, huh, Concetta?"

"Yeah, it does, Howie. Kids write me for an autographed picture and add, 'Send one of Bobby, too!' Like we're the Italian Romeo and Juliet, or something. Someday those good folk in Hollywood will print a factual story. It'll be such an event, they'll throw a big ticker-tape parade down Broadway!" I couldn't stop blabbing.

"So, Bobby's out, Neil! Let's think of another name . . . wait a second . . . of course! Frankie, who else?—Frankie Avalon! Frankie's the biggest teenage idol in the country! Besides, he's my friend. The kids'll love it!"

"Don't forget, Con," countered Neil, "Fabian's real big, too!"

"Neil," I said, impatiently, "how many girls in Brooklyn do you think have boyfriends named Fabian? C'mon you guys, it's *gotta* be Frankie! Okay by you, Neil? How about you, Howie?" It was okay by both of them.

So okay in fact, that we three would soon enjoy our second gold record together.

*   *   *

July 8, 1959
Bloomfield, New Jersey
4:15 P.M.

"Oh, my God! Kill it!"

"Shut up, Georgie!" I grumbled to my brother. "If you don't say anything nasty, maybe Mommy and Daddy won't think it's such a catastrophe. The girl just made a little mistake, that's all."

"What girl?"

"The girl who mixes the dye at the beauty parlor. I just told her to give me a few highlights. It was supposed to turn out dark auburn—almost brown."

"Oh, boy! Are *you* in luck! What grounds! You can sue that salon for a fortune! Show up in court with that flamin' red hair, and the jury will see with their very own eyes how America's Singing Sweetheart became Newark's Swinging Street Tart overnight! The damages are incalculable. I don't know how to tell you this, Connie Francis, but you just blew your whole career!"

He couldn't stop roaring, the sophomoric dope!

"Will you clam up, Georgie? You know Daddy doesn't notice things like a person's hair color."

"Very true. But, what about Mom?"

"Mmmm . . . I almost forgot. The woman notices everything. She missed her calling—she should've been a spy. She must've been Mata Hari in another life. But Mom's not the problem, you know that. She never makes any waves, 'cause if there's a dispute—and when isn't there?—she's caught in the middle of it."

"But when Daddy sees you, he's gonna have kittens. And then you're dead, Connie Francis. Because, automatically, it becomes two against you," Georgie pointed out accurately.

"Tell me something I don't know, Georgie. Ssssh—let me handle this one. Don't say a word. Oh, hi, Daddy, hi, Mom." I tried to sound casual and bright, avoiding direct eye contact. "Did I get any calls?"

"Mr. Scheck called and Aunt Marie called, too," said Mom. She was carrying thirty brown bags into the kitchen from the supermarket so she hadn't seen my hair yet. Then Daddy walked in.

"What the hell happened to you?" exclaimed my astonished father. "Just tell me somethin' fast, PLEASE! Tell me that goddamned thing's a wig! It *better* come off your head!"

"You really don't like it, Daddy?" I asked in mock surprise, carefully patting it down all over.

"*Who* the hell did that to your hair?" Daddy persisted.

Georgie stepped in and answered for me. "Don't blame Louis Pasteur. He died."

"Yeah, he died, all right!" yelled Mom. "He dyed your crazy sister's head!"

"Real cute play on words, Ma. Clever. What do you people want from my young life, anyway? Why the big production number over a little rinse?"

"*Non mi fa scumbare!*" (Don't embarrass me.) "You look like Rita Hayworth in that Sadie Thompson movie. Everybody Down Neck's talkin' about you as it is!"

"It'll look lighter in a little while," I said unconvincingly. "It's only four-thirty. It's still sunny in the house."

"Okay then," Daddy suggested, "let's all sit around and wait until it's dark outside. Then if your hair still looks like this, go find yourself a street lamp, stand under it, and sing 'Lili Marleen.'"

Georgie had a more profitable proposal. "Are you kiddin', Dad? Where's your imagination? She could do a heck of a lot better than stand under a street lamp with that hair! She could flag down sailors— maybe the whole fleet! You'll make yourself a bundle, Connie Francis."

"Who sent for you anyway, Georgie?" I said. "Stick to your law books, will you? You're all getting worked up over nothing! It works just like shampoo," I lied. "It rinses right out!

"You know, you people are a real joke! Especially *you*, Daddy! When I'm collecting social security, you'll still want me to look like I got off some boat at Ellis Island."

"Grow up, will ya?" Daddy snorted pleasantly. "Now get in that bathroom and wash that goddamned red shellac outta your head. What did ya do—forget ya got 'Bandstand' tomorrow?"

"Who's going to see the color on TV?" I resisted unsuccessfully. "It won't look *that* different in black and white."

"And what about Dick Clark?" Daddy snarled. "You think he'll be watchin' you on TV from his *house*? He'll be standin' right next to you in the goddamned studio! *He* can see the color, can't he? Dick Clark still thinks you're sane—he don't know you."

"Dick won't notice it. He's a man, and men don't go around noticing things like that. Except *you*, Daddy!" I said forcefully. "You'd notice an ingrown toenail on my foot on a ski trip!

"Besides, Dick's my friend. He's my confidant, really. You know that, Mom. I tell Dick everything about my boyfriends, my career—everything. Even if he notices, he'd never say a thing to embarrass me. He's too much of a gentleman. He's not *you*, Daddy!

"Anyway, if I get a chance, before the show, I'll ask Dick. If he says he doesn't like it, it'll take a while, but I'll let my natural color grow back."

"I knew it, George! I knew it wasn't a rinse! It's dyed, George!" Mom yelled, pointing an accusatory finger at me. "Forget singin', lady! Haunt houses instead! You'll do a lot better. I *knew* it was dyed, George! She thinks we were born yesterday!"

"Okay, okay, so it won't rinse out," I conceded. "I've told you, Dick won't notice it. It's not a monumental change—like I grew an eye in the middle of my neck or something! Furthermore, even if he *does* happen to notice, he'll like it. He married Bobbie, and she's blond, isn't she?"

July 9, 1959
American Bandstand
WFIL-TV
Philadelphia, Pennsylvania
4:15 P.M.

"Oh, my God! Kill it!" shrieked Dick Clark, pointing at me on national TV as I stood there mute,
immobile, and shattered.

You too, Richard? I thought.

Dick Clark must have taken a poll that day, because
by week's end we received a thousand letters of indig-
nant protest. Dick's word was law—the world agreed
with him. America was disappointed in the new, updated me.

"What are you lookin' to be—like the rest of those
kooks in show business?" snapped Daddy. "What did
I tell ya? I always said you had no brains! Do yourself
a favor, will ya? Go out and buy yourself a turban!"

"She don't need no turban," Jitters put in her word
of advice. "She can just put a big A&P bag over her
head!"

"It's only because *Dick* said he didn't like it,
Daddy. That was embarrassing. If he'd liked it, there
would've been only three negative votes in this country—and they would've all come from this address—I
can tell you that! Besides," I continued, "everyone
tells me that on camera, lighter hair makes your fea-
tures appear softer—"

"You're not sellin' records 'cause of your good
looks, sister," Daddy informed me encouragingly.

"You're so kind and gracious, Daddy. That's what
you'd like to believe, isn't it? God forbid some ninety-
four-year-old man in Shreveport might think I'm
cute. Anyway, TV never did me justice. I've always
hated the way I look on TV."

Daddy shed some constructive light on the subject.
"Yeah? Doncha know why that is?" he said, puffing
away on his ten-cent cigar.

"No. What is it exactly?" I asked, interested now.

"The reason you hate yourself so much on TV is 'cause in your *head*, you think you're better lookin' than you really are."

A person could burst. Every time he acted like this, he reminded me of his identical twin, Edward G. Robinson. And I couldn't stomach that crummy cigar.

Well, at any rate, there must have been *one* fellow who thought I was a pretty cute trick—the chap who drew the svelte Connie Francis cutout doll with the legs that went all the way up. He made me look like a brunette Anita Ekberg on stilts.

"Georgie! Daddy! Ma!" I cried out enthusiastically, opening a huge carton. "Look at what's going on the market this week! God, how exciting! It's the Connie Francis cutout doll book! Isn't she cute? Look, guys!"

"Well, then, who's *that* supposed to be?" Daddy asked innocently.

"It's the cutout doll of *me*, Daddy. Isn't she adorable?"

"That artist has some imagination!"

"Compliments are sure doled out like rations in this house!" I carped.

"Look, Connie Francis, just let me say one thing." Georgie grinned widely. "I never met the doll before, but she's some knockout! Get me her phone number at least, will you?"

"*Et tu, Brute*," I sniped back. "There's no hope for my life in this house!"

Despite the plaudits of my immediate family, in that week in May of '59 the market was flooded with Connie Francis cutout doll books, complete with a gorgeous, fur-trimmed, glittery wardrobe the likes of which I'd seen only in a 1950 Betty Grable movie. And Connie Francis diaries, too. And scrapbooks, autograph books, record carriers, coats, scarves, sportswear, T-shirts, jackets, posters—the works.

"And, what's all the rest of the junk in that big carton?" Georgie inquired.

"It's not junk!" I objected. "They're all different Connie Francis products! They'll be in stores all over the country this week!" I thought the nerd would die laughing.

"I'm going to step on your throat, Georgie!"

"Only in America!" he howled. "It goes to show you, you can sell a gullible public anything!"

"I never bought any of your albums, either!"

15

Yiddishe Momme

August 12, 1959
Bloomfield, New Jersey

"Was that you and your father arguing *again*, Queenie?" scowled Mom as I stared blankly at the test pattern on TV. I was rocking back and forth—*davening*—as I always do when I'm in deep thought.

I was brooding again, my eyes glazed; I tried to turn Daddy off in my head, but I was just too steamed.

"What's wrong with you, anyway?" Mom asked. "Are you in a trance, or what? That was your *father* you were just talkin' to, lady!"

"I know," I sulked. "No one ever lets me forget it, either."

"Why do you always have to argue with him over the stupid songs you're gonna record?"

"They're not stupid, Mom! Of all the things I have to do, choosing the right song is the most important. And now he wants me to do an entire album of *all Italian songs!* Stuff like 'O Sole Mio,' 'Mama,' and 'Come Back to Sorrento.' "

"Only to you, it's important. Not to anybody else," she informed me.

"You'd better check that one out with the main office, Ma. 'Cause MGM records happens to think it's running an international company on my record sales."

"Yeah, just *you* they need!"

"Believe me, Ma, I wish I had a fresh head like yours."

"You'd be a lot better off with my head. Ever since you became a big shot, you're a real wet blanket! And that temper—it's the worst! How'd you ever get to be Sicilian, anyway? You were always bad, but now . . . who can talk to you?"

"Do you know what Daddy's problem is, Ma? The man thinks he's a regular genius. Daddy thinks that when Tchaikovsky died he left *him* all his talent in the will! What a hardhead! But he's Calabrese—so what can you expect?"

"He's done okay by you, lady. Maybe all those people in the business in New York kiss your behind, but in this house, you're nothin', Queenie."

"Now tell me something I didn't know," I sighed.

"You used to be such a good kid. Now you're not even friendly to people anymore."

"I'm always friendly to people I meet. Maybe you'd like me to stop total strangers on Broadway and ask them to lunch. Okay, Mom. I'm sorry. Tell me about these Gothic reports you've been listening to. *Who* said I'm not friendly?"

The question was clearly superfluous. It was my mother's usual source of information—my Aunt Marie. "Who said I'm unfriendly, Ma—as if I don't already know."

"Everybody—that's all!"

"Everybody's too many people. I can't handle everybody today. Let's just start off with a few thousand people, okay?" It was the same song, eighty-ninth chorus.

"Here comes your father," Mom announced. "Don't start in with him all over again over those jerky songs. Just record 'em! You make a big ceremony out of everything you do."

"You know, the both of you are really rich! *He* lives and dies the music business, and *you*—you want me to pick out a song like *you* pick out a head of lettuce at the A&P!"

"Lettuce is more important. You can *eat* lettuce," Mom said with predictable Gracie Allen reasoning.

Daddy approached me for still another harangue of the day, his face a study in steely determination. "If you don't do that goddamned Italian album in London, you can pick out your own songs from now on! I don't wanna be involved anymore!"

"I should be so lucky," I retorted. "Besides, that's self-deceptive on your part, Daddy. Let's face it, the record business is your whole life. The answer is still *no!* And that's the end of that tune! Period! End of subject!"

"Why do you knock yourself out talkin' to her, George? It's like hittin' your head against a brick wall. She used to be so different—such a nice kid."

"You know, Daddy, it's too bad Hollywood miscast that epic movie. You missed your golden chance!"

"What movie?" inquired Mom, puzzled.

"*Mutiny on the Bounty!* Forget Charles Laughton, Ma. Your *husband* should've played Captain Bligh. I don't know why I bother to argue with him. Look, Daddy, if I have to hear just one more time about that ridiculous album, I'm leaving home and joining Ringling Brothers!"

"Go ahead," encouraged Mom. "You'll have a lot better life ridin' on top of some elephant!"

"Daddy, you're a real Renaissance man, aren't you? Why is it that you're under the myopic delusion that every person born in America is Italian? There *are* people in this country who call macaroni 'pasta', you know. What about all those good folks in Texas and Iowa who've never ever *seen* an Italian? For that matter, what about all the people right here in Jersey who can't speak a blessed word of Italian—like *me*, for starters? The kids will laugh me right off 'Bandstand.'"

"Who the hell's talkin' about the kids? Or do ya wanna play the Brooklyn Paramount with Alan Freed forever?"

"Look, Daddy, the whole world came to these shores to assimilate—but you decide to set me *back* a century!" I clenched my fists for emphasis.

"For your information, kid, Italians are the largest single ethnic group in this country—there are twenty-five million of 'em who understand some dialect. If you want to broaden your appeal and reach an adult audience who hardly knows you and those dumb rock 'n' roll songs—if you wanna play places like Vegas or the Copa—you'd better take my advice!"

"And one Italian album is going to make all these miraculous milestones occur like overnight, right, Daddy? Is that what you think?"

"No! That's what I *know!*"

"Look, Daddy, forget about it! The only Italian songs I know are those old songs Grandma taught me when I was little. . . . Oh, yeah, and I'd forgot! All those curse words you and the neighborhood guys like Louie the lug say all the time. The FCC would ban the darned LP!"

"Don't be a wise guy. So you'll learn Italian! When has learnin' somethin' new ever been such a big deal for you?"

Then I tried a new tack—I appealed to his marketing sense.

"Okay, let's see if this makes any sense to you. Why is it that Italian-American singers—big names like Perry Como, Tony Bennett, Vic Damone—to say nothing of Frank Sinatra, don't make Italian albums? It hasn't seemed to wipe out their careers, has it?"

"Because, dummy, when *they* made it, there *was* no rock 'n' roll! They were stars with the grown-ups, who bought the records right off the bat. The grown-ups today still think of you as a rock 'n' roll artist. Just one solid hit record like 'Mama' and you've got it made with the adults."

"But kids buy the records, and they don't buy that

kind of stuff! You've got some real pipe dreams! Whatever you're smokin', save some for me too, will ya? (I could use it.) I wouldn't be surprised if the next thing you want me to record is a Jewish album!"

"How did you know? See? Once in a while you *do* use your brain! It's been on my mind for weeks now!"

"A person could die in this house," I mourned.

"Look, stupid, that's what I came back to talk to you about. You know a lot of Yiddish. And the Jewish people like you. Don't forget a Spanish LP, too!" With the blink of an eye, Daddy would always dump projects of monstrous proportions in my lap and then head for the hills.

I threw both arms up in the air in futility and left the room muttering, "This is the day I'm gonna blow my brains out!"

"Well, do it outside," Mom requested. "Your father wants to take a nap on the couch—the noise'll wake him up!"

I'm twenty years old, my disgruntled adult mind told me. I'm financially independent. I have ten people who work for me now. I'm even called "President" on those six corporations (That lousy Infernal Revenue Service!). Why is it still so vital to me to receive Dad's stamp of approval on each and every decision I make? I wanted to give myself a good swift kick.

But I didn't want to hurt myself. So, like the obedient child I still was, I went Down Neck to my old Italian neighborhood and visited every Italian record shop open for business. Who wanted to listen to Daddy if I didn't do his dumb albums?

I asked all the shop-owners if they would help me with a project I knew nothing about. I asked them for the names of songs they felt would appeal to Italians who had come to the United States during that mass migration of which my grandparents were a part, those weary immigrants—five thousand of them a day—who waited in silent apprehension and a sense of foreboding on those endless lines at Ellis Island;

then, once embraced by our shores, began that long
march that helped shape a nation.

I requested songs that would appeal not to those
who spoke educated Italian—they weren't the people
who, out of necessity, left their beloved Italy—but to
the peasants who had migrated from south of Rome in
order to survive in a new land of golden and unprecedented opportunity, just as poor Jews, Poles, Irish,
Germans, and so many others had migrated from
other lands.

I wanted the songs I chose to evoke nostalgia, to
have special significance for these people. I wanted
their children, who would call themselves "Americans," and *their* children, too, to hear and learn the
most beautiful and romantic music in the world—for
the Italian language bespeaks music and love itself.

I asked everyone who looked Italian (which was everyone) to name his or her favorite Italian song. I
stopped people on the street, in the meat markets and
fish stores, and in all the little bargain shops along
Ferry Street in Newark.

The next day I repeated these same activities in
New York's Little Italy. I casually strolled into all the
little record shops with their blaring outdoor speakers.
"*Hey, paisano! Mi chiami Connie Francis, ed io canto
canzoni*," I told the shop owners. ("My name is Connie Francis, and I sing songs.") "What's your favorite
Italian song?"

That day I made a list of the best-loved Italian songs
of the people from the regions of Naples, Calabria,
Bari, Sicily, songs of passion and pain and life, and
love of their beautiful Italia, songs they carried in
their hearts when they embarked on that distant jour-
ney to a new alien land. For it was this music which
would remain at the core of their existence always.

On the third day, I returned to my old Jewish neighborhood. I visited the rabbi and his immediate family,
with whom we'd been so close. Some of their friends
and other family members were there, too.

Like Italians, many Jewish people, when they're involved in a controversy or even a casual tête-à-tête, do not *talk*—they *yell* at one another, gesticulating all the while. Normal American persons observing these people would think they quarreled continuously; they wouldn't have understood that it was all just off-the-cuff dinner conversation.

That's why I remained almost phlegmatic all during the big *tzimmes* that occurred that night during the normally solemn Seder. Everyone was bandying about song titles and battling wildly and enthusiastically about which songs I should include.

I asked them not for the names of Hebrew songs (with the possible exception of "Eli Eli") but for songs in Yiddish, the marvelously audacious, tongue-in-cheek language of the Jewish-American people. I decided to sing them in Litvak or Galitzianer, the two main Yiddish dialects.

Even after everyone had settled on their favorite "top twelve" songs, they continued to quibble about the correct pronunciation of the Yiddish words. It was really comical to me, reminding me of Italian, with seventy-five different languages within a language.

Sheila Shapiro, the rabbi's sister-in-law, said: "Oh, Connie, 'Yossel Yossel' is a must! It's got to be my very special favorite!"

Her husband, Seymour, had his own opinion. "Don't be a lox, Sheila! The only reason you're so crazy about that one is 'cause it's your lazy brother's name!" I almost choked on my matzo.

"What do you mean, lazy? Joseph's a very gifted sculptor!"

"So from this he's gonna earn a living?" said Mr. Shapiro. "Let's face it, Sheila, with sense your brother's not loaded."

"For your information, Seymour, my brother's going to be a famous and sought-after sculptor one of these days."

"You should live so long. Let's face it—a *shvare arbeiter* [hard worker] he's not."

"Look, folks," I intervened, "could I maybe choose a song about someone in the family who's a little more popular?"

Their married friends, Rhoda and Sol Goldman, also had something to say. "Connie's right! Not *that* one! As far as I'm concerned, there's only one song that's a *must* for this album!" Rhoda Goldman urged, as she danced, dreamily transported, spinning about the room, as if holding an imaginary man, and singing:

> "Oh, how we danced
> On the night we were wed . . ."

"Spare me, Rhoda, will you?" her husband Sol interrupted graciously. "You want I should have congestive heart failure by reminding me of that miserable night? It makes me nauseous already! My *mazel* I didn't get killed in a car crash before I got to the temple."

Then Mr. Goldman got *me* involved by asking me, as if I were a foreigner, "Connie, do you know what a Jewish wife makes for dinner every night?"

"I know, Mr. Goldman, I know," I answered precisely on cue. "Reservations, right?"

"How'd ya know that?"

"Because I'm ten percent Jewish—on my manager's side! Didn't you know that? I hate to break this news to you, Mr. Goldman, but every Borscht Belt comic has done that joke since I was three and a half."

The Rabbi's wife said, "Connie, it's important that you do two particular Yiddish songs about mothers. Mothers, as you know, are very valued figures in Jewish family life. My personal favorites are 'Yiddishe Momme' and 'Momele.' I'll teach you how to say the words properly, but some of them you must sing in English so that non-Jews can understand and feel the meaning of them, too."

There was great tenderness and a touch of melancholy in her voice as she lit the Shabbas candles and sang. "Those songs will move people—especially Jewish women—to tears." She smiled softly, misty-eyed. "You see, Connie, it saddens me that so many daughters of Jewish mothers like those described in these songs feel so guilty and confused that we're fast losing these values. I sometimes fear we already have."

"Well, I guess that's true of every religion and nationality."

"I suppose," she said pensively, "but not necessarily. Not all mothers are the same, you know."

"I know what you're saying about devoted mothers, because I have one of them. They're actually a dying breed, aren't they?"

"Yes," she whispered faintly, "I'm afraid they are."

I wanted to sing the colloquial, down-to-earth music of the people. The Jewish people, warm, nostalgic and emotional, have one foot firmly planted in the past; steeped in cherished and valued tradition. So I wanted to select music that had special meaning for them as Jews. That day we chose songs like "Belz, Mein Shetele Belz," "Oifen Pripetchick," and "Wus Geven Is Geven."

In those three eventful days, I collected almost a hundred Jewish and Italian records and lead sheets. Finally, my list dwindled down to the twenty-four songs I felt I would need for both albums—those songs requested most by the people I asked and those I felt I could sing the best.

And so what began for me as still another musical "accommodation" to my father resulted in a very special relationship between myself and two diverse, yet very similar, ethnic groups. It was undoubtedly the single most significant factor of my adult career.

Because of the recordings of these several albums of ethnic Italian and Jewish songs, a tacit bond of loyalty emerged—an indefinable respect rarely accorded an artist—an unspoken blending of the hearts that never wavered, never diminished, never failed me, even during all the long, lean years. And deep inside, even way back then, I knew that the most precious legacy my father had given me was a true "sense of the people."

16

God Bless America

August 26, 1959
Savoy Hotel
London, England

"C'MON already, Con!" urged Pidge, "Make tracks! Do you wanna be late *again!*"

"Pidge, my stomach thinks my throat's been cut. I'm calling room service *right now!* We've gotta eat *before* that fancy-shmancy reception! Who can eat that fake food?"

"Con, this whole EMI *megillah* is in your honor. Is being late gettin' to be a trademark with you, or somethin'? You do ten times what a normal person does in one day! I can't take this job anymore! I'm gonna quit! People will think you're like some flaky movie star! C'mon, Queenie, move it—or you'll be late again as always."

"I'm *not* always late, Pidge! It's just that everybody else always arrives exactly on time," I reasoned. "Besides, if you're gonna criticize me, never confuse me with the facts—you know that!"

"Someday I'm gonna go sane from this job. God! How boring *that* would be! . . . Psst . . . Hurry up!

". . . It's Mr. Scheck . . . and he's lookin' real nervous. . . ."

"So, what else is new? . . . Oh, hi, George" I said nonchalantly. "How's the weather—crummy again, right?"

"It's time already, Concetta!" he said, tapping his foot and trying to focus on his watch. "It's *time!*"

"Wait a second, George. You gotta hear something hysterical. . . . Today, an English cab driver told me that if you wanna see summer you have to be in Britain on August thirtieth between twelve and two in the afternoon. Is that a riot?"

"Concetta, stop doing shtick! The limo's *gotta* be here by now! And, I *mean* it this time. If you're late one more time I'll take you over my knee and spank you—just like I did the first time we came to London!" he cautioned, definitely miffed.

"What was *that* all about, Con?" Pidge asked, only mildly interested.

"Oh, nothing monumental, Pidge. It was one of my first appearances on TV here—an in-depth, Mike Wallace profile type thing. Before the show, the host wanted to know if there was any particular subject I wanted to avoid, because—he *said*—he didn't want to embarrass me.

"'That's very nice of you, sir. I'm a neophyte at interviews, so thanks. . . . Let's see . . . yes . . . there really *is* one subject I'd like to avoid, and that's the subject of money, sir. Every reporter in the British Isles seems to ask me how much money I earn. Money isn't my God—it makes me feel very guilty sometimes, 'cause England's a poor country, and to flaunt my earning capacity is in poor taste. Don't you feel that way, sir?'

"'Indeed, I do,' he agreed, 'that's one subject we'll want to avoid, isn't it?'

"'Well, it's just plain ol' bad public relations—don't you think—offensive to people. They resent a twenty-year-old earning an absurd amount of money, 'cause performers are paid more than anybody's worth, anyway.'

"Two minutes before airtime, he reaffirmed his position—that I was perfectly correct in avoiding any discussion of money. I should've known from that supercilious attitude that he was a fake guy, Pidge—a real empty suit!

"Then guess what! Right off the bat (he couldn't wait for the cameras to roll), what do you think the first thing the crafty twirp asked me? Are you ready for *this?*

"'Since your meteoric rise to prominence, Miss Francis, is it true that you earn the astonishing annual sum of what's purported to be five times that of the *President* of the *United States of America*—your President Eisenhower?'

"I should've belted him right on the spot, Pidge! But, it was TV—so I had to be a lady. So, all I said, calmly, was 'Would you run that by me one more time, sir?' and he did. I was absolutely livid, Pidge. Then I said, 'Sir, may I tell you something as a friend?'

"'Yes,' he answered, feigning interest, with a cocky little smirk on his face. 'And what would that be, Miss Francis?' It was an invitation my inner brat couldn't resist, Pidge.

"'You sir, are a clod, a con artist, and a snake! You probably could crawl under that studio door over there—with a knapsack on your back—you louse!'

"'He was dumbfounded, Pidge, but so was I! I couldn't believe what I'd said. I thought George Scheck, the Wreck, over there would have kittens, but I was really bent out of shape."

"So, how long did the interview last?" asked Pidge, terribly interested now.

"It was at least a half-hour interview, I think, but it took only about four minutes in all. Then I said . . ."

"You said *more?*" asked an astounded Pidge.

"Uh huh. I said, 'It's obvious to me that I'm merely the latest guest to be added to your casualty list, sir!

And, as a visitor to your lovely country, I'm offended. You, sir, are *not* a man of your word!'

"'Well, you're certainly letting your presence be felt here, Miss Francis,' he said ceremoniously. 'Be sure to visit us again, won't you?'

"'Of course, sir,' I said, sarcastically, 'someday if I really wanna punish myself for some great guilt!' And then, I just marched off the show, Pidge!"

"Oh, my *God!* What about your mother! And, what about poor Mr. Scheck! They must've had a stroke! My *God!* What happened!" asked an aghast Pidge.

"Don't ask, Pidge. I thought it was a plucky decision myself, but everybody—even EMI—was real mad at me!"

"You must be kiddin', Con. If you were the only guest, what did the host *do* for the rest of the show?"

"I let *his* mother worry about it, Pidge—I went home! He was a real nothing of a guy!"

"Oh, Con—my *God!* What did your mother say?"

"She never says—you know that—she yells! In the limo she just started to curse at me in Italian. (I wouldn't even repeat the words for your young ears, Pidge.) Then she took out her rosary beads—what else?"

"Well, what about Mr. Scheck—he must've *died!*"

"You could be right, Pidge. All the way home it sounded like we were at *somebody's* wake! Mr. Scheck became a deaf mute—the man uttered not one word! And, neither did Jitters (only because she couldn't pray for my soul and yell at me at the same time)!"

"So, what happened on the way home?" a wide-eyed Pidge asked.

"Well, the driver was trying real hard to be nice. You could cut the air with a knife, so he kept asking me the usual dull stuff like how I got my start—how is it in show business, stuff like that—you know."

"Then what?"

"Well—this is the real clincher, Pidge. You know how meek and timid Mr. Scheck seems, right? Well, don't let that veneer fool you for a minute, because that night the man became Victor Mature—like in *Samson and Delilah*. Are you ready for *this* one?

"As soon as we got back to the Savoy suite, Mr. Scheck couldn't wait to take off one of his great big shoes, and he spanked me with it real hard over his knee! And, guess what? My own mother didn't lift one finger to help me! All she kept muttering was, 'Your father and I shoulda done this a long time ago!'"

"Little, quiet Mr. Scheck . . ." she reflected, ". . . hard to believe, Con. What did *you* do?"

"The usual, Pidge—you know. I started throwing the pencils from my tin can all over the room."

"Did any of them hit you or Mrs. Franconero, Mr. Scheck?"

"No, of course not—she just threw them at the ceiling, at every wall, on the bed . . . like that. . . ."

"So, then what happened, Mr. Scheck?"

"What happened is, I said, 'Goodnight, Concetta. You and your pencils have a good time together!' Then I went to my room and slept like a baby," he said, momentarily reminiscing.

Suddenly, remembering the time, he shouted, "Connie! Hurry up, already—before I reenact that whole scene! The limo's *gotta* be downstairs by now! I am staring directly at the second hand of my watch, Concetta! And, I'm timing you! You've got exactly three minutes—*that's all and no more!*"

"Oh, for godssake, George, give me a break, will you? What *am* I—an egg?"

August 26, 1959
Savoy Hotel
London, England

At my last recording session in England, I was singing the final song from my Christmas album, appreciating fully the magnificence of the best string sound in the universe. The session took place as usual at the immense old church EMI used as a studio. The last song I sang on that sultry August day at four in the afternoon was "I'm Dreaming of a White Christmas."

I suppose EMI wanted to create the proper ambiance for the song, because during the last eight bars of what we knew was "the" take, from the three-story-high ceiling of that huge studio, snowflakes (thousands of teeny-weeny little bits of white paper) came tumbling down all over me, the orchestra, the charts—everything. I ran into the control room and gave Norman Newell, the Director of EMI, a great big hug. Sue me! I love thoughtful surprises!

August 27, 1959
Luxembourg, Europe

The day was dying; the night was being born as the Lufthansa plane touched down abruptly in Luxembourg, jarring me out of my troubled thoughts.

All during the trip I'd felt a pervasive sense of aloneness, felt as if I'd never sing another love song or ever have anyone but Bobby in my thoughts. I was beginning to feel as if "love" was only a word that appeared on a lot of lead sheets.

I thought to myself: My whole life I've been adored and idolized—I wondered how it would feel to be just plain ol' loved. Idealized, of course—but more importantly, just loved.

We'd come to Luxembourg and Cologne to do record promotion for my American recordings. We were greeted by two congenial gentlemen, two of the top DJs of Radio Luxembourg, Pete Marshall and Tony Prince.

The history of Radio Luxembourg is impressive, indeed. The fifty-year-old hundred-kilowatt station is the largest on the European continent, with a daily listening audience of at least six million. Even today, people tell me about how it influenced them. My hairdresser Libby told me that, as a child growing up in an orphanage in Scotland, Radio Luxembourg was her only real link to the world outside. It sprawls and wends its way easily throughout Russia and the rest of the European continent, to Morocco, Algeria, Tunisia, and many other places. And, as much as the Russians detest the idea, it stubbornly transmits the music of the West to an eager legion of devotees—to the millions of people captive in their own countries.

Withstanding most of the efforts of the Communist world to jam its airwaves, it has shown no respect for all the iron curtains and Berlin walls "Mother Russia" has unsuccessfully erected around her. Radio Luxembourg still stands as a monument to freedom on the European continent.

After a very short while in Europe, however, I realized that any attempt at promoting my records—especially in Germany—was a dead-end street. On my first visit to a non–English-speaking country, I became aware of the total lack of real interest in my music. I wondered why—but not for too long.

In those first few days I did a great deal of listening, observing, and learning, trying to discover what it would take to create a hit record in a place so different psychologically, philosophically, and historically from any place I'd ever visited.

In America our popular music was uneducated, freer, almost raw. The German recordings I heard were definitely superior—the finest technically in the world—but far more restricted, structured, and regimented in style and content.

I bought almost all the top 100 hit records in Germany over the previous two years. I discovered that in a country of only fifty million people, a huge hit was capable of selling two million copies, and that a German singer named Freddy frequently sold two to three million records of a single release! That was equivalent to the sale of eight to twelve million records on one hit in the States. I was astounded at the size of this new, yet-untapped, foreign marketplace.

I noticed another interesting thing—no American artist at all appeared on the German charts, save for a lonely Elvis who happened to be stationed in Germany. There were certain jazz artists who were well known, but they lacked the mass appeal to generate sales of any significance. Not a single American artist on any of those charts—the thought churned about in my mind.

The trip was a total revelation to me. I had always believed American music was an international export, but it wasn't—not by a long shot. In Britain, South Africa, New Zealand, Australia—all English-speaking countries—the charts were chock full of hits by American artists. It wasn't difficult to comprehend the reason for the lack of popularity of Americans, or foreigners of any kind, in Germany.

The reason had to be the language barrier. In Europe, people still bought songs, not gimmicks or sounds as they did in the USA. And songs have words, and words are potent.

Many songs—in fact most of them—became hits because of lyrics—words of emotion that communicate our innermost feelings, feelings we would have difficulty expressing were it not for the writers of popular songs.

How could anyone in these countries get excited about love songs they didn't know the meaning of? It was small wonder there were no English or American records on the charts.

I learned, too, that Germans, like Americans, are very nationalistic, that it was mainly German songs, composers, and artists that sold there. But what sales! And there was another curious thing. Their biggest hits seemed to be unsuccessful attempts at duplicating that unique Nashville country sound—a poor man's imitation of something that simply cannot be duplicated in New York, Los Angeles, or anywhere else.

"George," I said after a couple of days, "it's great here on the continent, but we're leaving. A kiss on the hand may be quite continental, but language is a girl's best friend."

"What are you talkin' about?"

"About the fact that we're wasting time here trying to promote a song in English. We'll come back again, but when we do, we'll speak to the people in their own language! I know what I have to do as soon as we get home!"

Before returning, Pidge, George Scheck, Ray Ellis (a gifted American arranger I worked with in London), and I stopped off in Paris. We stayed at the resplendent, old-world George V Hotel.

One look at the room service charge for the breakfast Pigeon and I ordered (twenty-five dollars), and I winced. Pigeon wasn't as cool—she gasped loudly. Then she told the pompous waiter, "Wait a minute! I think I need my glasses 'cause I'm lookin' at telephone numbers here."

She looked in disbelief first at the bill, then at me, then at the haughty waiter at least three times before she said, "For this kind of money, a family of four could eat for a month in Forest Hills!" The waiter was impervious to her remarks and quite cheerless.

"Sir," I said, trying to get a rise out of him, "the next time we call room service, could we just *rent* breakfast?" He remained impervious and cheerless.

"Hey, wait, gendarme!" Pidge shouted. "Room service forgot our coffee! But look, mister, before you bring it, I'm calling your boss for an estimate!"

As he left, Pigeon said, "This place is just a little too fancy for our blood, Queenie."

"Not so, Pidge. We're an asset to the establishment—we add tone to the place."

That evening George and Mr. Ellis told Pigeon and me they were taking us to Gay Paree's Lido nightclub. I remembered the name vaguely from somewhere, but

Pigeon and I were ill-prepared for what was to be our first all-nude female review.

Pidge and I were seated at our table with George and Ray Ellis like two innocent babes-in-the-woods, when what should appear before our wondering eyes but a stageful of about twenty nude-as-a-kumquat, long-stemmed, silky-haired, zaftig cheries—the ladies of the Lido line.

I found my eyes riveted on forty immovable breasts that had never been introduced to a bra in their lives! Pidge was flabbergasted! I was speechless! George Scheck and Ray Ellis were mesmerized!

Both Pigeon and I were stunned by the sordidness of the whole scene. The very first thing that popped into my mind was my Aunt Tessie. I remembered how appalled she was with Daddy for allowing me to sing at all those church socials. I'd have given up Marilyn Monroe's body just to get one look at her face in this den of depravity.

"Pidge, I'm in a state of shock! Did you *ever* in your life. . . . George! Ray! Why didn't you at least *warn* us? You make us come to a review like *this* in these frumpy Mickey Mouse prom dresses!"

"What about me?" asked Pigeon. "I feel like a fat dwarf! It's downright depressin'! I shoulda worn my tight black toreadors."

"*Gurnisht helfin,*" George Scheck predicted, in a near trance.

"What does that mean, Con?"

"It means 'nothing would help.' Why do I always have to teach Jews Yiddish?"

Meanwhile, Mr. Ellis and George Scheck remained transfixed; they had no time or interest in our small talk. Pigeon looked as if she were mourning the passing of a loved one.

"I wanna go home," she wept.

"Look Pidge, don't feel so bad. Who *needs* this? It must be the pits being a sex symbol!"

"I'd like to give it a shot, anyhow," grieved Pidge,

smoothing down her Jane Eyre dress. I tried to cheer her *and* me up.

"Pidge—just take a good look at them—what've *they* got that we haven't got?"

"Have you got a week or so? I'll tell you all about it," Pidge replied encouragingly.

"You know what it is, Pidge? The secret's all in the packaging! It's like when you go to the supermarket—they can make even Post Toasties look glamorous—at least on the box, anyway."

"I couldn't be packaged like that if Santa Claus did the job personally!"

"Look at it this way, Pidge. What do these girls *do* with their lives? They just stand up there on that stage with those vapid Huntz Hall expressions on their faces. They don't have the talent of a gnat! They don't act! They just about walk! And, they don't sing, either!"

"You want they should sing, too? Besides, who's lookin' at their faces? Con, don't these girls have *parents?* My God! Do their mothers know what they *do* for a living?"

"Forget about their *mothers,* Pidge! What about their fathers?"

"*Your* father? At dawn—he'd rather see you die before some firing squad! I'm just totally flipped out—my *God!* The sight of so many *fallen* women up there on one stage!"

"Pidge, where are *you* looking?"

"I'm lookin' right up there—at the stage."

"I hate to tell you this, Pidge, but so far, I don't see a darn thing on those floozies that's fallin'. Where?"

"They're all *courvehs* (whores)! That's what my mother would say. I hope every *one* of them gets chapped hips!" prayed a disgruntled Pigeon.

"Ssssh, be quiet, girls!" said George Scheck, somewhat annoyed, but still in a daze. "You're missin' a real good show!"

"What show, George?" I asked, sharply. "Where do you see a show? Why can't we just whisper, George?

Are you afraid you might miss some of that great Eugene O'Neill dialogue up there, or what?"

"Don't act like a silly child. It's an excellent review. We'll wait till the show's over."

"George, you can wait here till Chanukah if you want. *I'm leaving right now*. Goodnight—for Pidge and for me!"

"Con, we've all gotta leave. We gotta get up at the crack of dawn to make that plane for New York. You've got seven hundred commitments at home, including the new session and 'The Perry Como Show.' What songs are ya gonna sing on that show?"

"Oh, there's only one song to sing—'God Bless America.' It'll be a super song for the show!"

October 1959
Hollywood, California

"Who the hell is Francis O'Conny? Okay, okay, Connie Francis, whatever the hell her name is. Whadda you think I do, Scheck—sit up nights and memorize the names and telephone numbers of these flash-in-the-pan singers?" An irate Irving Berlin was speaking long distance from the coast to a conciliatory George Scheck.

"C'mon, now, *tatele*," George Scheck stroked, "relax. You'll meet Connie when she comes to the coast. She's a nice kid. Just relax, Irving."

"I'll give you relax! If she's such a nice kid, why's she tryin' to wipe out Kate Smith overnight? Look, Scheck, I don't know her and I don't *wanna* know her! I'm puttin' both you *and* that teeny-bopper on notice. If she thinks she's gonna gussy up my beautiful 'God Bless America' with—"

"You haven't even heard the master yet, Irving!"

"What I heard of that little runt is enough for me! That 'Cupid Is Stupid'—what crap! I'm gonna do everything in my power to stop that record! Besides, all the rights belong to the Boy Scouts of America!"

"Good! The Scouts need all the help they can get. So, they'll make a little *gelt*, too."

Mr. Berlin was not pleased. "Guilt, not *gelt!* Guilt, she should have—for screwing up a generation of kids with the garbage she sings. Not to mention our airways! You're talkin' about a lotta kids and a lotta country, Scheck! If she thinks she's gonna louse up my 'God Bless America' with those goddamned triplets and that sledgehammer drum like she did to poor Harry Ruby's 'Who's Sorry Now?' then she's got *me* to contend with! When am I gonna hear the thing?"

"On the air, you'll hear it. MGM doesn't keep Connie's records a secret. Rest your heart, Irving, it'll be fun to see a tune of yours on the charts again."

When George Scheck received the first test-pressing of "God Bless America," he had it delivered by messenger, posthaste, to Mr. Berlin's desk.

"It stinks! No, wait! I'm being too nice!" he reacted. "It's that same rock 'n' roll crap—just how I thought she'd do it! It makes me so nauseous, I wanna throw up!"

"*Vay iz meer*," George Scheck murmured softly. "Irving, by any chance, did you see the statement the mayor of San Francisco released as soon as he heard the record? He was so impressed with "God Bless America" that he taped a message that's broadcast over KOBY. Every show, every day. I'll read it to you. It says: 'This is Mayor George Christopher. I am tremendously impressed with Miss Connie Francis' recording of "God Bless America," and I'm grateful to know that our young people will be exposed to its beautiful and stirring lyrics.' How about that, Irving? You'll see—three, four weeks from now, 'God Bless America' will make the charts."

Mr. Scheck was right. "God Bless America" hit the *Variety* charts on November 1, 1959, at number 28 and the *Cash Box* charts on January 2, 1960, at number 36, at which time Mr. Scheck received a call from its renowned composer.

"Tell her I'm sorry I lost my temper, Georgie—she

should understand," he said a lot mellower. "I'm a little out of touch with the market today."

A week later when "God Bless America" hit *Variety*'s Top Ten in record bestsellers, Mr. Berlin gave Ma Bell another dollar.

"Georgie, whadda you think? Talk to her. Maybe she'll do it on TV. Go ahead. Ask her."

He did, and I tried, Irving. But, Perry Como wouldn't let me, God love him.

And for that reason, something very special occurred, something that proved to be the most significant milestone of my adult career.

17

Mama

MAMA,
Until the day that we're together once more
I live in these memories
Until that day when we're together once more
MAMA, my MAMA *

November 12, 1959
Francon, Inc.
New York City

"PLEASE, George, Daddy," I persisted, "I *love* that song! I get goose bumps each and every time I sing it!"

"Mr. Francis, maybe you can talk some sense into her head," pleaded an exasperated George Scheck. "She *cannot* do 'God Bless America' on 'The Perry Como Show,' and that's that—period! Naturally, Perry closes the show, and *he* feels that the song is a show closer. Please, Mr. Francis, *you* tell her."

Then the undisputed reigning president of the Italo-American Perry Como Fan Club, George Franconero, chimed in. "Perry Como's one helluva nice guy," Daddy stated flatly. "He's no show business kook! The man knows what the hell he's talkin' about! So you'll sing somethin' else. What's the big deal?"

I knew I had my work cut out for me. "Don't you see what I'm trying to tell you people—that even though Kate Smith's a beloved singer to you grown-ups, the kids don't know who she is. And most of them don't know 'God Bless America,' either. I mean, sure, they've heard it, but they've never really listened to those inspiring lyrics before. Nobody ever sang it in *their* idiom—*their* language!"

"What language did Kate Smith sing it in— Korean?" Daddy cracked. The man was missing the whole point.

"Look, number one, 'God Bless America' is the perfect song for a Perry Como audience; number two, it's on the charts, which means the kids are buying it; and number three, it's a positive thing for the kids to feel patriotic about this country."

"You wanna do somethin' patriotic? Hold up a big flag, and sing somethin' else," said my sympathetic father.

"Okay, Daddy, okay! Then *you* come up with another blockbuster like 'God Bless America'—one that will really touch the people. Because that's the kind of audience Perry Como has! You *do* that, Daddy, and then we'll talk."

"How many times do I have to tell ya? Just do a number from the goddamned Italian album! Perry'll like it."

"Oh, of course! The Italian album! How preposterous of me to let that slip my mind! What other number would *I*, as an American artist, choose to sing on American TV?"

"I hate talkin' to dumb women. Sing 'Mama' for chrissakes."

"And then you can do another song, Connie——

maybe an up-tempo song—from the same album,"
George Scheck said, agreeing with Daddy as usual.

"How wonderful! It'll be 'The Italian Hour.' Only
we won't be broadcasting from Abruzzi, folks—we'll
all be at NBC in New York in the New Land. I can
see it all now. Down Neck and in Little Italy—maybe
even in South Philly and the North End of Boston—
I'll knock 'em dead! But in case you haven't heard
about it, there's TV in Paducah, now, and *there* the
only Italians they've seen are on 'The Untouchables'!"

"What you know about show business, sister, you
could shove in a cocktail olive," Daddy said re-
spectfully.

"I just wanna know one thing before I give in.
Who's got the concession on the earphones in Helena,
Montana? Or maybe NBC's sending in a UN interpreter to tell them what I'm singing about there?" I
was getting nowhere fast—par for the course.

"Does a major TV shot sell records fast, or doesn't
it?" Daddy asked, clearly perturbed at my denseness.

"It's the best way to sell 'em," I conceded. "We all
know that."

"Do you think that if a couple sees someone on TV
they like, they just might plunk down a hundred bucks
in a nightclub to catch that act in person?" Daddy
baited me still further.

"Of course."

"Well, you know those folks you were talkin' about
in Montana? They never seen the inside of a real
nightclub in their lives! At the Copa or in Vegas
they'd look like lost war brides. Ya know who goes to
the Copa and Vegas, doncha? The Italians and the
Jews—*that's* who! And the Jewish people love
everything Italian—food, music, Italians, and Italy,
too!" Just keep it up! Pull one of your usual stunts!
Open your big mouth, and get yourself into a brawl
with a nice guy like Perry!"

"I *still* say it's too ethnic! But don't mind me—I'm
just the girl with the microphone. Oops! I almost for-

got—I'm just an *Italian* girl! I relinquished all rights to an independent idea at birth!"

"Connie, you can have ideas," George Scheck placated. "Just don't tell them to anybody but your father and me, okay?"

"No, it's *not* okay, George! Just look at poor people like Judy Garland and Marilyn Monroe who let others run their careers. They're like little wind-up, automaton dolls! You wind 'em up, dress 'em in something pretty, and they smile and perform for you. Then when the show's over, they get put back in some drawer—scared to death and totally dependent upon somebody else. I'm convinced of it now! If you're a woman with a mind of your own, you get penalized! It's contrary to all state, federal, and international law!"

"You talk like a real jerk," said Daddy. "Just act like a lady, do your songs, and leave your two cents out of it. Nobody's interested! What are ya gettin' to be like—one of them pain-in-the-ass suffragette broads?"

"No, Daddy. But we're in big business now, and you still want me to be shy and retiring—right?"

"That's right!" decreed Daddy. "Because men don't like it—*that's* why!"

"Well, it doesn't choke women up, either! And they *should* resent it a lot more than they do!"

"What the hell's the matter with you?" growled Daddy in surprise. "I don't even understand what the hell you're talkin' about anymore!"

"Thank you, Daddy, for the only compliment of the year—from *you*, anyway! Look—I listen to everything everybody has to tell me. Then I do what *I* feel I should do, that's all. I'll sink or swim by my own decisions, not somebody else's. If I turn out to be wrong, at least I can live with that."

"So be a monster—you'll make yourself a ton of enemies. You're gettin' to be some diplomat, sister. You should run for office."

"Well, that one takes the cake! I hope somebody's taping this! *I* know, Daddy! It must be in the genes! That's it! You've transmitted your tact genes to me!"

Daddy had no time to listen to nonsense. "Look, are ya tellin' me you're *not* gonna sing 'Mama,' or what?" he asked menacingly.

"Why? Do I have a choice?"

His response was all too predictable. "No, you don't! What's right is right! Perry said 'God Bless America' is out, so it's out! And that's that, sister!"

Who wanted to live with the man if I didn't do his Italian song?

November 18, 1959
"The Perry Como Show"
NBC-TV
Rockefeller Plaza
New York City

"Maybe we should cancel Carnegie Hall. What do you think, Mr. Francis?" a forlorn George Scheck asked tentatively. "It's Wednesday, and they've sold less than a hundred tickets. She can't sing to an empty house Sunday night. It's embarrassing."

"Naah, ya can't cancel," Daddy said calmly. "The people who *did* buy tickets will be disappointed."

"Why didn't you let me stay home today?" railed Jitters. "I'm nervous enough, as it is. We were better off when we had nothin', George. Now there's always some kinda trouble—and all the time, over stupid things like this!"

I walked briskly into my dressing room at "The Perry Como Show." "Hi, you guys! They just checked my makeup. And wardrobe put some flesh-colored net in the front of my dress, see?" The room had all the ambiance of an Italian wake. "What's up, gang?"

"Not ticket sales," said Scheck. "You know, Mr. Francis, I heard that not too long ago, when Joni

James played Carnegie Hall, MGM papered the whole house."

The words caught my ears, conjuring up the memory of that depressing five-hour wait outside the office of MGM's president as he sat "in conference" with Miss James.

"MGM papered Carnegie Hall for Joni James!" I cried out in amazement. "Well then, they can paper it for me, too, can't they? Can I help them pick it out, George?"

"Pick *what* out?" asked a puzzled George Scheck.

"The *paper!* You know how I love interior decorating. Can I help them pick out the wallpaper?"

George Scheck stood doubled over, convulsed in a rare display of wild guffaws.

"Connele, 'papering the house' doesn't mean wallpaper hangers and glue and scaffolds! It means they give the tickets away for free so at least the place *looks* full!"

"Oh," I whispered, not a little disappointed.

"Okay, here's what we'll do. We'll wait one more day, Mr. Francis, and see if anything happens," suggested George Scheck. "Hey! Connele! The show's on the air in fifteen minutes. C'mon, you're running late again!"

"Is Perry Como gonna announce my stage name tonight, George?" I said truculently. "Because I'd prefer it if he'd just call me Concetta Rose Marie Franconero. We may as well go the whole Italian route!"

"Take a look at the front of your dress!" Mom said suddenly. "You look like Dagmar! It's too low in front. You can see everything!"

"See *what*?" I yelled. "They've got me covered up to my neck in net! You can't see any cleavage at all!"

"Yeah, sure! Only if you're blind!"

"Oops, I lost my head again! I almost forgot! Breasts are dead in America! Italian girls who sing 'Mama' can't even *own* cleavage!"

"Why doncha just shut up, and sing the goddamned song!" said Daddy, cheering me onward as always.

As I stood backstage in the wings adjusting the horsehair crinoline beneath my simple dress I felt an anticipatory tingle deep inside me. I didn't understand why then; I was so opposed to performing the Italian numbers.

A makeup person was dabbing my nose and forehead with a large powder puff when George Scheck tiptoed up behind me, covered his mouth furtively, and delivered his ritualistic preshow pep talk: "Sell, Connele!"

"You don't ask for much, do you, George? I'm doing songs I don't want to do—and on TV yet. Ugh! It's such a mechanical medium. Even with the audience, I still feel as if I'm playing to a piece of metal. Oh well, bye, George! I love ya! I'm on!"

At the conclusion of my first fiery, Italian song, "Scapriciatiello," I was startled and caught totally off guard when the audience rose to its feet shouting a chorus of bravos in wild abandon. Wave upon undulating wave of unprecedented TV cheering engulfed me.

The whistles and the deafening claps continued for so long that it was difficult for me to begin the second song, the ballad. But long ago I'd learned an old show business trick that whenever you want an audience's attention, if you speak or sing very softly, they're compelled to listen. And that's what I did.

When I began the tender opening strains of "Mama" there was a perceptible hush; an electric crackle swept through that studio.

> "When the evening shadows fall
> And the lovely day is through
> Then with longing, I recall,
> All the years I spent with you."

As I neared the end of the song, I was misty-eyed,

so caught up in the significance of the words that I was unaware of the presence of another living soul. I felt as if I had just been to confession. And I knew my heart had expressed itself well as I reverently sang the final words:

> "MAMA, until that day when we're together once more
> I'll live in these memories
> Until the day when we're together once more
> MAMA, my MAMA."*

The tumultuous, deafening roar that greeted "Mama" is what show people call a TV "happening"—one that I shall never forget. The outpouring of love that I felt from that audience caressed and flooded my senses. And like that moment almost two years before when Dick Clark first played "Who's Sorry Now?" on "Bandstand," I knew instantly that this moment too was special—but in a very different way.

I experienced a totally new, almost celestial oneness with my audience. It was as if we'd shared something very special, as if we'd both been touched in some secret, uncharted place we'd never been touched before.

Daddy was right about something else; Perry Como is a gracious gentleman in every sense of the word, and he allowed me to submerge myself in the many rounds of thunderous applause far longer than he should have.

Perry was originally supposed to do a voice lead-in into a commercial, but he was unable to speak over the seemingly endless cacophony emanating from the studio audience. Finally Perry walked over and put

---

* "Mama," music by: C.A. Bixio; English lyrics by: Harold Barlow and Phil Brito. Copyright 1941 by Bixio S.A.M., Milan, Italy. Copyright renewed. Copyright 1946 by Southern Music Publishing Co., Inc. Copyright renewed. Exclusive rights for the United States and Canada controlled by Southern Music Publishing Co., Inc. Used by permission. All rights reserved.

both arms around me. Then he merely pointed to the camera, signaling the control room to begin the commercial without his lead-in.

"That was beautiful, Connie," he said to me privately.

"Was it really, Perry?" I answered lightheadedly.

"Just listen to those people! That's all the proof you need. You're really on your way, now," he said kindly. "But be calmer, honey. Learn to take this business with a grain of salt. Enjoy it! If you don't, it's not worth it. Good luck, little girl."

Backstage the two Georges were in seventh heaven. Eleanor Scheck and Georgie were beaming, too.

"Well, that's it, kid," Daddy gloated, his eyes shining. "After tonight, you've got it made. You can write your own ticket in this business now!"

If ticket sales were a concern earlier that day, that changed fast. By the next afternoon, Carnegie Hall was completely sold out, with people already scalping tickets. I found it hard to believe that one song could affect so many people so deeply. I realized as never before what a great big kind heart America has, and how much we Americans, as a people, can be touched by anything that rings true and tugs at our heartstrings.

> November 22, 1959
> Carnegie Hall
> New York City

"Will you look at that crowd out there!" Daddy exclaimed triumphantly, peeking out from behind the backstage curtain.

"You should see what's doing in the street!" declared Aunt Marie excitedly. "Every Italian in Newark must be here tonight!"

"I'm so excited, so happy! This is the best night of my life! I can't wait to go on stage! Where's Mr. Scheck, Daddy?"

"How do *I* know?"

"Well, go check."

"Leave him alone. He's probably tied up with somebody, or else, he's on the phone again."

"But intermission's half over. I go on in ten minutes. I want to see him, Daddy—especially tonight!"

"What for? Since when do you need somebody to hold your hand?"

"I'm not nervous, Daddy, you know that. I just want him here, that's all. It's our little secret. He always says something special to me before a show."

"Then tell me what it is, and I'll say it."

"No! George has to say it, Daddy! I just want George to say 'Sell, Connele!' Hurry up! Go look for him!"

Seconds later, as I was giving a last minute cue to the guitarist, there was a flurry of panic and I heard subdued, frightened whispers among those standing backstage.

"Hey, you guys, what's going on? Is there a fire in the house? Somebody—where's Mr. Scheck? Has anyone seen Mr. Scheck? Where the heck is my father?"

Just then my conductor Joe Mele approached me. "He'll be all right, Connie," Joe said to me grimly. "Don't worry, he'll do fine."

"Who'll do fine?" I responded, alarmed now.

"Mr. Scheck," said Joe. "Take it easy, baby, everything will be okay."

"I *know* everything's okay! I just saw Mr. Scheck in my dressing room! Answer me, Joe, please!" I begged. "What in God's name is happening here? I can't go on till Mr. Scheck says 'Sell!'"

"Connie, try to stay calm! Listen to me, honey. Mr. Scheck won't be here tonight." I stared at him wordlessly. "A few minutes ago he was rushed by ambulance to the hospital. I think he's had a heart attack."

I sobbed and screamed simultaneously in Joe's

arms, unable to believe that this could be happening to George on the most important night of our lives.

"I want George," I cried childishly. "I want him with me *now!* Please, Joe, I can't go out there like this, not knowing what's happening to him!"

"You'll do fine," Joe said halfheartedly. "I've gotta start the bow music, Connie. We're on! Good luck, baby!"

That evening I gave the best, most professional performance of my life to date. It was the first time I recognized just how extraordinary a sanctuary the stage and my audience are to me—a chimerical, yet very real, refuge—the only escape I'd ever be able to count on with any certainty.

In years to come, the graver my offstage problems the more I wanted to leave them behind me and enter that other world. And the more I needed to do that, the more I embraced in song and with great love and warmth my audience, and they, in turn, wrapped their arms around me. To this day, that remains true.

The stage and the people were the only reality I needed. The rest—even the most ruthless demands—I accepted or tolerated just so that I could perform. Performing was always sheer bliss for me—my magic.

To hear the tuning up of a twenty-eight-piece orchestra and the opening tympani salvo of a bold, well-written arrangement, to bask in the glow of a soft pink spotlight, to soar on the wings of that natural "high," and to know the sense of total control is something I don't think anyone but a performer can experience. All this the stage has never failed to bring me.

But most especially, it was reaching people—that, most of all, was what my life was all about. The heady exultation of experiencing the simultaneous love of thousands of people was a thrill so overwhelming that I knew, even then, that little else in life could match it—that any kind of life beyond the footlights would be, for me, of little consequence—unthinkable, really.

*   *   *

December 1959
Bloomfield, New Jersey

"Look at what Connie just got from Europe, Marie," said my enthusiastic mother. "Look at this beautiful silver trophy! It'll look nice in the living room, won't it?"

"Forget the living room!" Aunt Marie responded excitedly. "Where did she get it—in London?"

"No, in England," Mom corrected.

"Wow!" exclaimed Aunt Marie. "Will she say hello to any of us poor slobs anymore?"

"Why? What is she—a big deal? Look, Marie, as long as she's healthy and eats good, that's all I worry about. All this runnin' around she does is nerve-racking. I don't sleep nights—I'm always worried about her."

"Just look at *this!*" Aunt Marie examined the over-sized cup. "'World's Outstanding Female Vocalist!' And look at what this poll here says: 'Number One: Connie Francis—26,617 votes! Number Two: Doris Day—3,513 votes!' We'll show those highfalutin folks out there in Hollywood a thing or six!"

There was one thing no one in my family or in the immediate world could show Hollywood—and that was how to make me good in the movies! Fortunately, Miss Day recovered speedily from that ignominious defeat and continued to reign as Hollywood's queen. She was a superstar in the movies, all right, which was one achievement I would never toot my own horn about—not with a straight face, anyway.

Yes, '59 was another golden year on the treadmill called success, as MGM presented me with its own award: a golden album that signified the sale of fifteen million records. It read: "To Connie Francis—who has sold more records than any other MGM artist in history." And they threw in a spanking new gold Cadillac, for good measure.

By year's whirlwind end it was winner-take-all for me in almost every sense of the word. *Billboard,*

Cashbox and "American Bandstand" once again called me their Best Female Vocalist. And that year was special for still another reason: on national television, I'd shared the honors with my male counterpart, the Best Male Vocalist of the year and an old friend— Bobby Darin.

18

#1 with a Heartache

Twinkle twinkle, Superstar
Fame and fortune took you far
Everybody envies you, the #1
Night and day the records play
But since the day he went away
Life ain't no fun
The songs you sing about him
Keep coming back without him
The Queen of Charts is the Queen of broken hearts

#1 WITH A HEARTACHE
Hear the girl singing on the radio
With every play your heart is breaking so
#1 WITH A HEARTACHE
You sing your song, and the whole world sings along
His love is gone, but the music goes on *

> January 3, 1960
> Ed Sullivan Theater
> New York City
> 9:00 A.M.

MY throat was parchment-dry as I stood riveted, facing Bobby, at the opposite end of the narrow, cold,

---

* "#1 with a Heartache" by Neil Sedaka/Howard Greenfield. © 1976 Entco Music.

hospital-green corridor. We simply stared at one another, as if caught off guard by a chance, unexpected meeting.

Then, very slowly, Bobby walked to where I was standing, his eyes never leaving mine. Slowly he wrapped both arms around me, burying his head in my neck, and rocked back and forth. For history's longest moment, neither of us uttered a sound, each remembering another cold early January day four years earlier.

Suddenly and desperately, we clung to each other, our eyes filled with tears, our hearts with a complexity of resurrected emotions we thought had begun to fade a long while ago. Then Bobby stepped away, extended one hand, and in a tender, husky drawl said, "Hi, honey."

"Hello, Bobby." Trustingly, I placed my hand in his, and instinctively I put my head on his shoulder. Then, very slowly, we walked toward the smoke-filled rehearsal room, a barely perceptible smile of serenity on our faces, our veins filled with the narcotic of a lost love.

In retrospect the day was deceptively simple, the kind of day of which dreams are made—dreams, retarded by hapless illusion. We were like two young lovers, totally oblivious to the approval or reproval of those around us, our faces mirroring what was surely written on our hearts—each of us rediscovering all the old feelings, deep and warm and uncluttered; each luxuriating in that endearing bond, felt and given. And remembering, too, all the youthful hurts.

Neither Bobby nor I would ever be found guilty of "traveling light." The Sullivan people teased us, saying we had the two largest entourages of any performers they'd ever witnessed on their show.

Stealing every possible moment away from the many watchful, intense stares, we spoke at a fevered pitch, listening more intently than either of us had listened to another living soul in a very long time.

I felt that I could say anything to Bobby without

having to go into long explanations, or to choose my words carefully, or to hint or hedge. I knew he understood it all.

All the things we thought and felt, and tried in vain to make others understand, came bursting forth in torrents. At times, when he talked, it was like hearing myself speaking, played back on a tape cassette. I listened to my own private, confusing, bottled-up thoughts handed back to me all crystallized on a sparkling silver tray—thoughts I'd relegated to some remote corner of my mind reserved for unsolved puzzles.

We both agreed that it was one of those things no one ever warns you of when you enter that glittery world called show business, that throughout your career you will be forced to concentrate on yourself, as if you were a rare and very costly *objet d'art*.

No one tells you about the constant selling of yourself, the never-ending striving for self-improvement, or the hours spent studying yourself dispassionately before a mirror. Or, more impersonal than that, of having four strangers study you with clinical detachment, discussing ways to deemphasize all your "bad points," talking about you as if you were a mannequin in a department store window and not a human being with feelings that can be hurt.

No one mentions that, although certain questions shock and pierce your sensibilities, you must nevertheless remain gracious and sweet while you answer them. Nor do they tell you how the harsh words of critics, especially those you know don't like you very much, render you powerless, and how some of those words are forever written on your heart.

Nor do they let you know that there are any number of people out there—some of whom you've never met—who are rooting for you to fall flat on your face, or that almost every time you make a decision, big or small, you'll make someone happy and someone else unhappy and even angry.

No one speaks of the relentless pursuit of that next

hit record and the next and the one after that; no one tells you that you're only as good as your last chart record, or that you'll make some "lifelong" friends who'll always be there for you—so long as you're in the Top 10.

They never tell you, either, of the same unending questions—questions about each thought you think, each feeling you feel, each dream you dream, each fear you fear—or of the vulnerability you feel when you constantly open yourself up for criticism. Those probing, intense questions that cause you to dig too deeply inside yourself, propelling you toward self-absorption, self-preoccupation, and self-centeredness.

How can you be anything else but, when people hang on your every word, blowing their importance out of all sane proportions? And, because of that, how easy it is to forget that others have thoughts, feelings, and dreams of their own—thoughts that might be valuable, if only you could retrain yourself to listen to what others have to say, to "think outside yourself" again.

And, most of all, they never tell you that, strive as you may, perfection is, in the end, unattainable—like some kind of stratospheric sopranic note completely out of your range. We spoke, too, of being slaves to an image, sometimes not of our own making.

"I've made so many enemies, Connie—real enemies. People who really honest-to-goodness hate my guts; they groove on this type of scene. Sometimes I don't even know why. In normal life, real life, sure— sometimes you fight with people you don't like, but no one bothers to really hate you, to want to do you dirt. Sometimes, you even find yourself hating back."

"Yes, Bobby, I know that. I say to myself over and over again, Connie, you're getting a little callous, you're getting a little too good at business, contracts, stuff like that. And, I become frightened that I'll forget how to be soft and warm and feminine."

"It's a drag, honey. You find yourself thinking about people in terms of what they can do for you.

Not too often, but often enough. It makes for a far-out viewpoint of life. And, naturally, you think, If *I'm* doing this, how about those people who surround me? Do they really give a damn about me?"

"Well," I said, a little hesitantly, "that's one problem I don't have. I'm sure the people around me care very much. But, even so, sometimes the pressure is so tremendous I just want to escape to some Lewis Carroll fantasy world where no one ever heard of Connie Francis."

He smiled warmly and said, "Where's that, baby?"

We found we shared—and were both alarmed by—our uncontrolled and incessant drivenness; we always did so much more than anyone else would have dared to ask of us.

Each of us was painfully aware, too, that our views of life had to be distorted, because people rarely leveled with us anymore. Almost everyone had some kind of vested or potential interest.

It was ironic how we felt exactly alike about one particularly disturbing aspect of our lives that gnawed away at us—how some of our *shtick*—the idiosyncrasies and excesses in which we absently indulged ourselves, even when they led to the infringement of good manners or common sense—was beginning to be perceived by those around us as further proof of our success and the power that goes along with it. And we spoke of how easy it is to abuse that power.

We spoke, too, of loneliness—how that emptiest of emotions was the most terrible kind of poverty.

"Bobby, sometimes the more people there are around me, the lonelier I feel."

"Yeah, I know—like most times," he said softly, staring ahead at nothing and playing with the topaz ring on my finger.

We exchanged all our hitherto unspoken fears, both big and little, a thousand very private, fragmented thoughts, revealing all the harmonies and dissonances of our chaotic existences. And, even in silence, we understood it all—possibly better than anyone ever would or could.

Just prior to our stage entrance, we stood backstage holding hands in a dreamlike floating state, looking out upon that theater, so full of shadows of the past, so steeped in memories of each other.

Neither of us felt like who we were—two young people orbited into prominence by communicating the romantic thoughts and dreams of an entire generation. We felt no different than the starry-eyed kids who bought our hit records. And we were both surprised when Ed Sullivan announced on network TV: "I shouldn't tell these things out of school, but when these two youngsters—Connie Francis and Bobby Darin—started out they were kids around Tin Pan Alley, and they used to go together. He was her fella. And I think it's started all over again because today, even though he had only one hour's sleep, he went out and got her a pizza. Will the two of you sing together?"

We nodded.

"Fine," continued Ed Sullivan the matchmaker. "And now, for the first time in Tin Pan Alley and in recording history, these two are gonna sing a duet together."

Bobby smiled broadly and said to me: "What'd you say your name was again, lady?"

THE SONG: Cole Porter's "You're the Top"

TOGETHER: You're the Top, you're the Colosseum
              You're the Top, you're the Louvre Museum

CONNIE: You sang "Mack the Knife" and they
              did your life—like WOW!

BOBBY: I flipped my lid when you first did
              "Who's Sorry Now?"

CONNIE: You're the Top

BOBBY: Thank you, thank you

CONNIE: You've got ladies sighin'

BOBBY: (Name one.) You're the roar on the Metro Lion

TOGETHER: But next to you, I'm a worthless shoe, a flop

BOBBY: 'Cause Connie, if I'm the bottom, You're the Top. (Shall we go around again?) You're the Top, you brought back all the old songs.

CONNIE: You're the Top—you've made all those gold songs

BOBBY: (I've gotta pay taxes yet.) You're "My Happiness," you're a big success, my friend

CONNIE: You're a *Newsweek* cover, "My Dream Lover," the livin' end

BOBBY: You're the Top, methinks you've won every title

CONNIE: No, no, no, no, You're the Top, you're the nation's idol

BOBBY: (My hair's not long enough.)

TOGETHER: But next to you, I'm a worthless shoe, a flop

CONNIE: 'Cause Bobby, if I'm the bottom

BOBBY: No Connie, if I'm the bottom

TOGETHER: 'Cause baby, if I'm the bottom, You're the Top.

Later a fan magazine would write:

When they sang together on Ed Sullivan's TV show no one would have guessed their story. They looked like what they were—a couple of kids sharing the spotlight they had both earned—a couple of kids proud of their Italian ancestry, devoted to their families (for whom they both bought houses in Jersey), determined to make even more of their already dazzling careers. No one would have guessed that not so very long ago this couple of kids were very deeply in love.

Not so very long ago (and maybe it was over an ice cream soda in a drugstore on Broadway), he'd said, "Connie, let's get married in 1961. I'll have a million dollars then and I won't have to say 'sir' to anybody." She said—well, she didn't say anything, but she thought: "Ask me now, ask me anytime, I love you so much."

The way she felt then had been so simple. They'd be walking down Broadway, maybe in the middle of summer, with the crowds milling around like nite bugs, and she'd think it was paradise. They'd look at each other and smile; he'd squeeze her hand and she'd tell herself: This is happiness, this is all I ever want. . . .

January 3, 1960
9:30 P.M.

When the show was over, I stood outside the dressing room in that same spot of the corridor where we'd seen each other when the day began a millennium ago. I watched intently, as if invisible, while Bobby stood there with almost weary urbanity, surrounded by a group of people, signing an autograph or two.

And as I watched, I felt totally estranged from him, as if he were a performer I'd watched on TV a hundred times, whose face I'd seen in a thousand magazines, whose voice I'd heard each time I turned on my radio. Only a name I'd read in gossip columns, like some stranger I'd never met before and would possibly never meet again—nothing more, nothing less.

It was a rather haphazard, almost phony, show business good-bye—quiet, undramatic, devoid of theatrical fireworks; no klieg lights, no fanfare, no theme music, no tears—not at that moment, anyway. As his lips brushed my cheek, he said, "Tear down the Cloisters, C.F.! Hollywood's waitin' on you."

Then abruptly, he turned to face Daddy, his stern, direct gaze belying the casual, on-top-of-the-situation remark.

"Oh, by the way, Mr. F.," he said, "quit talkin' 'bout me to all those movie magazines, will you? My fans don't like it much."

Then, with the alacrity and finality of a slamming door, Bobby stepped out of my life again. And the long, full day—like a scratched 45 carelessly rejected—was over as passively and cruelly I slipped back into my seasonless and loveless tinsel world.

19

Hooray for Hollywood

Hooray for Hollywood,
That screwy, ballyhooey Hollywood,
HOORAY FOR HOLLYWOOD *

> January 1960
> Sunset Strip
> Hollywood, California
> 12:45 P.M.

"Tinseltown, U.S.A.! I ask you, Constance, is this town faaabulous?" said Bruce, my slight, blond public relations man from Rogers and Cowan.

"Yes, Bruce, it certainly is!" Sandy Constantinople, my new, older gal Friday, answered obligingly.

What's so great about it? I thought to myself sadly, as I sat on the floor in the back of Bruce's pink foreign sports car. I'd become sick to my stomach as we'd wended and weaved our way down the serpentine curves of Benedict Canyon toward the famous Strip.

"Contessa! Why on God's good earth are you sitting

on the floor?" Bruce reprimanded. "*Stars* don't sit on floors, dahling! Sandy, you tell her."

"Connie, what is *this* all about?" Sandy asked, as she turned and cast a look of disapproval in my direction.

"I'm nauseous, Sandy," I groaned, "from all these curves in the—"

"Tsk, tsk, tsk, Constance," clucked Bruce. "I'm nauseous means you cause nausea, you evoke it in others. Now we don't really mean to say that, do we? 'I'm nauseated' would be more appropriate, dahling."

"Okay, Bruce," I blinked. "I'm nauseated . . . from all the curves in the—"

"Tsk, tsk, tsk. Tacky, tacky," admonished Bruce. "Stars don't get nauseated, Contessa! You tell her, Sandy."

"This one does, Bruce," I said, setting the record straight. "Could we stop for an Italian lemon ice over there? It'll settle my stomach. . . . Then I can sit on the seat again and make everybody happy, okay?"

"How many times this morning does this make, Sandy?" asked a supercilious Bruce. "You mean this is only the *third* stop? Really, princess, my wire terrier gives me less trouble on the road. Oh, very well. . . ."

"Bruuuuuce," I whined, injecting a note of suffering into my voice as I licked my lemon ice, "how come everything out here looks so fake?"

"What do you mean?"

"Well . . . it's not like—real, Bruce. It's not like Brooklyn, Newark, Belleville—any of the places I've lived. . . ."

"I'll just bet!" Bruce replied.

"You know what I think it is? There's no dirt! That's it! Everything's too clean! And, plasticky—like a backdrop! And, everything's like one shade—a sick-looking-washed-out-pastelly-type color. And there's another thing, Bruce—"

"There is?"

"Uh-huh."

"Really, Connie!" Sandy said. Then, trying to appease Bruce: "Connie's been in L.A. before—it's just that she's a bit nervous about her interview with Miss Parsons at the Brown Derby. She knows how important it is for her Cloisters date."

"I'm not nervous, Sandy—you know that—I'm just interested, that's all." Then to Bruce I noted sympathetically, "It's a sin for you people out here, isn't it? Nothing is near anything else. How do you guys conduct business? When do you find the time? All you do, day in and day out, is zip around on those hideous freeways in your convertibles. I mean, you got great tans, but how do you guys earn a living? I could never live like this."

"Probably not," Sandy lamented. "If you couldn't make twenty-six and keep forty-eight appointments a day, you wouldn't be able to handle it."

"Whatever," said Bruce absently, ignoring my banal criticisms. He had more important things to fret over—like priming me, for the twelfth time, on our upcoming luncheon interview with Miss Louella Parsons.

"Listen, dahling, I hate to keep harping on the same silly nonsense, but this interview with Louella is extremely important to your Cloisters date. Let me see, did I tell you everything?" Bruce pondered. "Wait! Oh, Lord! I can't believe I almost forgot! I could wring my own neck! There's one thing I completely neglected to mention—and it's vital!"

"What is it?" I asked.

"You, Contessa,"—he paused dramatically, peered over his left shoulder, and winked—"you, my dahling, *adore* Stephen Boyd!"

"I do?" I asked innocently.

"Yes, Miss Connie, you think he's faaabulous."

"Could you run that by me one more time, Bruce? Stephen Boyd . . . let me think about that one a minute."

"If you think, think Stephen!" Bruce instructed.

"Okay . . . let me see . . . Stephen Boyd. Gee, Bruce, the only time I think I saw him was in the movie *Ben Hur*, and I was so busy drooling over Charlton Heston, who had time to look at Stephen Boyd?"

Connie and George Hamilton on the set during the filming of *Where the Boys Are*. On location during the filming of *Follow the Boys:* from left to right, Russ Tamblyn, Paula Prentiss, Janis Paige, Dany Robin, Connie, and Richard Long.

Right: A recording session with Arnold Maxim, president of MGM records *(photo by Gerald Engel). Below:* A pensive moment while recording an album of Burt Bacharach songs.

A birthday party for Louis Armstrong on the set of
When the Boys Meet the Girls.

Connie with her French fan club in 1963.

Connie has entertained audiences throughout the world, singing to people in their own language; above, in Spain, left, on her German TV special; opposite and above, accepting a gold record in Japan.

Connie visiting U.S. Air Force troops in Vietnam.

Connie and her family in earlier years. Connie dancing with brother George. Connie dancing with her father on the occasion of her parents' fortieth wedding anniversary.

Right: Connie and her longtime manager, George Scheck. *Below:* Connie surrounded by members of her fan club.

Connie and son Joey, on a trip to London.

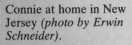

Connie at home in New Jersey *(photo by Erwin Schneider)*.

"For heaven's sake, Contessa!" Bruce shouted, close to panic. "Whatever you do, don't say that to Louella! Besides, stars don't go to the movies—they go to screenings. Now, don't forget, La Connie, not a single breath about anyone but Stephen!"

"How come?" I asked, still in the dark.

"Because Stephen is Louella's fair-haired boy, that's why! If you want to get on Louella's good side, you'll merely mention that Stephen is divine, that's all. We're simply mad about the lad—true?"

"Nothing's true out here, Bruce. That's what I mean by fake—you got fake interviews, fake trees, fake fruit, fake weather. Even the way you guys talk out here is fake—what a sin—what pressure. . . . Newark was never like this, was it, Sandy?"

The Brown Derby
Sunset Strip
Hollywood, California
2:00 P.M.

"Constance," Bruce hissed, his patience strained, as we left the Derby, "when Louella brought up Mr. Boyd's name, why on earth didn't you tell her how insane you are about him? You missed your golden opportunity, dahling."

"I couldn't do it," I said. "I would've choked on my cottage cheese and fruit salad. Cottage cheese and fruit salad—yuk! Why wasn't I born Swedish and svelte? A grain of rice shows up on my hips. . . . Oh, yeah, I forgot! That's another thing I don't like about this place—"

"There's more?" he asked in an irritated voice.

"Uh-huh. Don't you have any fat people out here? I don't think normal people live here. Everybody used to be an extra in the movies. What a way to live—"

"Are you through, Connie?" Sandy stopped my flow of conversation. "Because I wouldn't want to interrupt you when you're on a roll."

"Thanks, Sandy. No. I'm not through. Bruce . . ." I paused reflectively, "it's so sad, isn't it?'

"What's so sad?"

"The business—everything. I mean, everybody's waiting for that big break that might never come. Or else, everybody wants to look younger than they really are. They don't grow old gracefully out here. You know what I mean?"

"Actually, no . . . whatever." Bruce brushed away my comments like so many gnats. "Well, let's be thankful for small things, La Francis. At least, you're not a dummy! You saved yourself when you told Louella you'd think about doing a Jimmy McHugh tune in an album. Louella and Jimmy are like this." He winked and crossed his index and middle fingers. "Very close."

"Why wouldn't I do a Jimmy McHugh tune? Jimmy's a great writer. If I think back, I probably did one already. . . . Bruuucce," I drawled, "can I tell you something as a friend?"

"Connie," Sandy put in, "why don't we just dispense with any further critiques? Bruce will think you don't like it here—"

"Your values are all topsy-turvy out here, Bruce," I interrupted. "It's no wonder you people are so insecure."

"Really, Connie!" Sandy said, a deep frown creasing her forehead.

"You know, Constance," Bruce said, in a huff now, "I can't believe you and I have the same town in mind."

"How come?" I asked.

"You can't be serious!" he went on defensively. "Hollywood's faaabulous! It's God's country, that's all. What's so great about New York, anyway? Do you think New Yorkers are happy?"

"No, they're not! But at least they're alive! They have to be, just to survive for a day out there! And New York's still real—they've got dirt there!"

"In abundance, I'm sure," Bruce countered.

"And, that's another thing about New York—people don't rent everything there. The people here rent everything. It doesn't matter if they *own* things or not—just so it looks like they do."

Sandy began speaking, but her voice broke.

"Don't feel bad, Bruce, but it's the truth. You got rented houses, rented jewelry, rented furs, rented cars—even rented people!" I mused. "I wanna go back to Jersey—"

"Not now you're not, La Francis!" Bruce said. "Hollywood's waiting to welcome you in style! Too bad you won't have time to change out of that dreadful little polka dot number you're wearing. But, we can't be late for this shindig. We've got KLAC and KMP—"

"What shindig?" Sandy asked, suddenly alert.

"At the Cloisters! Every star in the theatrical galaxy will be there to welcome the Contessa—"

"Oh, no!" Sandy shouted in alarm. "Connie can't go to a party in her honor in that Sunday-go-to-meeting shirtwaist thing she's got on! She must appear in something far more dramatic—more sophisticated—more Hollywood!"

"Sorry, my lady—no time. Next time the Contessa will have to plan her day better."

"Don't worry about it, Sandy," I said soothingly. "Calm your nerves. We'll go in, we'll have a diet soda, say hi. It's no big deal."

> The Cloisters
> Sunset Strip
> Hollywood, California
> 6:00 P.M.

"What a bash! I knew we should've changed your dress!" Sandy moaned. "How embarrassing—you look like Shirley Temple in *Good Ship Lollipop!* And, in the company of all these fantastic-looking people. Oooooh—there's Joan Collins and Tuesday Weld!"

"Look at these people, Sandy. They look like apart-

ment buildings! They grow the people out here the
way they grow the fruit. Don't they have any short
people—?"

"Ooooooh! There's Michael Landon!" Sandy exclaimed. "What a gorgeous hunk of a man! Go introduce yourself, Connie!"

"Forget it, I don't wanna hang out with men who
are prettier than I am."

"Well, at least you look wholesome. . . ." Sandy
said half-heartedly.

"Sure, I know, Sandy—like a refugee from the
Pillsbury Bake-Off, right?"

"Look at all the furs and diamonds dripping off
everybody. Couldn't you just drown from all the furs
and—"

"Speaking of drowning," I interrupted, "I need a
drink! Hey, Bruce, could I have a diet soda?"

"Connie's very shy with men—it's her insecurities,"
Sandy revealed. "I wish you'd introduce her to one of
these gorgeous men—"

"Bruce, don't mind Sandy—she wants me to fall in
love every time I sing a ballad."

"Just don't forget that old saying, Connie," advised
Sandy. "Faint heart never a fair lady won. Which
means, in essence, you're going to have to be a lot
more aggressive if you're going to win the heart of one
of these incredible—"

"Sandy, you sound like a valentine! The only thing
I'm gonna win around here is the Gabby Hayes look-
alike contest."

"Connie," persisted Sandy, "if you'd begin caring a
little less about record sessions and a lot more about
makeup and clothes and hairdo sessions, you'd be a
lot better off."

"If I don't do those record sessions, who's gonna
pay for the makeup and hair and clothes?"

"Ooooooh, look!" Sandy said excitedly. "There's
Edd 'Kookie' Byrnes from 'Sunset Strip'! He's breath-
taking!"

"Pull yourself together will you? You're eyeing the man like he's a midnight snack!"

"Don't be a child. Oooooh, there's Warren Beatty! And Troy Donahue! How exciting! They're absolutely magnificent! Really, Bruce, I'm quite serious about this—we've *got* to do something about Connie's non-existent love life."

"Sandy," I said defensively, "there's only one thing wrong with my love life."

"What's that?"

"I need another person, that's all."

Suddenly Bruce whisked me across the room. "Hello, Miss Malone," he said obsequiously. "Miss Malone, would you please say hello to Connie Francis. Contessa, meet Miss Dorothy Malone."

"Hi, Miss Malone! Gee, I loved you in *A Summer Place!*"

Bruce's face was ashen as he whisked me away. "That was Dorothy *McGuire*, pet! You're succeeding in giving me a vile, loathsome headache! Now don't blow this next introduction—her daddy is a big, big man! Runs a beaucoup big studio. You've heard of—"

"Save your breath. I met her already. She's affected—she has an attitude. Know what I mean?"

"Not actually."

"Well, like I got the feeling that when she's petting with a fella she's really wild about—she cries out her *own* name! Do you know what I mean?"

Bruce blinked.

"Bruce," I said soulfully, "don't you have any real people out here?"

"What do you mean, real?"

"Like real—you know, people who get head colds, psoriasis, sinus trouble, stuff like that. People with some imperfections."

"Imperfections!" Bruce scoffed. "You want imperfections! In L.A.! Like what?"

"Right about now I'd settle for a split nail, a chipped tooth—anything, Bruce!"

"Tsk, tsk, tsk. Stars aren't blessed with things like that, Contessa! We'll just have to ship you back to Newark for that sort of nonsense, dahling. I'm sure you'll find exactly what you're looking for there, won't she, Sandy?"

"Sandy knows what you mean, Bruce, 'cause she's from Newark too, only she forgets a lot. If I could be in Newark right now, do you know what I'd do first thing, Bruce?"

"I haven't the foggiest," said Bruce, dully.

"The first thing I'd do is look for some Italians!"

"Tsk, tsk, tsk . . . you'll simply have to look a little harder, La Francis, because there's Frankie A—"

"Frankie! Thank God! (Thank you, God—and I mean it!) What a sight for sore eyes!" I cried out enthusiastically as I pulled Sandy across the room.

"C'mon, Sandy! I'll introduce you to Frankie Avalon and Fabian! Thank God you guys are here! Hi, Frankie! Hi, Fab!" I shouted, bussing each one on the cheek. "Frankie, imagine if Pigeon knew you were here, she'd die! C'mon! Let's go call her! Where's a telephone?"

The Cloisters engagement was nothing to write home about—Hollywood *wasn't* ready for me yet! But one first emerged from that ill-fated trip to the coast. As a direct result of that big bash, I soared right to the top of the charts. That was me, all right! Yup, I was voted Hollywood's Number One Worst-Dressed Personality of the Year!

20

Everybody's Somebody's Fool

or

How a Number-One Double-Sided Hit Was Born

EVERYBODY'S SOMEBODY'S FOOL
Everybody's somebody's plaything
And there are no exceptions to the rule
EVERYBODY'S SOMEBODY'S FOOL*

> February 1960
> Bloomfield, New Jersey

"WHAT'S all that, Sandy?" I asked Sandy Constantinople, as I lay sprawled on my tummy on the lavender quilt of my lavender and white, early Levitz bedroom. I was completely surrounded by a menagerie of assorted stuffed animals as I signed my new 8 x 10 glossies.

"Hey, Sandy! Did you see my new eight-by-tens? Great, huh? Take a look at this one! Mom must have had it touched up by Leonardo da Vinci! What's all that stuff?" I asked again.

Sandy was carrying a huge bale of gift-wrapped packages; there was a telegram in her mouth.

"It's the usual, Connie. But this is nothing!" Sandy reported with difficulty. "While we were in L.A., over two hundred belated birthday and Christmas presents arrived."

"Ooooh, I love presents! What's this one?"

"It's a koala bear from your fan club in Australia and a whole carton of Bazooka bubblegum. Three hundred and sixty-five pieces—one for every day of the year—from your Milwaukee fan club," Sandy was still clenching the telegram between her teeth.

"How cute!" I said, removing the telegram. "How did they know?"

"They read—that's how they know! You tell the fan magazines too much. And you're too approachable. After that disastrous party in L.A., I should think you'd want to project a more sophisticated image to the public!"

"Here we go again. I should've left the telegram where it was. Sometimes you can really be a drag, Sandy."

"A drag! You're doing it again! Super! Dreamy! The end! Groovy! All that Heidi phraseology! Throw it out the window! You don't need it anymore—it belongs to another life! . . . What's the telegram about?"

The telegram was from Howie Greenfield. It read:

> There once was a girl named Concetta
> Whose friend tried in vain just to get 'er
> He tried ninety times, spent all his dimes
> Should he take out a loan or forget 'er?

"Hi, Howie. Whatcha doin'?"

"Watchin' a Frankenstein movie. Jack Keller's here—I've been writing with him. You got my telegram, right, Concetta?"

"Yeah, Howie, I did. Cute telegram . . . and effective, too. I called. Did you write that country tune yet for my next date?" I asked eagerly.

"That's what I've been trying to call you about. Jack

and I wrote it together. It's real country, Con, and it's called 'Every—'"

"Solid!" I interrupted. "What's it called?"

"You did it again—you always step on people's lines! It's a terrible habit of yours!"

"My mind's always racing, Howie."

"That's no excuse—it's a rude and annoying habit. Everyone says so."

"Okay, okay, already," I said impatiently. "So what's it called?"

"It's called 'Everybody's Somebody's Fool.'"

"Love it! Hit title! You know how I am with titles. What's it like?"

"It's a love song, what else? It's the end, Con—you'll love it!"

"What's the name of it again?"

"'Everybody's Somebody's Fool.'"

"Well, you're right on target, Howie," I sighed. "I have to say that much for you. Story of my life. . . ."

"Of course it is. Every song I write, I write about you, and what's currently happening in your life. Didn't you know that?"

"No, Howie, I didn't. That's cute. Tell me more about the song."

"It's a country ballad, real groovy. A Laverne Baker–type blues ballad."

"Well, for Germany—incidentally, Howie, Germany's a tremendous market—I need something more regimented. I would sing too much off the beat on a ballad. I need something very precise—very definite—right on the beat."

"Like what—'Deutschland Über Alles'?"

"You're cute, Howie. No! Like 'Heartaches by the Number.' That's it! Like 'Heartaches by the Number'! Go ahead, Howie, tell Jack to play it up-tempo like *Heartaches!* Hurry up! I'm late!"

"Jack's asleep on the floor in front of the TV set."

"Well, shut the TV set off and wake Jack up and tell him to play the song! C'mon, Howie, I haven't got all night! I gotta write in my diary and open presents

yet! And *Photoplay*'s coming over here to shoot a pajama party with my girlfriends and Dion—you know,
from the Belmonts. C'mon! Let me see if the ballad
works up-tempo! Wake Jack up!"

We tried doing the song like "Heartaches by the
Number." It worked well.

February 1960
Bloomfield, New Jersey

"Connie, here comes your father," Mom hissed under her breath, as she stood at the kitchen sink
washing pots. "Go ahead—*you* tell 'em! I don't wanna
start up with him again."

"What, Ma?" I asked absently, reluctantly looking
up from my ritualistic morning crossword puzzle in the
Newark *Star Ledger*.

"Stop doin' the damned crossword puzzle and tell
your father to change his clothes! He looks like a rag-
picker."

"What's the difference what he looks like? How bad
could the man looook . . ."

Then I looked up and saw Daddy. He was wearing
his uniform—his black-and-red flannel plaid shirt and
his I-don't-know-what-color slacks, looking even
scruffier than usual.

"You're right, Ma. Daddy! Mom's right! What is it
with you? I bought you an entire closet full of designer
clothes, and you still look like a *caffone!*"

"Where the hell am I goin'—to a ball? I'm goin' to
take some sausage to Joe Koczat at the bank in Newark, then I'm goin' to Phil the fishman, and then I'm
goin' to Melody Mike's. I wanna see how the Italian
album's doin'."

"Connie, tell him!" Mom urged.

"Daddy, do you have to walk all around Newark
looking like an accident waiting to happen? It's embarrassing!"

"You two women are nuts," Daddy said. "I'm glad

you got nothin' else on your mind to worry about except my clothes—"

"Daddy! You still ride in that old crate—that Mickey Mouse car! Buy yourself a car, for godssake! You get ten percent of my record royalties, that big consultant's fee from MGM, and one-third of my publishing companies. That's big dollars! But no one would ever know it—you still look like a *shlump!*"

"I read in the papers yesterday you're goin' out with that jerky rock 'n' roller? Is that true?"

"I've seen him twice."

"You always did go for weirdos. You got some taste, sister. Why don't you ever bring anyone around whose normal?"

"I did, in high school. Stevie Cohen. He's studying to be a doctor now."

"Then he must've just *got* sane. When you brought him around, he was still a kook!"

"And what was so wrong with Scott?" I asked.

"He's a nice guy, but he's divorced."

"So?"

"Whatta ya need *that* aggravation for? He's got kids. . . ."

"So?"

"So, you don't need nobody else's problems."

"You're so cold, Daddy."

"No, I'm not. I'm just talkin' common sense."

"Your father's right," Ida echoed. "Besides, if people see you with a divorced man, they'll take your Catholic Entertainer of the Year Award back!"

"Daddy, Mom, forget that. Do me a favor, will you, Daddy? Make Mom happy. And make me happy, too. Go inside and change your clothes. People will think you're an orphan. I can just hear it. 'Oooooh, look at Connie Francis's father—just *look* at the way he looks!' They're gonna throw a benefit for you, and I'm the one who has to listen to all the stories. . . ."

The same day
Melody Mike's Record Shop
Newark, New Jersey

"Hey, George, I can't keep that Italian album in stock," Melody Mike told Daddy, who was making one of his thrice-weekly visits. "It's sellin' like hot-cakes!"

"Yeah, I know. That's another idea of mine my jerky daughter didn't want no part of."

"George, I meant to ask ya—is MGM gonna issue another Italian side as a follow-up to 'Mama'?"

"How come?"

"Well, this here number, George—it's a real oldie, but I've been selling three, four copies a week of the lead sheet, week in and week out, for years now. Here—give your kid a copy. Maybe she'll like it."

"*My* daughter? She wouldn't know a hit if she ran over it with her car—that Queen Mary she drives around in. What's the thing called?"

"'Tango della Gelosia.'"

"Aw, that's all she's gotta hear, Mike! Does it have an English name? 'Cause my daughter won't do it if she thinks it's too Italian."

"Yeah, it says here in small print: 'Jealous of You.' Tell 'er it's called 'Jealous of You.'"

"Lemme hear it. If it's good, I'll tell her it was *your* idea. She don't listen to nobody no more, 'specially her old man."

When Daddy came home, he carelessly flung a battered old 45 and a lead sheet on the kitchen table.

"Here, throw this on the flip side of that country tune you're cuttin'."

"But, I've already got that *other* great song, 'The Millionaire.' It's a Howie Greenfield–Barry Mann song."

"I don't care if Chopin wrote it—it stinks. Here, listen to this thing."

"What is it?"

"'Jealous of You.'"

"Where'd you get it? Who sent it?"

"No publisher. I got it Down Neck, at Melody Mike's."

"Oh, by the way, how'd he say the Italian album is doing?"

"Okay," Daddy said grudgingly.

"Just okay?"

"It's doin' pretty good." As usual, it was like pulling teeth. God forbid, he should make me feel secure.

"In Newark. Only *pretty* good in Newark? I'd better check that out with Sol at MGM. Are they doing enough promotion—record store displays and stuff? Gee, I don't know . . . Sol Handwurger is my man up there. He always does such a good job for me. Let me make a note of it. So this new song—what's it like?"

"What's the difference? Throw it on the other side. The country thing's the hit, anyway."

"Can we own part of it?" I inquired.

"What the hell's the difference?"

"Maybe George can make a deal."

"What are you, a publisher now?" Daddy barked. "Just do the best goddamned song and leave the publishing up to Donnie Kirshner. That's the trouble with people—they get too greedy."

"You're right. Besides, you've gotta give the jukebox operators a decent flip side. So what kind of song did you find?"

"It's Italian," he said almost inaudibly.

"I can't read lips, Daddy. Run that by me one more time."

"It's Italian," he murmured."

"Italian! Of course! What a shock!" I cried. "Why don't you give it to Phil Brito or Carlo Butti? Better yet, why don't you just abandon your family and go *live* in Italy? Why do you languish away here in America when all of Calabria awaits you?" I shouted, stamping my foot. "*This*, Daddy, is carrying my heritage to idiotic lengths!"

"The hell with ya—do whatcha want. You sure can pick 'em, sister." Daddy shuffled out the door.

I did his dumb song. Who wanted to listen to the man if I didn't?

April 7, 1960
Olmstead Studio
New York City

"I don't even have to hear the playback! It's a smash!" I shouted after the second take, grabbing Howie Greenfield and jumping up and down. "I *knew* it, Howie! I knew it as soon as I added the organ! Hey, hey, hey! You *did* it, Joe!"

I gave Joe Sherman, the arranger, a bear hug, almost knocking him off his feet. Then I grabbed him by one hand, Howie by the other, and made a beeline for the staircase leading up to the control room, scaling the steps three at a time.

"Run that thing, Val! I've got goose bumps! *Toca la canción, mi amor!*" I beamed, planting a kiss on the forehead of my Spanish engineer, Val Valentine. Then I noticed Arnold Maxin, the President of MGM Records; he did not look pleased.

"What's the matter, Arnold?" I asked. "You look like your dog died."

"You're not serious, are you?" Arnold asked gloomily.

"Not serious about what?"

"About releasing this thing—'Everybody's Somebody's Fool'?"

"Why not? I've never been so sure of a side in my life!" I said. "It's a monster!"

Arnold Maxim disagreed. "'The Millionaire' is the monster."

"Arnold, now that I was stupid enough to waste your money and cut 'The Millionaire,' I can tell you that it's a certified dumbo song—a real loser!"

"Not for my money! As far as I'm concerned, it's the A side, Connie."

"It's not even an L side, Arnold," I pouted. "It's

the worst! And, it ain't never gonna see the light of day!"

"Connie, it's tailor made for you!" said Arnold decisively.

"Thanks a lot, Arnold. I love you, too. I ain't got no money, ain't got no gold, but I got more heartaches than Fort Knox can hold! C'mon, Arnold. A Hall of Famer it's not! Howie, tell Mr. Maxin how you feel. Tell him 'Everybody's' is the smash!"

"I don't care either way, Concetta," Howie replied magnanimously. "I wrote both songs, so I can't lose!"

"Howie," I said, gritting my teeth, "you're pressing your luck—"

"Okay, okay, Concetta. Don't get your Italian temper up. Mr. Maxim, how come you don't like 'Everybody's Somebody's Fool'?"

"'Cause it's country, that's why! The country people will hate it! You're never gonna break that country market, Connie."

"So what?" I shrugged. "I don't sell country, anyway. I never have. And as far as the pop market is concerned, 'Tennessee Waltz' didn't destroy Patti Page's career, did it?"

"That was a decade ago—there hasn't been a female country hit since."

"So? All the more reason to release it. Anyhow, a good country tune breaks through in any market, any time, any year."

"Really? Like what?" asked Arnold skeptically.

"Like 'Heartaches by the Number,' like 'Singin' the Blues,' like 'Bye, Bye, Love.' Should I continue on into the next century?"

"Mr. Francis," Mr. Maxim pleaded, attempting to enlist Daddy's support. "You tell her. Tell her the song's a dog."

"No, it's not—it's good, Arnold," Daddy said. "Besides, don't talk to me about country music—I always loved country. I'm the one who sold Connie on country in the first place. Now she loves it, too. Anyhow, as long as she puts 'Jealous of You' on the flip side, so she's got an Italian follow-up to 'Mama' to help the record in metropolitan areas, I don't care."

"Howie, *you* tell her," Arnold pleaded.

"It's all the same to me," said a lackadaisical Howie.

"Connie, please!" Arnold pleaded. "Everybody in the business will laugh at you!"

"I don't want a verbal karate match with you, Arnold. 'Everybody's' *has* to be the side! That's the name of that tune! Period! End of subject! Besides, it's perfect for me to put foreign lyrics to, for Germany and the rest of the world."

"What are you talkin' about?" asked Arnold.

"It's just an idea I have, Arnold. You really are upset, aren't you? *Why?*"

"It's a decided risk, that's why! Why do you have to take risks anymore?"

"Because I'm alive, that's why! So long as you're alive, you take risks!"

"This isn't your run-of-the-mill risk, Connie! It's a death wish—career suicide!"

"My contract, Arnold—what does it say in the teeny-weeny itsy-bitsy print about releases? Am I allowed to pick my releases, or am I not?"

"You know you are."

"Okay, then, that's it! 'Everybody's' is the A side! 'Jealous' is the B side! And that's all she wrote—over and out! *You* happy, Daddy?"

"Yeah. 'Cause I was thinkin'—the next time you do Perry's show, maybe you could sing the Italian song and play it on the accordion, too."

"That's the best yet! Why *me*, God? Why do I have to fight the whole world? Daddy, do you know what a loser is? A *loser* is a healthy Italian girl who plays the accordion, *that's* what!"

Daddy just grumbled and shook his head slowly from side to side. But I wasn't through. "And, while we're on the subject, Daddy, let me say one last thing about accordions. I fervently pray that every accordion ever manufactured in America, Italy, Hungary, Romania, and the rest of the universe gets run over by one big Mack truck!"

June 1960
Hollywood, California

"Why *won't* Deutsche Grammophon release 'Everybody's Somebody's Fool' in Germany?" I asked Arnold Maxim long distance for the third consecutive week.

"Because Heinz Voigt in Hamburg says that the German lyrics are unintelligible, that's why."

"That's funny. I used a Berlitz teacher in town who lived in Germany for a while. Maybe I should redo it with a teacher who's *from* Germany. Maybe that Berlitz teacher here in Hollywood couldn't detect an American accent—and the Germans can."

"I don't care if Mr. Berlitz drove to the studio and taught you the words himself. Germany says your record's bad."

"It's a perfect side for Germany—and the rest of Europe, too! I don't care what *anybody* says!"

"You're right about *that*. Hamburg agrees with you that the song's terrific. In fact, they're releasing it by somebody else—some German artist's cut it."

"MY SONG?" I screeched. "They can't *do* that! It's my idea—my baby! I won't let them do it, that's all!"

"Wanna bet? They're releasing it right away."

"I'm going to check with legal, Arnold," I said in frustration.

"So go check."

I checked and they could and they did. In fact, for the German market Deutsche Grammophon released five different versions by five different German artists of "Everybody's Somebody's Fool." Each week I watched those German charts, and none of the versions became a hit in Germany or anywhere else. I also checked something else with MGM's legal department. Then I called Arnold again.

"Arnold, call Hamburg *now*, and tell them to release 'Everybody's Somebody's Fool,'" I demanded.

"How many times do I have to tell you—they won't!" Arnold was annoyed with me now. "They *hate* the thing!"

"They'll get over it—besides they *have* to! It's in my contract."

A few days later, Arnold Maxim telephoned me again.

"Heinz Voigt in Hamburg says your record's embarrassing," he reported. "They say you'll ruin your career in Germany."

"What's to ruin? I don't *have* a career in Germany! *Tell* them to release it!" A few days later, Arnold called still another time.

"Hamburg says if you insist on releasing that thing in their country—what's it called again in German?"

"'Die Liebe Ist ein Seltsames Spiel.' It means 'Love's a Funny Game.'"

"Whatever. Hamburg says if you insist, they're going to lop off the entire first verse! They can't even understand what the hell you're singin' about!"

"So tell them to lop it off—who cares? It's a long song, anyway. Now let's talk about Japan and the rest of the world. . . ."

Daddy's "Jealous of You" made the Top Twenty, and rose to Number One in New York and most metropolitan areas. It also was the song responsible for making me the Number One Best-Selling Female Artist in Italy.

The song remained Number One there for a long time, and stayed on the Italian best-selling charts for the better part of a year; CGD records happily reported that they were keeping their Italian pressing plants open on a twenty-four-hour-a-day basis. And "Jealous of You" became the best-selling foreign record in Italian history.

"Everybody's Somebody's Fool" earned a gold record in America, England, New Zealand, and other foreign countries. It was the best-selling record of my career. It reached Number One on the pop charts and Number Two on the rhythm 'n' blues charts. But Mr. Maxim was right about one thing. It reached zip on the country charts. (Ernest Tubb recorded it for the country market and had a Top Ten hit.)

"Everybody's Somebody's Fool" was the first song I recorded in six languages, a practice I maintain to this day. It became the Number One song on the European continent for the year. And *I* became the recipient of Radio Luxembourg's prestigious Golden Lion Award, as the most programmed vocalist on the European continent—the only time this award was won by a non-European.

My German version of the song became Germany's best-selling record that year and remained so for many years. Even today, I enjoy the honor of being the best-selling female artist—German or foreign—in German recording history.

The moral of the story is one I live by. Unless you can be proven unequivocally wrong, if you have a dream—if you truly believe in something with all your heart—you will do yourself a grave injustice if you let another living soul dissuade you from your purpose, destroy your dream.

PART THREE

PART THREE

21

Yesterday When I Was Young

Seems the love I've known
Has always been the most destructive kind
That is why I feel so old before my time

Yesterday the moon was blue
And every crazy day brought something new
    to do. . . .
So many wild pleasures lay in store for me
And so much pain, my dazzled eyes refused to see

The thousand dreams I dreamed, the splendid things
    I planned
I always built to last on weak and shifting sand
I lived by night and shunned the naked light of day
And only I am left on stage to end the play*

November 7, 1974
The Westbury Music Fair
Westbury, Long Island

I looked about my spacious dressing room, actually seeing it for the first time since opening night, forty-

* "Yesterday When I Was Young" (Hier Encore). English lyric by Herbert Kretzmer. Original French text and music by Charles Aznavour, © 1965 and 1966 Editions Musicales Charles Aznavour, Paris, France. TRO—Hampshire House Publishing Corp., New York, controls all publication rights for the U.S.A. and Canada. Used by permission.

there had been no time. And not having enough time was such a good feeling, but much too rare these last three years since I'd stopped singing, become Joe's wife, and hopefully a mother.

Tonight I had time to think. So much had happened since those first few cyclonic years when every new day brought another milestone. I'd filmed *Where the Boys Are* in the summer of 1960, and when it was released on New Year's Eve at New York's Radio City Music Hall, it became the biggest teenage film ever, and literally altered the face of Fort Lauderdale, Florida. The title song, written by Howie and Neil, became Number One in fifteen countries and in nine different languages. And then there were the succeeding teenage films, and the eleven hilarious Copa years beginning in December of 1960, when I was the youngest performer ever to star at that club during the winter season. During that first engagement, Newark's Mayor declared the day I turned twenty-two Connie Francis Day, and invited all of Newark's teenagers to celebrate at the Essex House, where he handed me the key to the city.

And the many awards, here and abroad—*Billboard*'s Top Female Singer for seven consecutive years, *Cashbox*'s Most Programmed Female Vocalist 1959-1964. Favorite Female Recording Star of Hawaii, the Philippines, Germany, Hong Kong, Italy, Australia, New Zealand, the European continent, Mexico, Austria, Japan, the Netherlands and India.

My first ABC-TV Special, my first book, *For Every Young Heart*, written especially for teenagers. The year I became Miss Coca-Cola, and was featured on "This Is Your Life" and "Person to Person."

Then came the seven exhilarating Las Vegas years, when I appeared at the Sahara, culminating in an award in 1967 as Best Female Entertainer in Las Vegas. . . . The command performance before Queen Elizabeth, the many foreign tours, being named Queen of the Venice Music Festival in Italy, the Olympia Theater in Paris, the mob scenes at the airports of Tokyo, Australia, New Zealand and South Africa. . . . The unforgettable memories of entertaining the troops in Vietnam, the excitement of filming "The Ed Sullivan Show" live five times a year in this country, for our troops in Berlin, at the Guantánamo Naval Base in Cuba, and then at the Moulin Rouge in Paris.

My weekly radio shows on Radio Free Europe, the Voice of America, and Radio Luxembourg; the honor of being chosen along with Bing Crosby as Female and Male Entertainers of the Century at Canada's '67 Expo.

I reminisced now about my two short-lived marriages, and how I had swept the failure of those marriages under the carpet; about the devastating nervous breakdown I had suffered after my second divorce; about how very much I wanted a baby. And I thought of how happy I was now that everything was back in place again.

I was at the Westbury Music Fair, a huge theater-in-the-round, about an hour's drive from New York City. This engagement marked the beginning of a tour for me of such theaters across the country. And I was having a super time. It was really great fun feeling like Connie Francis again for the first time in a long time.

I looked at the stacks of new glossy 8x10 photographs, and at all the pretty jeweled gowns made by my Paris-via-Brooklyn designer, Lisette, especially for this return engagement. And I looked, too, at the tall stack of fan mail lying on the makeup table.

I was savoring this rare time alone, reflecting upon the feelings that had resurged in the past few days; I felt alive and productive and valued. On that stage, I was in control of my life again, back in touch with myself. I was singing for the people again, and that's where I belonged—in the only world I'd ever known and loved.

I hadn't realized how much I'd missed it all. And though I liked very much being married to Joe, I wondered how I ever could have walked into any life that didn't include singing songs.

And the depression was gone—the gloom that had haunted me (and therefore everyone around me) after I lost the baby I was carrying—Joe's and my baby. Joe felt sorry for me, always moping around the house. And, as usual, he gave me the right advice. "Go, honey. Go sing some pretty songs. You always feel better when you do."

What a lucky world—this world of show business— where the rewards are extravagant, financially, of course, but in oh-so-many other ways. Just by doing what you love doing best.

I thought of the audiences and the way they personalize with you as if you were a member of their own family (and that's an honor); the way you can make them feel happy, nostalgic, romantic, even sad (if sadness is what they want to feel) just by sharing a God-given gift you really had nothing at all to do with.

Time to get the show on the road, I thought. Then, never wanting to waste a second, I decided to read some of that mail before everyone started piling in.

I picked up the letter on top. It was thick, as if it contained photos of me. Probably taken by a fan, I thought—it's a nice thing fans often do after attending shows. I opened the envelope in the same old way I usually do—with my index finger—and I made a paper cut in my finger the way I usually do.

Yup! They were photos, all right, but not of me. They were pictures of a truly beautiful four-month-old baby boy.

Also enclosed was a letter, and a clipping of a candid article my columnist friend, Earl Wilson, had written about me a week earlier. The article, called "I'd Rather Sing Lullabies," told of my going back to work because of the miscarriage and of my many fruitless attempts to adopt a child.

Then I read the letter—the letter that had me jumping with joy when my parents, my friend Francine, and my hairdresser Libby entered the room.

"You won't believe this, guys! This has gotta be the most phenomenal day of my life! Somebody write this date down! Don't forget! Look at this letter, gang! It says this baby is available for adoption! Mom, Daddy, look! Is this a doll? Is this the most precious thing you've ever seen?"

The letter said the baby was born in a slum area. His parents were too ill to care for him, and he was in a foster home with several other babies.

"I'm calling this lady *right this minute!* Frannie! Hurry up!" I shouted with characteristic impulsiveness. "Get me the phone! But first go tell them to hold the show a few minutes. Ask Rodney to stretch seven or eight minutes, too and tell Enzo he can sing till Friday night if he wants to! Tell him to sing *my* numbers, too! And ask them to stretch the intermission! Where's the darned phone, Frannie? Get me that lady!"

One word tumbled after the other: "Libby, put that steamer on! No, Libby, for godssakes! You people will *never* straighten out my life! Not the one for the gowns, Libs! The one for my *throat!* Frannie, is the lady on yet? Where's *Frannie!*"

"You gave her fifteen things to do," yelled Mom. "You told her to have them hold up the show! Who the hell can work for *you?*"

"Nobody's ever around when I need them!" I insisted.

"But you just told her—"

"Forget it, Ma! Hand me a phone! I've gotta talk with this lady! We're talking about a *baby*, you know! The phone, Ma!"

"Why doncha phone her while you're up on stage singin'?" Daddy asked. "I'm sure the audience won't mind." Then to my mother: "Your daughter's nuts. The older she gets, the worse she gets. What a screwball!"

"Sure! It's always *my* daughter when she acts nutty like this! Not yours! Mine!"

Then, like any well-trained Italian wife, she offered

her daughter a piece of wisdom. "You have a husband now, lady! Before you do *anything*, call your husband!"

I realized that, for a change, she was right. So I said, "Libs, while I'm doing my makeup, phone Dick Frank, and get me Joe, too—in the Bahamas! Hurry up!"

My husband had left that morning—just for that one day—to attend an important conference in the Bahamas. Joe had made a huge success of himself in the travel business, and I was very proud of him.

After countless calls, I was still unable to reach either Joe or our lawyer and close friend, Richard Frank. I heard a polite knock on the door and the old familiar, "Five minutes to show time, Miss Francis."

Shoot! It was too late to reach the Bahamas till after the show.

On stage I stepped into a dramatic circular pool of light to sing my closing number. But my mind kept leaping; flashes of thought wove themselves in and out of the meaningful lyrics.

>   YESTERDAY WHEN I WAS YOUNG
>   The taste of life was sweet as rain upon my tongue

(My baby's waiting for me! I'm gonna be a mother! Thank you, God! Thanks for everything!)

>   I used my magic age as if it were a wand
>   And never saw the pain and emptiness beyond

(Oooh, I know! That wallpaper I saw at the D & D building! The one they can print the baby's name on!)

>   I ran so fast that time and youth at last ran out
>   I never stopped to think what life was all about

(We'll call him Joey—what else! Perfect father! Perfect baby! Perfect name!)

There are so many songs in me that won't be sung
The time has come for me to pay
For YESTERDAY WHEN I WAS YOUNG *

The audience rose to its feet and applauded, and while the orchestra played the last few bars, I raised both hands high above my head, waved good-bye and shouted a happy, "Thank you, ladies and gentlemen! I love you! Good night and God bless you!"

While the exit music played, I skipped the usual second bow and dashed to my dressing room to make that very important phone call. But my staff and friends were buzzing around me with the usual after-show questions.

"Concetta, did I fade the spot soon enough on 'Exodus'? Are you sure you wanna take your bows in the dark? I don't like it."

"Connie, love, you promised to see your Brooklyn fan club president. She's here with her parents."

"C.F., enough echo on the ballads this show?"

Who cares? I thought to myself. I wanted all these people I loved to become Lamont Cranston, The Shadow—just disappear—because tonight there was something more important on my mind than sound and lighting.

No one understood that my baby was waiting for me to take him home and to give him more love, from more people, than any baby could handle.

I hastily peeled off my gown, which was drenched with perspiration.

"Take it easy, love," said Libby in her adorable Scottish accent. "You're breaking all the beads again. Two more shows, love, and you'll have no beads left. Here, let *me* undo it."

---

* "Yesterday When I Was Young" ("Hier Encore"). English lyric by Herbert Kretzmer. Original French text and music by Charles Aznavour, © 1965 and 1966 Editions Musicales Charles Aznavour, Paris, France. TRO—Hampshire House Publishing Corp., New York, controls all publication rights for the U.S.A. and Canada. Used by permission.

I quickly poured the Vita Bath into the tub and sat in the warm bath, splashing the water over my body with my hands.

"Where's a washcloth? Don't they believe in washcloths in these places? Not once do they ever—"

"It's right here, love," Libby interrupted softly.

"Where?" I asked impatiently.

"Right under your wee nose."

"Sure, now it's a wee nose. When it wasn't such a wee nose, Libs, I never used to perspire at all on stage. You know, before that lousy operation, when I could sing in air conditioning."

"I know, love. You've always said that."

"I wasn't happy with my cute, pudgy Italian nose, right? I had to be Hedy Lamarr! My father's right. I *don't* have any brains! Libs, please phone Joe and Dick again!"

"Francine just did, love."

"Without the air conditioning, Libs, it's a colossal pain! Wait till we get to Vegas! *Everybody* dies. The audience wilts. The orchestra succumbs. The maître d' drops dead and then I join everybody else! Call Joe again, Libs!"

"I just *did*, love."

I raced against time—dressing, signing autographs, greeting people—and repeatedly trying to reach Joe or Dick. I must have placed twenty calls to each of them—but nothing! The dirty stay-outs!

"Okay, gang! New game plan!" I bubbled to our married friends Francine and Mike Ferrante, whom Joe had assigned to stay with me. "We'll go back to the Howard Johnson's and call Joe and Dick from there. I don't care if I have to call them all night. I hope you guys aren't real tired, because *nobody* sleeps tonight—not till we reach one of those little boys to tell them about my baby!"

Later, in my room at the Howard Johnson's, while Mike went out to get sandwiches, I carefully removed the letter from the pocket of my new mink coat and placed it on the bed next to Frannie.

"Guard that with your life, kid!" I told her.

I removed my makeup and brushed out my hair. Then Frannie and I sat Indian-style in our robes on the bed. She had just suffered a miscarriage, too, and we talked about how much we both wanted a child. And every few minutes I telephoned. Finally, about 2:45, I reached Richard Frank.

"What's *with* you, Richard?" I asked exasperated. "For godsakes, where've you *been?* Never mind— forget it—it's not important. Listen, Dick, there's a *baby!* I got this letter in the mail tonight about a baby!" I was shouting, unable to contain my excitement. "Dick, he's a Gerber ad! I'm not kidding! He's absolutely the most precious baby you've ever seen in your life! And he's available for adoption!"

"Calm down, sweetheart," Richard Frank counseled in his most lawyerly monotone. "Do you see what I mean? You're doing it again. We talked about this at length just last week. *Don't be impulsive!* It gets you in trouble every single time."

The man was going on and on about my personality flaws, and *I* was discussing my baby! I was getting a little annoyed with Richard. "Okay, is that about it Richard? Then take this number down—it's important."

"Straighten out, will you, Connele? You're so damned hyper! How many times do Joe and I have to warn you not to be so rash? It's your worst fault. To-morrow's another day, Concetta. Relax."

"Look, Richard, just write down this num—"

"I *said*, sleep on it, Connie. It's three o'clock in the morning. What can I do at three o'clock in the morning? Tomorrow, when Joe gets back, we'll talk. We'll give it some thought."

"What, are you crazy, Dick?" I shouted in amazement. "It was *meant* to be! This is too incredible a coincidence to believe, but it's true! This child was born on June sixteenth!"

"So?"

"So! You *forgot!*" I said in disbelief. How could the

man forget that Joe and I were married on September
16th—nine months to the day before this baby was
born!

"The man upstairs is definitely trying to tell us
something. It's *beshtert!* Dick, I'm not kidding around
anymore. Take this number down! And first thing in
the morning, see this lady! Promise me!"

"For godssake, Connie, get your act together!
You're supposed to be a bright woman, but sometimes
I wonder. What do you *know* about these people?
Who sends a letter in the mail offering a baby? And to
a total stranger, no less."

My famous patience was just about running out.

"Look, Richard, do you wanna talk about it, or do
you wanna write the lady's number down?"

"I wrote it down," Richard Frank said with resigna-
tion. "Three times, I wrote it down."

But I knew Dick like a book—the man wasn't fool-
ing me. I knew from that patronizing tone that he
hadn't written down a darned thing.

Okay, Richard, I thought. It's no big deal. As
usual, I'll do it myself! First thing in the morning, I'll
just handle everything. Thank you very much, Richard. I love you, too.

Not wanting the letter to get all mixed up with the
mounds of other papers, mail, sheet music, tape cas-
settes, and the like that littered the small room, I carefully put it back into the pocket of my new fur coat.

I know what Dick's thinking. He's saying to himself,
"This is just more of her *mishugas*. Another wacky
idea!" Joe—come home, Joe. Okay, Richard—it's no
problem, believe me. If you don't call this lady, I'll
just do it myself—no big deal.

I was never to see the letter again—the letter that
was the only link between myself and my child. When
the police eventually returned all the papers that had
been in the room that night, all black from the dust
used to lift fingerprints, it wasn't with them. Not until
seven years later would Libby remind me that when I

left the Music Fair that night, I put the letter in my coat pocket for "safekeeping."

I double-checked the sliding glass doors with Mike, kissed both my friends good night, and bolted the hall door behind them. I left a very early wake-up call.

What a day tomorrow's going to be! The start of a brand new life for Joe and me! I drifted off, visions of bouncing four-month-old baby boys dancing about in my head. Who needs sugar plums? Not *this* kid—not on *this* joyous night!

I made a mental note of the date—November 7, 1974. The happiest and the most terrifying day I'd ever know. How would I ever be able to forget that incredible November night when the music died?

22

Scream, and I'll Kill You

November 8, 1974
Westbury, Long Island, New York
About 4 A.M.

"SCREAM, and I'll kill you!"

A searing pain shot through me. I was yanked by my hair and forced onto my back. I looked up. It took me a moment to understand. *My God!* This was no dream! He was black. There was a white towel over the lower part of his face. And there was a knife in his hand.

He released his other hand, which had been covering my mouth. He set the point of his knife at my neck. My blood froze.

"I won't talk," I whispered, half-dazed.

He shoved a towel into my mouth and tied the ends around my head. He put his hand through the top of my nightgown and, in a single motion, tore it away like so much paper.

I don't know how long it lasted—time is relative.

My face was wet with the sweat that had dripped from his face and body. I wanted to wipe it away.

I wanted desperately to throw myself into a hot, disinfected tub. There was a dim light coming from somewhere, probably from the half-closed bathroom door.

At first, his voice was soft, and not uneducated—not a black Harlem accent, but almost New England.

"Did you enjoy it?"

I'm gonna kill this bastard! This filthy, rotten pig! Wait a second—are you *crazy?* What are you doing? Think . . . just think a second . . . control that temper, Connie. Don't show him you're afraid—that's just what this animal wants . . . like an attack dog . . . no sudden moves. No sudden moves, Connie . . . calm, very calm.

"Well, it *was* a little sudden . . . I'm a woman . . . I need more time—you know. . . ."

The gag was looser; I could speak now. I was so filled with terror that my soothing, rational words shocked me as I spoke them.

Suddenly I was consumed by a demonic rage, powerful and indescribable. Rage . . . fury . . . I never knew the meaning of the words before—stop it! Stay calm! Be smart for a change—you *have* to. Don't make any mistakes . . . don't get this guy riled.

"Ever f——— a black man before?"

Twice a day, you filthy bastard! Where are your guts, Connie? You're supposed to be a fighter. This scum can't talk to you like this! I resisted the urge to lunge at his eyes. Stop! Think! Keep that Italian temper way down. Control, total control now. . . .

"No, uh-uh, I haven't."

Why is this pig tying my hands behind my back now? It's so tight . . . he must be on something . . . who knows what? His eyes . . . don't say one word to upset this bastard, not a single word. Choose your words, be nice to him, that's all. Oh, dear God in Heaven, what if this monster wants to *kill* me? How do you know? How can you tell? Remember Richard Speck in Chicago—remember that animal—remember how he actually killed all those poor kids, those eight nurses, and talked them into believing he wasn't going to kill them? Oh, my God, the towel's off his face . . . I can identify him now. Now he'll *have* to kill me—

"Did you see that movie on TV? *Cry Rape?*"

"Yes." He's saying that if I report this thing, a lotta good it'll do me. Like in that movie where they put that poor woman through hell. It's so cold in here . . . I'm freezing—

"How old are you, lady?"

"How *old* am I? Thirty-four."

"You don't look it. You're just a few years younger than my mother. I'm gonna be punished, you know. God will punish me."

Oh, dear God . . . my luck! He's a nut! Connie, *please!* If you don't panic, you can handle this . . . you're not a stupid girl. . . . Listen to the inflections in his voice—not what he's saying, but what he really means. Use common sense for a change . . . very high stakes here. . . .

"How old do you think *I* am?" he asked.

"Nineteen?"

"Right. Hey, lady, you're good, you know."

I'm *good!* You bastard! I'll rip your eyes right out of your filthy rotten head, you subhuman pig! In vivid detail, my mind dismembered him.

"Your money, lady! Give me all your money!"

"Let's see now . . . where did I put that wallet?"

Stop shoving me around, you piece of slime! Oh, please, dear God, please . . . it's not fair! Don't let it end this way. There's so much to live for. . . .

"Look in that top drawer, fella—I think it's right there. Do you see it?"

Oh, no! My wallet—what the *hell* did I do with my wallet? It's always right here! Oh, my God! Oh, no! I gave everything to Frannie! All the jewelry and the hundred dollars, too. Okay, okay, calm yourself . . . think a minute. Use your head now, be nice to him. . . . Think peaceful thoughts, Connie . . . blue skies . . . the ocean . . . calm. Okay, this better be your best performance.

"You're such a young guy. You've got a whole lifetime ahead of you. Why do you wanna do this—what you did tonight? Are you having trouble finding a job?"

"Why should I find a job when I can do this?"

A night's work of unskilled labor, huh? You piece of garbage! He yanked out all the drawers, frantically throwing them onto the floor.

Oh, no! Oh, no! Dear God, no! This can't be happening—not to *me*—not *now!* Please, somebody, tell me this isn't real, that it's a bad dream . . . the worst dream I ever had. Connie, your voice is shaking—keep your voice calm, soft. . . . Of all things, imagine this happening to me, with *my* temper. Keep your voice soft now . . . very soft. . . .

"I don't have any money. I'm really very sorry—not a darned penny. I gave it all to my girlfriend. . . . She has my jewelry, too. Hey, wait a minute! My topaz ring may be in that drawer on the floor over there. It's only worth about three or four hundred dollars."

I don't believe this! I'm apologizing! For *what?* "Go ahead. Why don't you take it with you? It's real pretty. You can have it."

That is all I can give you, you low-life, for this wonderful night—a lousy topaz ring, you miserable pig.

He's getting very nervous now. All he wants is the money. That's it. Period. I'm getting very scared . . . just look at his face . . . why is he sweating so much? I'm *freezing!* Don't look at that knife! Don't!

"There's a strand of pearls here somewhere, too." Don't underestimate this guy! Don't lie to him, he'll know it. . . . "I don't know if they're the real ones or not." . . . Sweetness and light, Concetta—he's only a man . . . be feminine . . . speak gently. . . .

"I have a mink coat over there—see it? It's brand new. I just got it a few days ago—I didn't even pay for it yet. Go ahead, why don't you take it? I bet your girl or mother will look real nice in it." What an idiot you are! Maybe he *hates* his mother!

"Yeah, sure, bitch. That's what you want me to do, isn't it? You want me to carry this f———in' thing all the way up that hill? Give me the f———in' money, lady! Now!"

If he punches me one more time I'll—I'll—you'll— *what? What?* Oh, please, please, dearest God! Help me! Help me just this once, and I'll be good the rest of my life . . . I swear . . . I'll be a good person!

He slammed my body into the dresser for the third time, and I fell hard to the floor. I'm really hurt . . . I know I'm hurt. But there's no pain, no pain at all. Where am I going to get the money? *Where?* Just stop and think a second, 'cause he's getting desperate. That's why *you* can't panic! If you do, he'll . . . no, no, no . . . don't think like that! You're okay, C.F. . . . just hang in there—

"Okay, you slut! You asked for it!"

He doesn't believe one word I'm saying. He's furious with me.

"I'm not lying, honest, I'm not! I don't lie—I wouldn't do that! I really have nothing else to give you—"

"Okay, you *whore!* I'm gonna count from one to twenty! If you don't give me all your money when I get to twenty, I'm gonna slice your f———in' throat from ear to ear! It'll be a pleasure, understand me? *Do* you?"

Instinctively, I didn't think about losing my life at all. Cut my throat? If he does that, I'll never sing again! Go ahead then, mister—kill me . . . you'd better. Never *sing* again! Ha! I'm better off dead!

He stuck the point of the knife into my neck. I felt the warm blood turn cold as it dropped onto my chest. Why doesn't it hurt? How can I convince this man? Please, God! I don't wanna die! Don't count, mister—

"One . . . two . . ."

Oh, Mommy, where are you? Help me, Mommy— please!

"Three . . . four . . . five . . . six . . ."

Does he know who I am?

"Seven . . . eight . . . nine . . ."

What if I tell him who I am? Would it help me? Could it be he just picked *this* room? Of course! That's it! Just another room . . . I bet he's never even heard of me . . . he's so young. What's there to lose? Nothing. Keep your voice steady and soft, be very humble, reasonable. It's just a meeting . . . it's a negotiation, that's all—

"Sixteen—"

"Look, fella, just let me say one thing. And then you do whatever you have to do, okay? You're holding all the cards, right? You probably don't know who I am. You're younger than I. I'm a singer. My name is Connie Francis, and I'm appearing right down the road at the Westbury Music Fair—" What am I telling him—that I'm a big shot? That he'd better not kill me 'cause they'll look harder for him? What does *anybody's* life mean to this animal? "I earn a lot of money. I might be saying the wrong thing to you— maybe you don't like rich white ladies. But the truth is, I never carry more than a hundred dollars with me. Even if we *could* find the money, it would be a hundred dollars—that's all. Do you think I would give up my *life* for a hundred dollars?"

I waited in stark terror for his answer.

I don't think it's gonna matter one bit. He's furious over the lousy money, over the lousy money. . . .

He threw me violently on the floor. Then, as if he had changed his mind, he pulled me up again brutally by my long hair.

He took the straight-backed chair that was in front of my makeshift vanity table. He positioned it facing the wall, between the two double beds. Then he pushed me down hard on it. He didn't let go of that knife for a second.

He tied my legs to the legs of the chair, with a cord, a belt—something. Then, fiercely, he jerked my arms behind me, crossing them over the back of the chair. He bound my hands together tightly.

With malevolent scrutiny he stared at my naked, trembling body. I was panic-stricken—like a criminal convicted of first-degree murder, waiting for a hostile judge to pass sentence. He shoved the chair backward with all his strength. I fell back onto my arms and hands, knees and feet in the air; I was looking up at the ceiling. My fingers, I knew, were crushed.

The jolt of pain that shot through me was the first truly intense pain I'd felt. I lay there on my back, trussed to that chair, listening while he roamed about the room, cursing and muttering to himself. I could barely make out the words. Maybe that was good. "I hate my mother."

Hate your mother, *hate* your mother, you crumb! Just don't hate *me* enough to kill me! My God! I have so much to live for. Hey, Joe! Daddy! Somebody! Take care of this guy for me, will you? He's way out of line!

He took one of the double mattresses and threw it over my face and body. Then he did the same with the other mattress. I can't see. Oh, God, I can hardly breathe! If I turn my head a little to the side, maybe I can still get some air. Maybe it'll be enough—maybe. On top of the mattresses, he threw three or four of my large trunks.

Oh, no! He's stuffing pillows under the mattress. Don't do that, mister! There won't be enough air! Oh, dear God, he's burying me alive!

Oh, thank you, thank you, God. There's still some air. Why is he going through all that stuff again? What the hell is the creep looking for, King Solomon's mines? Thatta girl, C.F., keep up that ol' sense of humor. You need it now, kid.

"I have to carry this f———in' thing up the hill," he continued to complain.

An eternity later, I heard the glass door sliding on its track.

"I'm gonna go, lady! You wait thirty minutes before you scream! Do ya hear me! Thirty minutes! Not before! If you scream too soon, I'll come back to this f———in' room! I'll do what I shoulda done in the first place!"

It's not time yet, Connie . . . you can't fall apart yet. Not now. You're not safe yet—not by a long shot—not with *this* maniac!

How are we gonna keep this thing quiet? We've *got* to, that's all. Joe will think of something. Oh, God! Daddy will go insane! Of all people! Where are you *now*, Daddy? My God, how will he ever be able to accept this awful thing!

And Mommy. Poor Mommy. I love you so much. You've gone through so much with me already. Two divorces—that breakdown—all the craziness that's been my life. Oh, Mommy, you don't deserve this at all—not *any* of it. You're such a good woman.

And, Joe, my sweet Joe. I love you so much. Oh, sweetheart, what can I say to you? I'll be all right, honey, really I will.

It's gotta be ten minutes by now.

Scream, Connie! Scream!

I screamed and I screamed. Then I paused to listen to the chilling silence. I heard the faint sound of an animal far away, baying pitifully in the cold November night. God, I knew how he felt.

Remember the old James Stewart movie, *Winchester '73*? Remember how Stewart was imprisoned in this tiny cage from which no one had ever come out alive? But *he* did. Remember why? Remember what the movie said? "You can't think of two things at the same time." That's what it said. So he concentrated his whole being on inventing, in his mind, that new rifle, the Winchester '73.

That's exactly what I'll do! Of course! Let's see now, what should I concentrate on? Lyrics! I'll think of lyrics—to happy songs. Sing from your heart, and you'll believe what you sing—always. What song, though? Come on, you're good at this, Connie.

> When skies are cloudy and gray
> They're only gray for a day
> So wrap your troubles in dreams
> And dream those troubles away

I don't know how, but somehow I got out from under those two large mattresses. *Now* I felt the excruciating pain. In my arms, my fingers, my legs, over my entire body. Don't think of that now—it's not important now. You can't think of two things at the same time. Impossible.

> Until the sunshine peeps through
> There's only one thing to do
> Just wrap your troubles . . .

I propelled myself across the room, inch by painful inch, alternately singing a lyric and then moving a bit, singing and moving, singing and moving. But with each move—the pain! Ignore it, I said. There's only one thing left to do—just *one*. *Get to that phone!* But, calmly, very calmly. You're not gonna get there any faster if you panic, Connie.

> Your castles may tumble
> That's fate after all

I'm here! I'm near the phone! Where is it? What happened to the phone? It must've fallen under the bed!

> Just remember the sunshine
> Always follows the rain
> So wrap your troubles in dreams
> And dream those troubles away*

Finally, I was parallel to the bed. My hands were still tied tightly behind me in back of that chair; my face was still looking up at the ceiling; all my weight was on my arms and fingers.

Somehow, I pulled the telephone cord with my index and third fingers until I reached the dial. I couldn't see the phone, but I could feel the holes in the dial. I remembered the room-to-room system I'd used a few times before, and managed to dial Mike and Frannie's room. My mouth was nowhere near the phone. I heard a man's voice answer—Mike's—and I screamed, "Mike! Michael! Help me! Please! I've been raped!"

It's daylight now. Everything will be back to normal soon. I'll be safe again. That man can't kill me anymore. Mike and Francine are running down the hall. They're struggling with the key to the room, but how can they get in? I double-bolted it from the inside!

"Shoot the door down! Please!" I screamed, frenzied. "Break it down, Michael! Help me! Please, Michael, help me!"

I heard nothing for an eternity. Then they returned with someone else, probably a night clerk. He tried to open the door, too, with a pass key, but it was no use.

Soon after, I heard other voices. The police are here. Oh, they're here. Thank you, thank you, God. . . .

Now . . . it's time now . . . it's all over. It's okay now. What's the difference anyway?

---

* "Wrap Your Troubles in Dreams" copyright 1931. Renewed by Shapiro Bernstein, New York. Used by permission.

When I heard the sound of the sliding glass door as it shattered, and the shouts of the policemen, I knew that any hope of containing this tragedy, of keeping this devastating thing within our family, was shattered, too. Soon the whole world would know. How awful! Dear God in Heaven. What a shameful, degrading thing!

An officer covered my naked body with a sheet.

Ed Yoe, Connie's Road Manager: "I was the third person to know. I was asleep in my hotel room in Westbury. The phone rang at six-thirty in the morning. This guy who said he was from the Daily News *wanted confirmation.*

"'Is it true Connie Francis has been raped?'

"'Buzz off, you sicko!' I hung up on him. But of course I couldn't get back to sleep. I called Connie's room at Howard Johnson's. The man who answered said, 'Detective so-and-so.' I knew then it was true.

"I got to the hospital just in time to see Connie being taken to the police station. She was wearing this light-colored nightgown, I guess it was. She looked wild-eyed, like someone who had been driven insane.

"They were trying to get her to drink something hot—coffee, tea—but she couldn't.

"When I came back to the theater later that day, everyone—the whole staff—was crying. The girls in the box office were making refunds, and they had tears in their eyes."

Days later, they told me Peggy Lee had called, and Rona Barrett and Earl Wilson and Sergio Franchi and Joan Rivers and Totie Fields and Dinah Shore. "Maybe Connie would feel better at my ranch? Would she like to stay with me at my ranch?" Dinah had asked. (Bless you, Dinah.)

Totie, after asking about what she could do to help, wanted to know from Ed Yoe in what room it happened so that she could check into it next time. That was my Totie, always making with the jokes, but still. . . .

The people who called, the celebrities, all said, "Is there anything I can do to help her?" There was no desire for publicity, for recognition. They called out of humanity, pure and simple.

November 8, 1974
Westbury, Long Island, New York
About 6:30 A.M.

Everything's hazy. Why can't they untie the ropes? The knots are so tight. Okay, okay, they're cutting them with a knife. . . .

The remainder of that day remains confused in my mind. The room was a shambles. All they could find to put on me was a lightweight robe and a pair of boots—nothing underneath. Funny, with all those beautiful clothes in that room.

As they placed me on the stretcher inside the ambulance, all I could say was "Oh, Frannie, what about my Joe? Call Joe!" Joe would handle this; he handled everything for me. He would take care of me, as always.

Then moments later: "No! No, Frannie. Don't call Joe!" I remembered Bobby Darin having to travel so far by plane when his mother died, and how awful that trip had been for him. I didn't want Joe to do that. But how much better it would be if he were here! I needed him so badly now.

In the examining room at the hospital, I lay on a metal table. It felt cold through my thin robe. My body quivered. The room was Spartan-bare save for a sink with a pedal, a clock, the metal table, and me.

I waited for an hour and five minutes. I shall never forget that feeling of isolation, of being completely shut off from the rest of the world.

I had never felt less like Connie Francis. But then

again, I had never felt less like a human being before, either. I was just another victim, reduced to a statistic you read about every day in the newspaper. But until now, the victims had always been other people hadn't they—faceless, formless people I'd never met.

I realized for the first time that I was covered in blood. Disassociatedly, I observed the cuts and bruises all over me; it was as if my body belonged to another person. On my elbows, the skin was abraded—so abraded, it would never heal. I felt dirty, defiled, ashamed, violated, helpless. I just wanted someone kind to hold me.

Finally, the doctor came in. He examined me without speaking.

Then: "I'm giving you DES so you won't get pregnant. And, here, take these antibiotics. Make sure you take them so you won't get syphilis."

I was shocked. Neither of those two possibilities had even occurred to me! Then the doctor left without another word. This was nothing new to *him*.

I will always recall the degradation I felt—so absolutely impure and unclean. I still had the man's sperm inside my body, and no one suggested I wash, even after the doctor had taken the slide. I didn't have the presence of mind to think about it myself until the next morning.

At the police station, lying there in misery, and in my yellow robe, one thought consumed me. "I'll make things normal again! I'll just do my show! Of course! I'll go right back on that stage tonight and do my show!"

All my life, when bad things happened to me, singing on stage seemed to make things right again. For me, a stage or a recording booth are the most natural places to be.

Now I remembered some of those bad times: When one of my husbands beat me so badly that the bruises couldn't be covered with pancake makeup, I did the shows. When I had undiagnosed typhoid fever, bled from the ears, nose, and mouth, and had a dangerously high temperature, I did the Vegas shows. Right before my nervous breakdown over my second divorce—that was bad—I did the Copa shows.

On every one of those nights, and on many, many others, I did my shows. Why couldn't I do them now? Just one more time? Why should tonight be any different? But it was.

I clung desperately to my plan; it was the only thing that got me through that day.

I don't remember how I got to the police station. I was taken to a room—still wearing that yellow robe, still unwashed—and questioned by two male police officers.

When the policemen asked me to tell them what happened, I just stared at them blankly, blindly. Then I cried hysterically, rocking back and forth in my chair like a baby.

While I alternated between periods of lucidity and periods of hysteria, I was fingerprinted, so the police would be able to tell my prints from any others they might find in the hotel room. Only later did it strike me as odd that I, the victim, was fingerprinted like a criminal.

How could I talk to these men? How could any man understand the self-loathing I felt—the disgust, the shamefulness of this awful thing that had happened? They couldn't; it was impossible. And I would not—could not—talk to them.

Finally, thank God, they left, and two women entered the room, two very gentle policewomen. I wanted to throw my arms about them and embrace them. I told them, sketchily, as much as I could bear to think of at that point.

For months—years—afterward, I would wake up in a cold sweat, shattered by the graphic memories, the horrifying, chilling details of those hours. I will surely live for the rest of my life—those thoughts—I'll never be able to block them from my mind. And I knew, even then, there were some things I would never tell another living soul. I never have.

"Did he say anything to you during the act itself, Connie?" Donna Alden, the kind policewoman on the rape squad, wanted to know.

I nodded and looked away, embarrassed.

"What did he say to you, dear?"

For a split second, I looked into her kind eyes and then away again. "He told me to move more," I barely whispered.

They took me into a room with a one-way mirror. I could see six or seven men—black men—in a lineup.

"Tell us something the rapist said to you, Connie," the policeman said.

"He said . . . he asked me, 'How old do you think I am?'"

Each of the men in the lineup repeated the sentence in turn: "How old do you think I am?"

Then, suddenly I heard his voice! Slightly New England! Incongruous. Not a black accent!

"That's *him!* Oh, my God! I'm sure that's him!" I screamed.

As the door to the corridor flung open and some of the men filed out, I saw him. There was no doubt about it!

I'll kill the bastard! I thought, as I flung myself at him, mindlessly screaming words I have never said before in public or in private. I pounded his back with both my fists and in each fist I felt like I had a knife and with each blow, I was stabbing him!

As he slowly walked away, I pummeled the air wildly. Someone pulled me gently away; someone took both my hands in his. "Connie, stop it, honey. He's a policeman—he's one of our people."

I *thought* it was he.

I turned and found myself in my Aunt Marie's arms.

"Oh, Didi!" I cried helplessly. "How are my parents?"

Didi was my pet name for her in the Neapolitan dialect; she was always Aunt Marie to me except when I was hurting. Since the time I was a baby, whenever I was in bad shape, I would call her Didi.

Aunt Marie held me in her arms while I sobbed. I knew it was hard for her to remain dry-eyed, but she was tough. "It's okay, sweetheart," she whispered over and over again. "It's okay. You're safe. We're here now. No one will ever hurt you again." How many times before and how many times again I would hear those words that simply weren't true.

And, then I saw my father. Facing him, I remembered the stern warning he'd issued so long ago: "Now that you're such a big star, no matter what, never give me any reason to be ashamed of you—not *ever!*"

I felt like a small child again, like a kid who'd stolen something valuable from the cookie jar. I felt vulnerable, apprehensive, as *any* child would feel facing her father after she'd done something really bad.

I looked at him, hesitatingly, waiting for those first important words. He just put both his arms around me, and I laid my head on his shoulder. He kept pinching my chin gently, the way he always did when I was in deep, deep trouble. The years washed away.

Finally, he said, "Let's get outta this joint, baby. There's reporters all over the place. C'mon, let's go home."

"*Home!* We're not going home; we're not going *anywhere!*" I shouted, feeling very strong. "I have an eight o'clock show! In fact, I have *two* shows tonight! It's Friday!"

"What are you, crazy?" he yelled. "You want people to think that this whole goddamned thing didn't mean a thing to you? Let's go! Don't act stupid."

"Daddy!" I said, half-pleading, half-determined. "I've *gotta* do my shows! I *must!* It's vital! Don't you understand, if I don't get right back on that stage tonight—I'll never go on another stage again! I know what I'm saying! Please, Daddy! I know what. You're all thinking, 'She's out of it'—right?

"I can do it! Watch my show tonight! You'll see! You'll *all* see!" I went on begging them, unmindful of my soiled robe, my wild, tangled hair, my lacerated and bruised body and face.

I didn't go on stage that night. In fact, a stage was something I wouldn't see again for several thousand nights to come.

Soothingly, my father said, "Don't worry. It won't be so bad. You're lucky Joe's the kind of guy he is."

Of course I am, Daddy. How lucky for me. I realize *you* would never understand, but *Joe* will. Joe's liberal, urbane enough not to think less of me because of what has happened."

It was a telling statement really. . . . Nothing ever changes, does it? We just *think* it does. For it was always that way—right from the very beginning.

23

My Buddy (I)

Nights are long since you went away
I think about you all through the day
MY BUDDY, MY BUDDY
No buddy quite so true

You know, life is a book that all of us study
And some of its leaves bring a sign
There it was written, MY BUDDY
That one day we'd part, you and I*

> March 9, 1981
> Our Lady of Blessed Sacrament Church
> Roseland, New Jersey
> 9:30 A.M.

THE strains of the song are playing, and for a brief moment I forget and I'm at a session listening to a playback. Or am I? Oh, no! I hope I'm not beginning to feel that panicky feeling—that same terrifying anxiety and isolation I felt just before I suffered that three-week breakdown in '71.

It happened then, too, because my mind needed so desperately to escape to a place of serenity—anonymity—any refuge at all from the unrelenting horror that had become my world. And so, very quietly, my mind detached itself, and I had slipped into a strange, dreamlike, twilight zone where mercifully, nothing real could touch me.

But, that option isn't open to me any longer; I'm solely responsible now for what happens to my family and to these people in my life who count most. I've depended upon them so much; now they're depending upon me—all of them.

They need me to be sure and strong and decisive again—the way I used to be before Westbury, 1974. I've got to try to make some sense of all of this, to bring some kind of order and reason to this world suddenly gone mad.

I held my prayer beads, but I wasn't praying. I was thinking of something I'd heard once—that God doesn't burden us with more adversity than we can handle. So, I know I'll be okay. I have to be. What choice is there?

Why am I always so hard on myself? Why shouldn't I feel disoriented? I haven't slept a single moment since this incredible day began—seventy-two nightmare hours ago.

I wonder now what—or who—could possibly hurt me again. Why do I feel so all alone? I suppose it's because it's just occurred to me that when my parents are gone, except for Joey—and it's not fair to depend on your children—I *will* be all alone with no immediate family.

No, of course it's not a session; it's Georgie's funeral—my compassionate, good-natured, only brother, Georgie. Oh, sweetheart, for as long as I live, I'll wonder what I could have done to change what happened to your life—a life that began so full of promise. It had to be a great deal more than I did.

True, I was there for you when you needed a special favor, a special contact, or money. But running around with a checkbook in my hand didn't compensate for the single most important thing I failed to give you—enough time; I was always busy doing all the important things that now seem totally meaningless. I'm sorry I let you down, sweet brother in Heaven.

I know you broke the rules, Georgie. But still, like an outsider, I ask myself: What could possibly have been *this* important to anyone? You brought joy into each life you touched. What enormous thing could have been worth the life of a sweet, devoted husband and father whom everyone loved? Well, almost everyone.

My brother Georgie is a casualty of my success; no one will ever convince me otherwise. But I'm not neurotic enough to blame myself entirely for this tragedy.

At least, that's what the psychiatrist told me not to do.

"Connie, you were a good sister," he said. "You should feel no guilt. You couldn't live life for him; you couldn't prevent the misguided decisions, the poor judgment. Nor could you change the things that happened so long ago in his childhood that caused him to do these self-destructive things. You merely did with your life what you had to do."

But I'm convinced that this isn't the case at all—I *know* I could have changed it if the timing weren't all wrong. But it was, so Georgie is a casualty. He got himself into such serious trouble—became involved with unsavory people my family, had always had the good sense to avoid—involved in a labyrinth of intricate schemes way over his head.

It's something I definitely would not have allowed to occur today. Why did it all have to happen during these last seven—no ten—agonizing years, when my will, my resolve, and my state of mind were so weak, and my life so desultory and unhappy. Today, it would be a far different story; I would never have let him die. I'd have found a solution—some way to make peace with whomever. But, what's the difference now? It's all over.

March 6, 1981
Hallandale, Florida
9:45 A.M.

The sultry March day began like every other March day in recent years. And then it became a day like no other that preceded it—or would ever follow again.

"Well, you have a choice, sweetface," I said to my good friend from the north, Anne Costellano, who was visiting me. "What'll it be, Annie? Shopping at Bal Harbour? The Diplomat pool? Or the Woodmont Country Club?"

Our robed, suntanned bodies were draped lazily over the sofa of my sunny Florida apartment as we read the *Miami Herald* and poured ourselves some pulpy, refreshing Florida orange juice. Our friend Rita, a guest for the night, was still fast asleep.

"It's up to you, Connie; I really don't care."

The average person observing this daily wintertime routine of ours would probably have exclaimed enviously: Now *that's* living! You can't die from a life like that!

But the average person would have been wrong; this wasn't living—not for me, anyway. Nor would it ever be. I learned long ago that you *can* and *do* die a little each day from the stultifying monotony of it all—that beneath this sybaritic existence the world saw was an emptiness no one could ever know. And then again, I'm not an average person.

Much earlier, after I'd sent Joey off to school, I'd fallen back to sleep. Why not? Was there any good reason to get up and face still another "filler" day—one more do-nothing, empty, unfulfilling day?

But at least it was safe behind this insulated wall of protection I'd built around me and mine. I had made a bargain with myself: If I was a good little girl and made no waves—if I did absolutely nothing at all with my life, called no attention to it—then nothing bad would happen again to me or my family. But that's not the way life works.

The phone rang; the phone always rings. Don't people sleep anymore?

"Connie, it's me."

"Good morning, Daddy," I said, still bleary-eyed. His voice sounded strange, tremulous; he'd said only three words, but I knew something was terribly wrong. Oh, God, I hope he isn't sick.

He'd left my mother in Florida only two days ago. But ever since his bout with cancer, I had palpitations every time he sneezed. This free-floating fearfulness of life had become a very real part of my personality in the last seven years. The undaunted, take-on-the-world Connie had died long ago.

"Daddy, you sound funny. Are you okay?" My throat was dry with fear.

"Connie, are you sitting down?" he asked hesitantly.

"I'm *lying* down." Now, I was filled with consternation. Nothing, but nothing, jangles my father's nerves; Daddy just rolls with the punches.

"What is it, Daddy?" I waited apprehensively for his next words. But there was only silence on the other end of the phone.

"Daddy," I repeated. "What's wrong?"

"An hour ago," he croaked, "your brother was shot."

"SHOT! GEORGIE! SHOT! OH, DEAR GOD! WHERE HAVE THEY GOT HIM? WHAT HOSPITAL IS HE IN? HOW BAD IS IT, DADDY?"

"He's dead, Connie. They've murdered your brother."

I screamed—a piercing, shrill scream. "DEAD! MY BROTHER'S DEAD!"

The magnitude of the terror that engulfed me was not a new feeling anymore; I'd experienced it three earth-shattering times before in the past few years.

Rita, hearing my outcry and the words I'd just screamed out, dashed into the living room and began sobbing. "Oh, no! Not this!" she cried. "Not this, too!"

On the phone there was only silence. My mother. I thought only of my mother. My hands were trembling so much that I had to ask Annie to hold them still. But my voice and manner belied that; I felt supernaturally calm—controlled—like some kind of precision automaton programmed not to respond to emotion of any kind. Finally, my father spoke again.

"Your mother, Connie—tell her Georgie's been in a car accident—that he's in the hospital or something—or you'll never get her home on a plane."

"I'll take care of it, Daddy," I said soothingly. "We'll be home soon—on the very next plane. I promise."

I stared, white-faced, at Annie. I found it difficult to breathe. I allowed myself a second's reflection. Just a second's.

"Annie, my brother is dead," I whispered. "Rita, we don't have to worry anymore; Georgie's gone now."

Annie looked dazed; she said nothing. Rita was hysterical. For me, this was no time to indulge in tears; there was too much to be done. I felt as if someone else had taken control of my body and mind, making me do all the necessary and correct things.

"Annie," I directed, as if addressing a secretary, "get me a yellow legal pad and a pen right away—in the drawer over there."

I made a two-page list of things to do, as if I were making a shopping list. I was my old efficient self, just as in days gone by. I phoned Tony, my right-hand man at the apartment where I spent my winter months. He worked there as a valet, but to me, he was an "everything else"; I could always depend on Tony. My words flowed calmly and evenly.

"Tony, I'm leaving Florida right now. . . . Yes, Tony, right now. . . . Please take my car and pick Joey up at school. . . . Tell him not to be concerned, but that something unusual has happened, and we're

going home to New Jersey. Don't alarm him—joke
with him a little. And Tony, have security downstairs
arrange for a station wagon and a taxi later—I'll tell
you the exact time when you bring Joey home from
school. Now, ask one of the boys downstairs to bring
up my trunks—no, no, not all of them, just two or
three of the large blue. When I leave for New Jersey,
you'll return my car to Avis. . . . I need you now,
Tony."

Tony asked me no questions—he never does; he
just tends to his own business and follows orders.

"Annie, snap out of it! Hurry up and dress! Throw
anything on and go to Mom's apartment right now!
Tell her Georgie's been in a bad car accident—that
he's in the hospital. No matter what, don't break
down, Annie! Even if she suspects he's dead—and she
will—*don't break down!* I'm counting on you, Annie.
Pack my mother's suitcases and bring her here just as
fast as you can. It's going to be a tough contract, but
keep her as calm as possible. I'll phone downstairs for
a cab."

Annie moved as if in a trance; Rita was still crying
uncontrollably and asking questions. I had no time to
respond. My mind was alert, my plans clear-cut.

"Eastern Airlines?" I asked, hurriedly. "When's
your next Fort Lauderdale to Newark flight? You say
you're totally booked? Okay, tell me when the next
flight leaves and the number of the flight. I *know* it's
booked, miss—I heard you! Please! Just give me the
time and the flight number. One-fifteen to Newark?
Thank you very much."

My clock said 10:30 A.M. I phoned a special friend,
Mr. Al Dunbar, at Eastern, and told him of the emergency on my hands—told him I needed four reservations on that flight to Newark. He said it was booked
solid. He'd have to call New Jersey to get permission
from the main office. He'd call back and let me know.
In a real pinch Al always came through for me.

Following my list precisely, I phoned my brother's
wife, my sister-in-law Arlene. There was no answer.

"Rita, stop crying. Cry later. Answer the doorbell. It's probably the trunks."

Rita and I began packing frantically. Not really packing—just throwing random essentials into the two large trunks.

"Get our winter coats, Rita. Joey's, Annie's, and mine. They're in the hall closet. And our boots. Then pack Annie's suitcases."

At 10:50 the doorbell chimed again. It was Tony, and he had Joey by the hand. Six-year-old Joey looked lost and bewildered.

"Hey, how's my little guy?" I said, cheerfully. Then I took him by the hand, excusing ourselves, and went into my bedroom with him. For my best friend, there's always time to talk. Gently I sat Joey down on the bed and kneeled on the floor in front of him. Joey always senses when I'm going to talk about something heavy; his face was somber. I clasped his little hands in mine. Until now, we had allowed no trauma to touch his life.

"Joey, Mommy needs your help, sweetheart. Today I need you to be a man, not a child. Something very bad has happened in our family. Uncle Georgie's been hurt very badly—in a car accident. We've got to go back home to New Jersey right away." It was one of the rare times I have ever lied to my son.

He looked at me oddly, not fully comprehending. "Is he really sick, Mommy? Is he home in bed in New Jersey?"

"No, darling. He's in a hospital in New Jersey."

"*My* Uncle Georgie?" he gasped, "My cousins' daddy?"

"Yes, sweetheart." Georgie loved Joey so much, and had felt a special obligation to him since Joe had left home. He wanted to be the second father Joey could always count on now that Joe had become a devoted, but once-a-week father. Recently, Georgie had enrolled his nephew in an Indian Guide program for the upcoming fall season, and planned to take him on weekly meetings and camping and hiking trips.

The phone rang.

"Please go inside with Rita, Joey. I'll tell you more later. Close the door now, honey." He balked about having to leave—he had a lot more questions—but he did as I said.

"Jim, you saved me a call. I can't have dinner with you tonight. I'm leaving for New Jersey . . . No, immediately. . . . I have no time to explain now. . . . My brother is dead—he's been murdered. Jim, I can't stay on the phone any longer. . . . Yes, you can come to New Jersey—no, not now—tomorrow."

When I hung up, I walked out of the bedroom to look for Joey, only to find him hiding behind my bedroom door; he had heard every word I'd said. He was sobbing softly, and there was true terror in his eyes.

"Mommy, why is my Uncle George dead? Who did this to him? Mommy, you mean I'm never going to see Uncle George again?"

"No, darling—only in Heaven."

He started to sob hysterically. Once again, I took him gently but firmly by the shoulders and sat him down on the bed. I kneeled before him and took his beautiful little face into my hands.

"Look at Mommy, sweetheart. Please concentrate, because what I want you to do for me is very important. I know how much you love Uncle Georgie. But Joey, you must not cry about it now. Please stop, darling. I need you today to do this very important and very special thing for Mommy."

He stopped crying and listened intently.

"We're going to play a pretend game, okay Joey? We're going to pretend that today you're sixteen years old, not six. Do you know what I need today? I need a big boy's help. I need for you to be just like Daddy, if he were here right now." Joey was so proud of his father. "Will you help me?"

"Yes, Mommy," he said through his sobs.

"Joey, listen carefully. This is terribly important. Nanny will be here any minute now. If you tell her that Uncle Georgie is dead, Nanny could die, too. You love her very much and you wouldn't want that to happen. Do you understand?" He looked puzzled; I guess I wasn't explaining myself too well.

"The shock of Uncle Georgie's death—the terrible surprise, I mean—could kill her. Now, do you understand how important it is to keep our secret from Nanny?" He understood.

"When we get home to New Jersey, when Mommy thinks it's the right time, we'll tell Nanny. Let's make this a kiss promise, okay?"

I kissed him on his little button nose. "We never break a kiss promise, do we?" He shook his head. No, never.

"You know how many times you've asked Mommy, Nanny, and Poppy, or Daddy to do something really important for you—something you wanted badly. Well, now I need something just as important from you. Think of Anthony and Kenny and how brave your cousins are going to have to be; it's their daddy who's gone—*you* still have a daddy. Will you keep this special secret from Nanny, darling—just from Nanny?" He calmed down a little, and he nodded, yes.

"I love you, Joey. Thank you, sweetheart, for being my grown-up man today and for keeping our very important secret."

He reassured me by patting me on the shoulder as he'd done since he was a small child. But in spite of the gesture, in my heart of hearts, I feared that no six-year-old, no matter how bright, could be emotionally mature enough to keep such a secret to himself—not for so many hours. But I hoped against hope.

I quickly telephoned a doctor in New Jersey who had treated me and my family, my brother and his family, and many of our good friends and relatives over the years. Over the past several years, he'd been treating Mom for a serious ulcer condition and a nervous condition, too. The events of the last years had taken a toll on a very strong, stable woman. Most other women would have been dead long ago.

On the phone long distance, it took a long, long

while before I could convince the nurse to put me through to the doctor.

"He's in the examining room," she said.

"Are you new, miss? Look, this is a real emergency—please!" I implored.

"Doctor," I pleaded, when he came to the phone. "My brother is dead! He's been murdered! I need your help! We're in Florida now—Mom and I—and Mom doesn't know about it yet. But in a few hours, Doctor, we'll be home. When she learns the truth, I'm going to need you to be there for me. Or if you can't, please have another doctor, or a nurse—anybody—to be there to give her some kind of injection."

"Connie, I'm really sorry about your trouble, but I can't come to your house."

"Doctor, did you hear what I said?" I cried. "I have a disaster on my hands! I know doctors don't make house calls anymore, but for godsake, have a heart. At least send someone to the house to help us— you're our friend."

"I'll send over a prescription of Valium."

"*Valium!* What good is Valium! She'll want to take the whole bottle!"

I was stunned; I'd always felt sure that in times of real sickness, crisis, and emotional need, our doctor would be our Rock of Gibraltar. He'd seen my family through so much, through all the bad years—the time I was hospitalized with typhoid fever, my emergency abdominal surgery, Dad's cancer, Georgie's liver problem, Arlene's nervous condition, Mom's illnesses, my bouts with depression. At first I thought I'd heard incorrectly.

"Doctor, please! Listen to me! You, better than anyone else, know my mother's poor condition. You know how close to you she feels—how she relates to you. Remember how you talked to her about Georgie when she trusted no one else? Please come! I'm begging you! I won't be able to handle this one alone— not with a Valium!"

"Call me when you get to New Jersey, and let me

know how she's feeling. I'm a busy man. I won't be able to come myself, and I can't send anyone else, either."

"What about your nurse, your associate—anyone?"

"I'm really very sorry," was all he said. I hung up the phone and cursed this good Christian.

If we weren't speaking long distance—if I'd been right there in the office with him—I surely would have done what I've never done to anyone before. I'd have slapped his face hard. I was nauseated and appalled by this man of medicine I'd had so much misplaced faith in; and I was very, very angry.

Maybe anger is a good feeling to have right now, I thought. Maybe it's healthier. Thanks, Doctor. Thank you very much. Thanks for eleven rotten years of you—you *and* your Hippocratic oath!

I called downstairs to security. "I need a cab and a station wagon downstairs in fifty minutes. No, no! Five zero—fifty minutes. Thank you, Roger."

I then called my driver in New Jersey, George Broeckel, and told him the news. He was shocked. "I haven't heard a thing on the news yet, Connie."

"Oh, you will, George—loud and clear. Count on it." I asked him to pick us up with the car and a station wagon at Newark Airport and to be careful not to reveal the truth to my mother when he saw her.

Next I called Aunt Marie.

"Hi, sweet potato pie. You lucky suntanned Florida girl, you! Don't you feel sorry for us poor folks up here in the north, shivering in our miserable boots?"

"Aunt Marie, I have no time to talk now. This is going to be a shock to you. Brace yourself. Please be at my home with Uncle Ray by four o'clock. Ask Mom's friend Pearl to be there too. Mom will need all of her friends today. Georgie's been hurt—he's been shot. Oh, Didi, he's dead! My brother's been murdered!"

There was a piercing scream—then disbelief and then a hundred questions through her sobs. But I had no time to answer any of them now. "Later, Didi, later."

The moment I had dreaded so had arrived. My mother threw open the foyer door and wrapped both her arms around me. She was crying hysterically. Her legs were trembling so that it was difficult for her to remain standing.

"Connie! Please, Connie! Tell me the truth! What's going on! My baby isn't dead, is he?"

"No, Mama," I lied. "But, he's hurt badly."

She ran into each empty room in search of a refuge, away from the insanity of it all. Finally, in helpless despair, she flung her body on the floor of my bedroom.

"Oh, *figlio bello*," my mother cried, her face twisted with grief. "My beautiful boy."

Kneeling, she rested her elbows on my bed and intertwined her hands in prayer.

"St. Jude, you know I ask for nothing for myself. I just pray to you whenever my kids are in trouble. I've made so many novenas to you, and you've helped me, St. Jude! Please, St. Jude! You know I never want anything for myself. I just want my two kids to be happy. God, help me! PLEASE!"

Rita and Annie tried to comfort her. I had to leave the room. If I gave into the pity for her that was consuming me now—if I put my arms around her and caressed her as I yearned to—the facade I was having difficulty keeping would surely crumble and then she'd know the truth. I couldn't handle that right now.

"Rita, Annie," she begged, "tell me my son isn't dead! Please! Please!"

"He's alive, Ida," they lied, their mournful eyes avoiding hers.

"When he was a little boy, whenever I had one of my bad migraines, my Georgie would sit just like I'm sitting now, at the edge of the bed, close to me. And, he wouldn't leave me no matter how many times I told

him to—not even to go out to play with his friends—
until he knew I felt better again."

I was standing just outside the door, silent tears
sliding from my eyes. It took all the strength I had to
regain my composure.

"Oh, Georgie," my mother screamed shrilly, "I love
you so much."

"Come, Ida, get off the floor," Rita said softly.
"Come and have some coffee."

But Mom just remained there on the floor. "I don't
believe this! Dear God, tell me this isn't true! How
much more pain do we have to suffer?" And then:
"Do you know, Rita, he comes to see me every day
before he goes to work? He never misses a single
morning. And he never gave me a minute's trouble—
the kind of trouble so many mothers go through. He
never once raised his voice to me. My baby! My son!
Figlio bello!"

I reentered the room; my face was almost expressionless. My friend at Eastern Airlines had just called
to tell me the reservations were confirmed. I knew I
could count on Al.

"Okay, Mom, let's go," I said firmly. "We're all set.
Everything's being loaded into the station wagon."

"Call Daddy first."

"I did, Mom. He's not home."

"Call Arlene!"

"I did. She must be with Georgie."

"Well, call the hospital then! Call St. Barnabas!"

"Okay. We haven't got much time, but I'll call."
And I made the call. I was afraid to fake it, just in
case she grabbed the phone from me and heard only a
dial tone.

"This is Connie Francis. Can you tell me if my
brother, George Franconero, was admitted to your
hospital this morning? Well, could he be in the emergency room?" Pause. "He's not there, Mom. He must
be in another hospital."

"Call Mountainside."

"I did."

"Call Clara Maass."

"I did."

"Call Martland Medical Center."

"You heard me, Mom. I just called there." Finally, we ran out of hospitals to call.

On the plane, I started to sit next to my mother, but she asked that Joey sit next to her instead. This is awful, I thought. Now he'll tell her for sure.

But, all my little son did during the long flight home was to keep patting her on the arm, kissing her, and telling her, "Uncle Georgie's going to be all right. You'll see, Nanny. Don't cry anymore."

No matter what my son does with the rest of his life, I'll never be prouder of him than I was at that moment.

Every few minutes my mother glanced at me, searching my face for some sign. But my face gave away no secrets.

I thought it would be wise to recollect some of the happy times of days gone by. My brother's dry wit and sense of humor were among his most appealing qualities.

The cheerful memories flowed willy-nilly. There would be no more of them in our lives for a long, long time to come. Surely, there would be none in my mother's life ever again—that is, if God allowed her to survive this latest and most calamitous of holocausts.

24

My Buddy (II)

Buddies through all of the good days
Buddies when something went wrong
Now I await alone through the gray days
Missing your smile and your song

How I miss your voice, the touch of your hand
I long to know that you understand
MY BUDDY, MY BUDDY
Your buddy misses you*

Even during the worst moments—the greatest crises in his life—my brother Georgie used to make me laugh. Not by telling jokes or by being a clown, but with his wry observations about people, and the special way he had of poking fun at himself and at me—very often at me. He never allowed me to feel more important than anyone else, or to take myself too seriously.

Georgie always called me by my full professional name, Connie Francis, the way small children often do when they first meet me. (My real name has never been changed.) It was like a private joke we played on the world. It was as if he were saying, "C'mon, cut it out. We both know who you really are. Will the real Concetta Franconero stand up?"

One day, Georgie came home and found a man who'd been writing strange and sometimes obscene letters to me for years. The man was hiding in the garage of our new home. We both knew his name well because he wrote almost every day. We knew he'd been in a mental institution on and off.

"What can I do for you, buddy?" Georgie asked.

"I'm Harry the Hairy Ape Brewster."

"Hey, Harry," Georgie said warmly, as if greeting an old friend. "Glad to finally meet you. What can I do for you?"

"I took the bus up from Carolina this morning to marry your sister. I have the floor plans for our home together. I sent a copy of them to her in the mail. Does she like the house?"

"Yeah, Harry. She thought the plans were cool."

"We're gonna be married soon, you know."

"She'll be glad to hear that. But she's not home now. We'd better get the papers in order for your marriage license. Why don't I take you down to the town hall, so you can fill them out there?"

They left in Georgie's car for the one and only commercial building in our little town. It was a small house that served as the town hall, the hall of records, the police department, the post office—you name it.

While Harry waited on a bench, Georgie went over to one of the police officers and told him in a low voice the entire story about this obviously unstable man.

"Look, this guy's a little weird. What are you boys gonna do about him?"

"I don't know. What are *you* going to do, George?" the officer replied.

Georgie looked at him oddly and said, "Well, he's all set to marry my sister; in fact, he brought the floor plans for their house together in Carolina. But I really don't think I should invite him to dinner. My sister's already been spoken for, and I don't think her boyfriend would like the idea very much."

The police put the man on a bus and sent him back to the Carolinas.

One hot summer Sunday, we went to a wedding of a friend. The tuxedos of the groom's six attendants were a wee bit garish—they wore shocking pink satin shirts with a purple lacy trim.

"What do you think of those shirts?" Georgie whispered to me in church.

"What do *you* think?" I whispered, suppressing a giggle.

"I think there'll be six gypsies in Newark who won't be going to their prom tonight."

When I told him I was planning to marry Joe, my third husband, he said, "Why don't you economize and buy yourself a drip-dry wedding dress?"

"I love you too, Georgie."

"Is Anita going to be your matron of honor again?"

"As a matter-of-fact, I'm thinking of asking her. Why?"

"Nothing. I just think it's a nice thing you keep doing for Anita. Everybody likes a steady job."

I remembered our closeness—how well we got along. After we lose someone close, the relationship seems more golden in retrospect than it actually was at the time. But in fact, my brother and I rarely, if ever, argued.

I shall never forget the night I was invited to the White House (with guest) for dinner and a performance by Red Skelton. My choice for guest was Georgie; he'd never been to the White House, and for one month in advance he was bubbling over with anticipation.

I went to Bill Blass and bought my brother a smart midnight-blue tuxedo, just right for the big night. For two hours before we were ready to leave for the airport to fly to Washington, Georgie kept checking himself in the mirror; he asked me about six hundred times how he looked. It got a little annoying, but I just kept repeating how nice he looked.

After the six hundred and first time I exclaimed, "*Again?* How do you look *again?* You look the same way you looked two minutes ago. It *is* the same suit, isn't it?"

"Oh, forget it! Never mind! I'm not asking you anymore!"

He really did look elegant that evening and we had a lovely time at the White House dinner and show. Just as we were about to leave, I stopped to introduce my brother to an old and dear friend of mine, Governor John Volpe of Massachusetts.

"John," I said, "say hi to my brother, Georgie. I don't think you guys have met, have you?"

"No, we haven't," the governor replied. "But it doesn't matter. I would have recognized him anywhere."

"How come, Governor?" Georgie asked.

"From that name tag you have dangling from your suit collar."

Lamentably, it was no name tag, but the *price* tag I'd failed to notice in six hundred and one inspections.

My brother wanted to strangle me that night. We laughed ourselves silly all the way home to New Jersey.

In '58, when I was beginning to earn large sums of money and Georgie was a prelaw student, I would send him a fifty-dollar check every week for pocket money. After six months, I learned that he never cashed a single check, so, for his nineteenth birthday, I bought him a sharp yellow Thunderbird.

Within four months he totaled it, as he had done with every other car he'd ever owned. He blamed the car. He said, "They stuck you with a lemon."

"No, Georgie," I said. "*You're* the lemon—you and the color of that car, which died of neglect and abuse."

*   *   *

I remember the day in '65 when I flew home from Boston to attend Georgie's Seton Hall Law School graduation. I hope I told him that day how very proud I was of him. I hope I did.

When he entered prelaw at Tuscaloosa University in Alabama, he didn't tell a soul for several months that I was his sister. It wasn't that he wasn't proud of me (he was)—but he wanted people to like him for himself and not because he was Connie Francis's brother.

But unfortunately he had to blow his cover when he appeared with me when I was honored on "This Is Your Life" and "Person to Person." Within a few weeks the entire campus knew who George was. I guess he became too popular too fast, because he left shortly after that and came home to New Jersey to enter Seton Hall University.

I don't think he was there six months when Seton Hall honored me with their Centennial Catholic Entertainer of the Year Award. I guess I even stole his thunder there.

There was one thing Georgie never had to worry about, and that was whether girls showed an interest in him because he was Connie Francis's brother. Georgie rarely dated, and when he did, he always came home early. He never drank, smoked, or did drugs.

Georgie also loved only one girl his whole life through. He had the stupendous good taste and good fortune to select one of my top ten favorite people in the world, Arlene Blind, as his partner for life.

Arlene's much more than a sister-in-law to me; she could have anything in this world from me, but she never asks—not ever. And that's when I love to do things for people most. She's the sister I never had.

Arlene is good and brave and strong; in spite of all she went through in the latter years of her marriage to my brother, she's one of the most up-front, put-together people I've ever known. She has more common sense than almost anyone else I know.

Although she often had cause for complaint, she never said a negative thing about my brother—not even to those people closest to her, her parents. She just worried for him, the way we all did. And she defended him, too. To me, she was the model of what a good wife should be.

Arlene bore the burden of Georgie's trouble alone, at least for a very long time; day by day, she watched my brother's life crumbling down around him. She *lived* it, while we had the luxury of being almost totally oblivious—until it was far too late.

But you'd never know a thing from Arlene, because she'd never say to a living soul something she wouldn't say if my brother were standing right beside her.

A week after his death we talked for a long while. She said to me: "I said so many times to George, 'You're such a great person, George, everybody loves you. It's really hard to find someone who doesn't. That's a very special thing to be. Why do you have to be superanybody?'"

She did everything in her power to make my brother feel like a real man, but, his troubles began too long ago—when we were both small children—for her to have made the difference she might have.

There's one thing I know for sure. I love Arlene very much, and she loves me. Like most people, we don't say it to each other often enough, but we both know it—we always know it.

Unlike even slight acquaintances who often used my name to get backstage to meet certain celebrities, my brother never did. Except in one case—and that was to meet his idol, Vic Damone. Georgie was so enthralled, so gaga over Vic Damone and that beautiful voice of his that he actually went backstage and introduced himself as Connie Francis's brother. It was a milestone. Arlene said she didn't think she'd ever see it happen again—at least, not until the next time Vic appeared in town.

That's why that night in July of '81 at Kutscher's Hotel in the Borscht Belt was such a melancholy night for me. It was four months after my brother's death, and Mom, Dad, Joey, Annie, Rita, and a few other friends had gone to see Vic Damone perform. Vic is a lovely guy and, as Frank Sinatra once said, "He's got the best 'pipes' in the business."

Well, that night Vic outdid himself. It was a very, very rare thing for me to go to hear someone else sing pretty songs, since *I no longer could.* But Vic is my friend, and I know how much Georgie liked him, so I wanted to see Vic for the two of us.

When I asked Arlene if she and the children would like to join us for the weekend, she said she couldn't bear to see Vic Damone without Georgie being there.

I had been out of the public eye for many years. Sometimes, people still made a fuss over me; sometimes they didn't even recognize me. On this particular night, Vic said something that I felt very deeply, something that made me very sad.

"We have a woman here tonight who possesses a truly rare magic and a voice like no other—a gift from God. Miss Connie Francis!"

The audience got to its feet and applauded, and for one wonderful moment, I had a feeling of déjà vu. How I loved the applause and all the attention! But after the applause died down, I said to myself, "Oh, Vic, if you only knew the truth—that, since that nasal operation in '77, I have no voice at all anymore." Reveling in all that applause, I felt like a fraud.

There was a buzz in the audience about my presence there that night, which lasted a long time. When Vic couldn't get on with his show, he good-naturedly joked, "Is it something I said?"

We all laughed. Then, instinctively, I motioned to Vic to hand me the mike. If I'd thought about it first I wouldn't have done it, because Mom looked as if she were enjoying herself just a little for the first time since Georgie's death. But it was spontaneous on my part.

I spoke into the microphone. "Ladies and gentlemen, this is the very first time since my brother's death that my family as a whole has been out in public. That we should be here at Vic's performance is as it should be. Because Vic, you were my brother's very favorite singer in the world. I mean, he was a real nutty fan of yours. He even used my name once to get backstage to meet you—something he never did. Thank you for entertaining us so royally tonight. My brother had very good taste, indeed."

It was true. My brother's sophisticated musical taste was much finer and more sensitive than my own.

Georgie was a C student in high school, which meant that he had to work very, very hard to get through law school. He would study till three or four in the morning, and he passed the New Jersey bar examination the first time around.

When he had flown to California for "This Is Your Life," he and Eleanor Scheck had had a long talk.

"How are you doing in prelaw, George?" she asked.

"It's tough, Ellie, it really is. I don't have my sister's smarts, you know. She's the one who got the A's in everything. I love my sister, and I'm really happy for her, but I think the Guy upstairs could have thrown me a bone."

Yes, Georgie, now I realize how very cold it must have been there in my shadow. . . .

25

The Wind Beneath Wings (I)

It must have been cold there in my shadow
To never have sunlight on your face
You were content to let me shine
You always walked a step behind

I was the one with all the glory
While you were the one with all the strength
Only a face without a name
I never once heard you complain *

THE Eastern Airlines plane from Fort Lauderdale touched down at a dreary Newark Airport—a thousand hours since takeoff. A grim-faced George Broeckel was waiting for us.

"George, where's my boy?" Mom shouted. "What did they tell you about my Georgie!"

"Nothing, Ida," he lied. "I wasn't able to get through to the hospital."

"Well, let's go there—right now! Please, George, take me to my son! I've gotta see him!"

"Mom, George will take you home first, okay?

Daddy's waiting for you there with Aunt Marie, Dolores, and Pearl—all your friends."

"George," I whispered as my mother paced the floor near the luggage carousel, "are there reporters and photographers around the house?"

"All day, Connie, but they were gone by the time I left for the airport."

"George, take Mom, Joey, and Annie home. I'll wait for the luggage and come home in the van. Wait till I get home to tell her anything."

In retrospect, I realized that I was too cowardly to be present—that subconsciously I was hoping they would tell my mother of Georgie's death before I reached home. She needed me, but I was so afraid.

When I got home, I found our large family room packed with friends and relatives. I dreaded this moment as I'd never dreaded anything before. But I soon learned that no one had yet told Mom that my brother was gone—they were waiting for me. All they'd said was that he was in a coma—that there was no point in going to the hospital, because she couldn't see him there.

"Connie! Connie!" she shouted when she first saw me. "Our Georgie's in a coma!"

"I know, Mama, I just heard." I saw a bottle of Valium on the cocktail table, and I fetched a glass of milk and asked her to take two of the little yellow pills.

"Oh, no! No! No! No! I don't want any of that stuff! Get rid of it! I wanna be wide awake, so I know every moment how my baby is! Don't even *try* to get me drugged!"

My dear friends Charlotte and Lou Sukoff had brought huge platters of food from our favorite restaurant, Stella's, in Queens, and were serving everyone. I was surrounded by all the people in my world I had come to love; yet, I was far away, on a remote, very private island—cut off from the rest of the real horror-filled world.

I gazed about the room and saw people whispering

to each other and trying to comfort my mother, but I heard no sounds. It was as if I were watching a made-for-TV movie with the audio shut off.

Then suddenly I snapped out of my trancelike state and took my mother's two dear friends, Dolores and Pearl, into the kitchen. I asked them to unplug all of the TVs and radios in the house and to make certain someone was there beside my mother at all times so that she didn't pick up the phone first and learn the news that way.

Then I approached my despondent father; he was sitting slumped and hollow-eyed on the sofa, his arms wrapped tenderly about my mother. She sat there in quiet desperation, her prayer beads in her hands.

"I don't believe this," she mumbled, half-dazed. "A car crash—I don't believe this happened to my Georgie."

"Daddy, can I talk to you?" I asked. When we were alone, I said, "Why haven't you told her that Georgie's dead?"

He stared blankly at nothing at all, totally unresponsive and oblivious to what I'd just asked him.

"The police had him lyin' in the snow for three hours, you know. I said to them, 'For chrissakes, take my son out of that cold snow!'" He continued to avoid my question.

"Daddy," I insisted, "*when* are you going to tell her?"

"I can't tell her. *You* have to do that—you and Arlene. Give her a few hours—give her a chance—and then you tell her."

"Daddy, will we have the wake tomorrow?"

"We can't. The police won't release Georgie's body yet," he said despairingly. To me, it was academic.

I walked over to my brave angel, my sweet little sister-in-law. We went into another room, and embraced as if this were the last time we were ever going to see each other.

The bond between us is deep and strong. We

clutched each other's hands; Arlene looked at me with the slightest brave smile on her face.

"There's nothing to fret over anymore, Connie, is there? No more to worry about." Then, after a split second; "Except what this horrible thing is going to do to my two boys."

"We'll get professional help, Arlene. For you and for Kenny and Anthony—I'll take care of that," I said consolingly. "I'll take care of you always, Arlene. Don't worry about that, please, sweetheart."

"I know you will. I know that."

"Arlene, where are the children now?"

"At my mother's."

"Okay, Arlene, I'll work it all out. I'm going into my study now. There are some things I have to do. There's no need for you to do anything at all. Go into my bedroom and cry if you want to, honey. Your children aren't here, so you don't have to be brave for anyone now."

"Connie . . . there's no money at all . . . the funeral costs. . . ."

"Oh, Arlene, please! Don't even say that . . . don't even think of things like that . . . please!"

On my way to the study, I passed the closed door of our walk-in pantry and heard a small voice crying. I slowly opened the door, to see my small son sitting on one of the pantry steps trying to stifle his sobs.

"What are you doing in here all alone, sweetheart?"

"Mommy, I don't want Nanny to see me cry." I looked at my child, and my heart was filled with a love so strong that I found myself choking on my words. "I'll tell you what to do. Be brave, and help your Nanny now. Go inside to her, be a big man, and hold her very close. Tell her how much you love her."

He did. He comforted her just as Georgie had done as a small child; he refused to leave my mother's side for many days after.

At my desk, I took the yellow legal pad, and once again made a list of things that had to be done. I knew that no one else could even begin to think of the many painful, heart-rending things that would have to be done.

I started to compose my list, trying not to forget anything. It was difficult; I had never been in charge of a funeral before. Suddenly Dennis Rappaport entered the study.

"Hi, Denny."

"Connie, honey. The FBI wants to talk with you. They're on the phone now."

"What do you want to discuss, sir?" I asked in a terse, no-nonsense tone.

"We'd like to ask you a few questions, Miss Francis, but whenever you feel you're ready to talk. We know how you must feel right now. When will you be able to speak with us?"

"You'll have to wait a very long time for that," I responded. "What are the questions? And for what reasons? You know the questions, I'm sure you already know the answers. My brother's gone. What's the difference?"

"I'm sure you want to help us learn more about his death—to bring his murderers—"

"Just read the newspapers when they come out—if they aren't already out. They'll contain all and everything I know."

"I'm going to put another agent on the phone. We'll have a three-way conference call," he went on politely. "Is that all right with you, Miss Francis?"

"Sure," I said, placating him.

"Hello, Miss Francis," the second FBI agent said in a pleasant voice. "Do you have any idea who did this thing to your brother?"

"Yes, I have ideas, sir, but they'll remain locked in my head—and in my heart—forever."

"Don't you want to help us find these people?" he asked naively.

"Help you? No, sir, I don't want to help you," I replied fiercely. "I want to help my family—what's left of it."

"Okay, then, just a question or two."

"Look, gentlemen, let's talk turkey, shall we? We all know this is an exercise in futility, don't we?"

The agent hesitated, embarrassed. "Well, that's not necessarily so."

I wasn't being fair; the man was merely doing his thankless job. "We're all big boys," I continued patronizingly. "We're supposed to be sensible people, so let's stop playing games."

"Okay," the agent said, "no games. Let me ask you just one question, Miss Francis."

"No, sir, let me ask *you* one question!"

"Go ahead."

"Do either of you gentlemen have any children?"

"Yes, we both do."

"Are your children in your homes now—happy and safe—tucked away?"

"Yes, they are."

"Well, so are *our* children. Let's keep them that way, shall we? Good evening, gentlemen."

I continued to write my list. It was too late now to do much today, and I wanted to be at my mother's side. Things to do for tomorrow, I thought. Let's see . . . today is Friday . . . Georgie's body is still with the police. Tomorrow's too soon . . . Sunday, we'll have the wake, just Sunday—one day. It's more humane. Three days of that ritual is almost barbaric. And Monday we'll have the funeral. Yes, the funeral.

The list read:

Call Galante's Funeral Home; speak to Joe Galante re: limousines, services, etc. Saturday, 9:00 A.M.—select coffin.

Call the *Star Ledger* to place obituary. Make request—instead of flowers, send contributions to Cancer Fund.

10:30 A.M. Select tombstone. What does Arlene want it to say?

Select a suit for Georgie.

Call Blessed Sacrament Church. Father Morel re:

services—what I'd like said about Georgie—not all religious—talk about the person he was, the way the Jewish people do.

12:00 P.M. See Father Morel re: services, read Georgie's favorite poem, "If," and play my song for him, "My Buddy." Also play the Lord's Prayer.

Buy guest book.

Call Henry's Caterers. Place order for next three days.

Call Jean and another waitress.

Call bakery—bread and Italian pastries.

Mary, Carrie stay with the children.

Call Dr. (Father) Lou Padavano—psychiatric consultation with Mom day after funeral.

Call cemetery re: family plot—go to see location—no muddy area.

See caretaker re: care of grave.

Call Essex Fells police department—road signs for cars near house.

Make a list of all . . .

Suddenly I looked up from my pad. Charlotte was frantically summoning me to the foyer. Just seconds before, my friend Marie Filipello had called from Philadelphia. Mom had picked up the kitchen phone before someone could reach it.

Marie said, "God, Ida! Oh, God! I'm so sorry—so very, very sorry! I just heard it on the news!"

"Heard what on the news?" my mother cried out.

She dropped the phone on the floor and shrieked: "HEARD WHAT ON THE NEWS? CONNIE! WHERE'S MY CONNIE? CONNIE, COME HERE! COME RIGHT HERE—RIGHT THIS MINUTE!"

I ran to her. "YOU'RE NOT TELLING ME THE TRUTH, CONNIE! MY GOD! YOU'VE ALL LIED TO ME!"

I threw my arms about her; Arlene was by my side. We each took one of her arms and led her into her bedroom. She kept falling to her knees; then she fainted.

When a doctor gave her smelling salts to revive her, she was panting, breathing so quickly I was scared to death. I sat her gently on the bed; Arlene and I knelt before her and I clasped her hands.

"Mama . . . Georgie . . . he's . . . Mama. Oh, Mommy, I can't say it, darling."

A scream emanated from my mother that was so eerie it didn't sound human. And then I heard: "DEAR GOD IN HEAVEN. WHAT HAVE YOU DONE TO MY FAMILY? AND WHY? WHAT HAVE WE DONE? OH, *FIGLIO BELLO*. MY BEAUTIFUL SON! MY GEORGIE!" Her face was a study in agony. My heart was broken; I held her tightly. I was completely devastated by this new, excruciating pain I felt. Nerves were struck I never knew existed.

My mother called to my brother, "I WANT TO BE WITH YOU, MY SON . . . I WANT TO DIE, TOO, SO I CAN BE WITH YOU, GEORGIE."

The doctor gave her an injection, but it seemed to have no effect whatsoever. It was then, seven years after the fact, that someone revealed something to me for the first time: "We'd better keep a very close watch on her" because of the attempt she made on her life the day I was raped.

I was shocked! Not *my* mother! Not my strong, sound-of-mind mother! I was distraught. My heart hurt so; I felt so totally helpless.

My friends and relatives just stood there numbly, in total despair—all the people Georgie had helped over the years—with their wills, their estates, their home mortgages, their marital problems. With all their legal problems, and their emotional ones, too. All the relatives he cared about and tended to, while I was singing in Las Vegas or making movies on the French Riviera. All the aunts he would drive to see each other because they didn't drive and they lived so far from each other. Like my good-hearted Aunt Tess, who loved him so dearly. ("Aunt Tessie, can I take you anywhere? Can I bring you something?") Each of us internalizing our own private relationship with Georgie.

I was crushed as I watched the reaction of our two good friends Pete and Dolores Federico, whose own son had died six years earlier. I stared in dismay at their wretched expressions as they relived their own horrendous nightmare. Dolores is a precious, good soul, and ordinarily very stoic. But she, too, screamed with my mother—recalling her own awful experience, and how my mother had felt for her and had been there in her hour of despair.

"How will Pete and Dolores live through this awful thing? Oh, my poor friends," Mom had said day after day after day, following their son's death. I watched Dolores and my mother embrace—two mothers with a common bond that could be surpassed by no other; Dolores (Dee) who had experienced grief every single day for the past six years while visiting and carefully tending the grave of her own young son.

For the next four hours, I sat on the bed beside my mother while she stared at a photograph of Georgie, Arlene, Kenny, and Anthony—a family photograph Arlene had given her at Christmastime, just two and a half months before. For four solid hours, she stared at the photo with frequent outbursts of hysteria. Then, even worse than that, the quiet kind of hysteria when she'd slip into that other world, which none of us could enter.

For the next two hours, until daylight, she lay on her side on the bed, her back toward me, her body racked by misery. I lay beside her, holding her closely as she clenched my brother's bronzed baby shoes in her one hand, the envelope containing his blond strands of baby hair in the other.

As I lay there, I felt someone lie down beside both of us and hold me tenderly. I turned around and saw my friend Charlotte. I thought of how our friends are always there for us.

I began the next day at 6:00 A.M., without having slept; there was so much to be done. At Galante's Funeral Home I really didn't care to hear our friend, the mortician Joe Galante, tell me why one coffin was superior to the other. "Whatever you think, Joe," I said numbly.

Arlene had said she couldn't bear to come with me to the funeral parlor to select a casket, but as I made my final decision, I saw her walk down the flight of steps to join me.

"*I* should be doing this, not you, Connie."

"It's all taken care of, Arlene; it's a very pretty casket. You've done enough—much, much more than enough. Let's go, honey—I have lots to do. Be with your children today."

We told my mother of my brother's death in two stages, on two consecutive days. That was a gross mistake on my part. To her, it was as if my brother had died twice.

It was impossible to keep the truth—that he'd been murdered gangland-style—from her any longer, because the next day people at the wake would be talking of it.

I sat her down tenderly and gently and, in the most circuitous way, I led up to the real cause of his death. I shall never forget the horror of that moment until the day I die. My soul felt fragmented in a thousand places. "MURDERED! MY BOY—MURDERED! NO! GOD, NO! YOU WOULDN'T DO THIS AWFUL THING TO US!"

She banged her fists against the mirrored wall of her bedroom, smashing it.

"THOSE FILTHY, ROTTEN BASTARDS! I'LL KILL THOSE SONS-OF-BITCHES WITH MY BARE HANDS! I—"

"Mother, stop," I said firmly. "Stop it, and sit down on the bed—right now! Listen to me, sweetheart."

I took both her quivering hands in mine.

"Listen to me, Mama," I pleaded. "Look straight into my eyes while I speak to you."

It was difficult to get her to focus her attention on the important words I had to say to her.

"I know, Mom. I know how you feel. I know how much it hurts, but . . . Look at me, Mommy. There isn't a single, blessed thing any of us can do or even say. Kenny and Anthony," I continued softly, "they are a part of Georgie that's left behind for you to love and care for. They're a part of your son. And, our Joey—he's been Heaven's noblest gift to us. You love them all very much, don't you?"

"Yes," she said weakly, "I love them."

"Well, Mama, then you must . . . *never* . . . *never* . . ."

"Yes, I know. I know that, Connie. I know I can't," she rasped. "Oh, my Georgie, *figlio bello* . . . my son."

All that night she sat up in bed, her eyes fixed on the photograph she held in one hand and the bronzed baby shoes she clutched in the other—just as she had done the night before, and as she would do for more than a year of nights to come.

26

The Wind Beneath
My Wings (II)

It might have appeared to go unnoticed
But I've got it all locked here in my heart
And I want you to know that I know the truth
That I wouldn't have made it without you

Did you know that you were my hero
And all the things I'd like to be
Yes, I flew higher than an eagle
But you were THE WIND BENEATH MY WINGS *

THE day of the wake I didn't leave my mother's side. She went to the funeral parlor one hour before the doors opened and she held my brother's eternally still, ice-cold body, patting his face gently. "It's too cold in here for our Georgie, Connie," she said protectively. "See? Just feel his face. Ask them to raise the heat."

There should have been services that day for my mother, too, because a large part of her died with my brother. The best part—the always-happy, always-smiling, always-dancing, always-life-of-the-party part. If it were not for the existence of my son Joey, I'm certain the part that remains today would be gone, too.

As I sat next to her at the funeral home, I remembered how she'd commiserated with other mothers she knew when their sons had been in deep trouble, or had died—long before her own son was in any kind of trouble. "How will she ever get through this? She'll never be the same."

And she was right. A mother never is the same. Of all the calamities that can befall a person, to lose one's child has to be the most devastating.

That night, we returned to the wake, and I sat in silent desperation beside my tortured mother. We greeted our many friends and relatives, and many of Georgie's business friends and acquaintances whom we'd never met, and who had come to pay their last respects to him and to us. I knew that they would come, and they did—almost all of them. There were two or three who should've been there that night, and were not. Only they know why not.

As I lay in my bed that night, feeling so utterly alone, it occurred to me that I hadn't been in control of things at all—that I'd merely been hiding behind a protective shell to keep from going mad.

I went to my Memory File and took out all the letters my brother had written to me while he was in law school and I was on the road singing. I sat up another entire night, checking frequently on Mom and Dad and reading each of the letters Georgie had written—letters written when his prospects of success as a professional man, and as a husband and father, looked auspicious indeed.

In one letter, written to me when I was twenty-two and earning $25,000 a week in Las Vegas, he closed with: "Write when you get work."

One letter said: "I thought I would've found out whether or not I passed the bar by now, but I won't find out until October 1st (breath). I am now a county investigator in the prosecutor's office for a cool $125 per. Withhold any financial requests for aid, however.

I have a badge and a gun just like Elliot Ness, but I still don't look like Robert Stack."

And after his honeymoon: "I thought your whole act in Vegas would fall apart when I left. But I'm glad to see you've finally learned to shoulder the burden of success by yourself. It's so refreshing to partake of Arlene's cooking after all that garbage we were forced to eat at the Monte Carlo room in Vegas. I knew there would be some saving feature in coming home." He signed the letter: "Love, The Enforcer."

He revered my parents and, even during the rebellious teenage years, accorded them a respect frequently denied other parents. He always viewed them with that rare humor of his—as if they were characters in a sit-com series.

In Las Vegas, I once received a letter telling of an incident concerning my mother that was par for the course. It said: "Ida pulled another cutie today. There was a mass for Grandma, and she went to the wrong church and sat through the entire mass. Of course, it never occurred to Ida that not one member of her family was present at the mass. Incidentally, I finished my exams last week. Forget about the minor fact that I couldn't come up with the right answers; I couldn't even *read* the questions."

I smiled through my tears; then I stopped reading because I was smudging the ink and I didn't want to erase one precious word. As I sat in bed, I dreaded the aftermath of my brother's death—that period after the first intense mourning when the full realization of the tragedy sets in, and only the emptiness is left.

There is one letter both Arlene and I want very much to find. She's hunted in every nook and cranny of her home for it; she's searched repeatedly through all my brother's possessions. It is a letter he cherished so much—it was given to him by my father on the day he graduated from law school.

Arlene never saw that letter, but she knew he kept it with him always.

* * *

Whenever I read, hear, or get the impression that people think of my brother as a clever wheeler-dealer—or a pernicious evil-doer—I ask myself: Where are all those hundreds of thousands of dollars he supposedly bilked from banks and land fraud schemes he was involved in?

Certainly none of it ever fell into his or his family's hands. *They* were not the recipients or beneficiaries of these staggering sums of money I've read so much about.

My brother didn't have the money to buy his own moderately priced home (my father made the down payment on it). He didn't have the money to pay for his own funeral; he didn't have enough money to buy many things.

Shortly before his death, I experienced a painful truth—the full realization of just how bad things were for my brother and his family. Arlene had never complained, so I had never known. Georgie hadn't said anything because he knew how many hundreds of thousands of dollars my father and I had spent (my father, three-quarters of all the money he'd saved in his seventy years) in a vain attempt to extricate him from his troubles.

But by the time we knew even a part of the facts, it was far too late. To this day, we don't know what actually occurred—we still have only fragmentary bits and pieces of the truth.

Just before Arlene and Georgie's fifteenth anniversary, I dropped in at their home and said: "Don't you guys have cable TV yet? . . . You're kidding. . . . Okay, I'm going to install HBO and give you a two-year subscription to it for your anniversary."

Moments later, when Arlene and I were alone, she whispered to me, "Connie, thanks a lot for the HBO offer, but I would prefer, and I know Georgie would, too . . . well . . . ah—he needs a pair of shoes."

The words stung. I was astonished, ashamed and aghast, as I thought of the six-hundred-odd pairs of shoes that were neatly arranged by color and type in the vast closet in my home, seven minutes from theirs.

I went out that day to buy him shoes in every color. A day later, I handed Arlene the latest in a series of large checks I'd given her. For days I berated myself mercilessly.

I later learned she never cashed a single one of them (I never check up on these kinds of things). But giving her the money brought me an ephemeral peace of mind and eased my conscience for a while. Soon after, however, I became engrossed again in my own joyless, insulated, miserable little world, which had been closing in on me for a long time now.

Just as I'd been shielded like a child from the media accounts of my rape in 1974, until the day the Howard Johnson trial commenced, I was shielded again from the blazing headlines about my brother's death. So much so that, when I began writing the chapters about my brother for this book, I asked my fans to send me whatever clippings they had about it.

I saw the glaring headlines for the first time a short while ago. For two weeks, I worked in a state of abject despondency. I read one old newspaper article published when Georgie's overwhelming troubles—and mine—were at their height. I read of this deplorable, reprehensible "crook" in a New York newspaper dated November 30, 1977. "CHARGE HE MASTERMINDED BANK FRAUD," it declared.

The sad truth of the matter was that my brother was never ingenious enough to mastermind even a purse-snatching; if there was a mastermind in any of the schemes, it surely belonged to someone else. My brother had true goodness, and he saw only goodness in others. But he had a desperate need for the approval, acceptance, and respect that had eluded him all his life, and this clouded and warped his judgment.

Georgie wasn't a criminal, but a victim. He was manipulated by people far shrewder than he ever was, people who took advantage of his deeply rooted weaknesses for their own personal gain. Tragically, doing anything at all for others gave him the feeling of self-worth that he lacked. He was used—in the worst sense of the word.

It was almost impossible to believe that, as a member of the bar, he could have been so deceived, so gullible, so misguided, and so abused and used.

But it happened, and because of the ensuing and very predictable catastrophe that befell my beloved brother, I am today a far different woman.

I've learned, the hard way, many sorrowful lessons. I have always been a trusting soul; when people told me something, I usually believed it. Seldom in my life had I been exposed to true malefactors—or if I was I must have been unaware of it.

But I've learned that truly evil people *do* exist—and they wait to prey upon someone with my brother's weaknesses. They make a career of it.

Now I've developed a thick, protective layer of skin and a new awareness of what life's about. It's tragic that it took my brother's death to teach me these lessons.

I've learned other lessons, too. In human relationships, we all "use" and need each other to some extent. That's normal and natural. I love being "used" by the people I love; I enjoy doing nice things for good people that they couldn't otherwise afford to do for themselves. And I "use" them in turn. When someone is part of my life, he or she had better be a hard worker. All the people around me—including my friends—work very hard.

In most healthy relationships, when people "use" each other, it turns out to be an even exchange; we do for one another. We give in different ways to one another; and that's as it should be.

But sometimes in a relationship, the giving is one-sided (and I'm not speaking primarily of monetary things). Nowadays, when I get the slightest sense that I'm being used or abused, I give absolutely nothing of myself. I fiercely protect myself, my family, and my worldly possessions.

My brother, even more than I, loved and trusted just about everyone he met. George wasn't street-smart; my parents didn't raise us to be that way. He was simply not sophisticated enough in the ways of the world to "mess with the big boys." He couldn't measure up to the nebulous, grandiose, pie-in-the-sky design he had created for himself. I sometimes think that when he died, he still believed in Santa Claus.

If Georgie was worried for his safety (and the newspapers I read only a short time ago told me he was), he never let any of us know it. He was always joking, teasing, happy-go-lucky and cheerful, as if he hadn't a care in the world. Now Arlene tells me that he never slept at night. He had good cause.

The headlines made many front pages in different capitals. They read like this:

STAR'S BROTHER HIT FOR SINGING ON MOB

Another read:

CONNIE FRANCIS' BROTHER RUBBED OUT BY MOB

In *The Herald-News* (Passaic, N.J.):

CONNIE FRANCIS' BROTHER VICTIM OF GANGLAND
HIT

And in London's *News of the World*:

CONNIE'S BROTHER MURDERED

And in our own hometown Newark newspaper, the *Star Ledger:*

DISBARRED LAWYER SLAIN GANGLAND-STYLE

The front page of the New York *Daily News Tonight* read:

CONNIE'S BROTHER SLAIN (WAS WARNED OF MOB CONTRACT)

I've forgotten much of my German, so I was unable to read the German headlines. Even in death, my beloved brother was still just Connie Francis's brother. It saddens me more than anyone could ever know.

Another lesson I've learned is to place an extremely high value on communication in relationships—on the expression (at the right time, of course) of any and all emotions that we feel toward another person, the positive and, especially, the negative.

I've always known the importance of communicating with my son, but now I search out his real feelings about anything and everything. I encourage him to express them even when I don't like what he's saying.

Every child occasionally experiences hate, anger, and resentment as well as love toward his parents; it's perfectly natural. If Joey is in the wrong, and says to me: "I don't like you today, Mommy," I'll casually reply: "You'll get over it, kid."

If he's really burned and says: "Mommy, I hate you!" I'll say matter-of-factly: "Right this minute, Joey, I'm not that crazy about you, either. But let's talk about why you feel the way you do, okay?"

If the communication between my father, my brother, and me had been honest, open and free, my brother would still be alive today.

I urge every parent: Open up to your children and allow them the same freedom of expression you would a most precious friend. Anger is a part of life and denying it, suppressing it, or harboring resentment will surely produce an unhealthy adult.

I recently heard—and it makes sense—that the breakdown of a human relationship occurs not so much because the words are misunderstood, but because the silences are misunderstood.

My brother, the "mastermind," left his wife and children penniless. I've invested wisely the small insurance policy they received from the company he worked for—and that he didn't even know existed. Their house is almost a hundred percent mortgaged, and Arlene was left owing a large debt to the IRS.

I was appalled to discover recently that, at the time of his death, this formerly respected attorney and good family man, who had begun climbing the ladder of success early and swiftly, was earning two hundred dollars a week as a salesman.

Today Arlene has advanced admirably in a job she enjoys, but her children are still her first concern. They still receive counseling, and understandably so. As we all know, other children, in their innocence, can be extremely cruel.

In April 1983, Arlene was married, and very happily, to Joseph Monaco—a good and true man who loves her very deeply. (I was her matron of honor and it was just that—an honor.) That night I was filled with an almost indescribable happiness for her.

My mother's future is a different story, for it lies in the past. They say the pain gets duller with time; I wonder if it ever will for her. So far, there are no signs that it has abated at all.

You see, there are mothers and there are mothers. My mom is a rare, totally selfless kind of mother, who has always been passionately devoted to her small family. Her whole life through, she's existed to be a good wife, mother, and person. She is all of these in spades.

This disaster should never have happened to her, of all people. She lives with it every waking moment of her life. She still cries at the mere mention of my

brother's name. All she has to do is look at his two
sons, and her eyes fill with tears. I remember the day
when Kenny, at sixteen, began wearing Georgie's
clothes. My mother held him and patted his face all
day long.

She visits Georgie's grave at least four days a week,
tending to it as she tended to him when he was a small
child.

Each holiday, each former occasion of happy cele-
bration, has now become a day of gloom and sadness.
Last Thanksgiving, she sat all alone in her car, while a
relentless rain pounded it for five hours, beside the
grave of my brother. She confided to Dolores recently
that when she's driving along, she closes the car win-
dows tightly so that she can scream freely without in-
flicting her pain on others in the privacy of her own
desolate world—a far emptier world now, with its
hopeless void.

She still attends her Thursday evening Novenas for
St. Jude. What does she pray to him for now? She
prays that she'll see Georgie again—that he'll appear
in her dreams as she sleeps. *When* she sleeps, that is,
which is not very often.

The other day, Joey saw her looking up at the sky-
light in our kitchen. "Are you looking up there for
Uncle Georgie, Nanny?"

She nodded.

"You're right, Nanny. I think I see him, too." He
probably did. And then: "Poor Nanny. Poppy and
Mommy are better. Arlene, Kenny, and Anthony are
better. When are *you* going to get over this thing,
Nanny?"

I wish I knew myself.

The other day, I read something I said a long, long
time ago, in 1958, when my world was young and gay.
The fan magazine quoted me as saying: "I don't know
what it is, but I must have some kind of guardian angel who watches over me. It must be, because nothing
bad *ever* happens to me."

But, life touches us all. Today, as in 1958, I sense strongly that there is someone special who cares very much for me sitting at the right hand of God, helping Him to pull all the right strings, helping Him make all the right decisions for me. Even when I make a very bad one, even when I make a gross mistake, that special someone seems to make it all turn out right. I sincerely feel this way.

And, I believe I know his name.

27

I'm Me Again

When all the easy times turned into long cold nights
I let myself take the blame
I felt so numb inside, I lost my sense of pride
Now I'm no longer ashamed

I'M ME AGAIN I've conquered all my fears
Now I'm at peace again crying happy tears
It's great to feel again that I love who I am

I'M ME AGAIN I've come back from despair
My heart is free again to laugh, to love, to care
I'm in control again, the only role I play is me

In all the years of need so few believed
Fair-weather friends walked away
It was a long hard fall, I thought I'd lost it all
Now I can stand proud and say

I'M ME AGAIN I've come back from despair
My heart is free again to laugh, to love, to care
I'm in control again the only role I play is me *

* I'm Me Again" © by George Scheck. Written by Alan Roy Scott and Ed Fox.

November 12, 1981
Westbury, New York

"This is the best gift I ever got," I told the audience as I held the child who'd been the only valid reason for my existence over the past long and hard seven years. As I looked into his beautiful, slightly bewildered face it was difficult to speak without choking on the words.

"You see this little guy here? With the red roses, the new suit and no front teeth? Well, his name is Joey, he's seven years old and he's all mine. And all this little guy did was turn my life around."

For two exhilarating months now, ever since I discovered that I had regained my voice, seemingly from out of the blue, I had dreamed of the magic of this moment. I was back singing for the people—on the same stage that I'd left for the last time almost seven years before. Seven years to the night I would have closed had the rape not occurred.

If it were not for Westbury and the tragedy I suffered there, there would be no Joey in my life. It's as simple as that.

December 6, 1974
Essex Fells, New Jersey

It was snowing heavily; my dear friends, Anita and Rico Barros, and Joe and I were in the family room. I sat before a roaring fireplace rocking back and forth, my mind somewhere in a world of my own—a prisoner of morbid fear in my own home, consumed by self-loathing and shame. My world had fallen apart.

Joe knew well the depths of my depression these days and he felt powerless to help me except in the only way he knew would make a real difference. It seems that the letter in my mink coat pocket offering a child for adoption, my only link to that lady, had been stolen by the rapist; but Richard Frank *had* written down the telephone number of the woman who wrote. And when Richard told Joe about it, they worked ceaselessly until that child became a reality in my life.

At 9:00 P.M. I answered the doorbell and there stood Richard Frank and Tony Foti, Joe's friend. Cradled in Richard's arms and wrapped in a large, bright red ribbon was that beautiful five-month-old baby boy who would forever be mine.

In the wee small hours of the morning Joe wrote a poem about that remarkable night in both our lives.

JOEY II's
ODE TO MOMMY

'Twas a few weeks before Christmas as best I can recall
That two wise men came for me, one short and one tall—

How happy I was as they drove me far away
Though I quietly wondered "Where's the reindeer,
       where's the sleigh?"

As we crossed a big bridge, I then realized that Saint Nick,
Was really Uncle Tony and good old Uncle Dick.

While the radio blared Christmas songs and Christmas bells
We finally stopped in a town called Essex Fells.

Could this really be for me?
No, I'm a poor boy; it just can't be!

Another disappointment, I thought, so just take it in stride,
And when I'm turned away, I'll hold my tears inside.

But then a big red ribbon was placed upon my chest
And I closed my eyes, and well, Mommy, you know the
       rest.

You were holding me so close, when I looked up at you,
I saw the tears in your eyes, then I finally knew.

That God's guiding light from far up above—
Had brought me to a mommy, who at last I would love.

So tonight, Dear Mommy, on my very first Christmas Eve,
When I know that I'm yours and will never have to leave,

Here's my Christmas message to you, 'cause that's all
    I have to give—
I will love you tonight, and always, and for as long as I
    live—
Thanks Mommy for finding me and Merry Christmas.

                                                    JOEY II

                          November 12, 1981
                          Westbury, New York

   It was a much publicized event. The rehearsals were
covered by all the television stations; the press came
from five different countries and loyal fans were there
from all over the world. Placards throughout the theater read "Welcome back, Connie," and there simply
was no more space in the dressing room for the bouquets of flowers that arrived.
   I was humbled by the total acceptance and unconditional love of the people. I always have been, and I
always will be, but somehow, this night, in particular,
was something special.
   I wasn't in the greatest voice by a long shot, but
who cared? Not I. Not the audience. And I knew that
before too long it would be back to normal, and I was
right.
   All the people I held dear to my heart were present.
All the people who cared. My talented and loyal conductor of twenty years, Joe Mazzu; my drummer and
good friend of nineteen years, Bobby Grauso; my

soundman, Tony Simonetti; George Scheck—all the people who came running back when I told them I could sing again.

And my out-of-show-business friends too, Anita and Rico Barros, Charlotte and Lou Sukoff, Lois and Bill Prokocimer, Fran and Adam Sadlon, Libby, my devoted fans and friends Pat Niglio and Barbara Clarke, Annie Castellano, and especially Anne Fusari, who long ago, had given up most of her friends and her social life in order to be with me, sometimes hours each day—hours when very often I had nothing at all to say. All the people who had experienced and shared so many of the peaks and valleys of the last two decades.

January 1975
Hollywood, Florida

"I can't, Dick! I can't do it!" I cried to Richard Frank, long distance. "How can I get up on a witness stand and bare the most intimate details of my life?"

"Because you must, Connie. We've *got* to sue, this will be an important case," pleaded Richard. "If Howard Johnson's loses, and they will, hotels and motels all over the world will become a lot safer."

"I don't have any causes these days, Richard. I just want to bury myself somewhere."

It was too painful not to, really. I remembered so well the first time Joe convinced me to go to dinner with friends. As I stood in the foyer of the small Italian restaurant on Mulberry Street in New York, a woman stared at me as she passed.

"That *is* her!" she told her husband excitedly. "That's the girl that was raped." And so, for seven years, I thought of myself only in those terms, negating all the fun and accomplishments of the years that preceded it.

August 8, 1975
Essex Fells, New Jersey

"I went up to the Howard Johnson's with a court order, you know," Richard Frank told me on the phone. "I took a photographer, a mechanical engineer, the manager of the Howard Johnson's motel, the attorneys for Howard Johnson, and an investigator from my office."

"So—what were your findings?"

"Connie, are you sitting down?—the place is a disaster. When we went to the motel and checked the other rooms the judge gave us the authorization to inspect, about half the rooms had defective sliding glass doors."

"Tell me you're kidding, Richard!"

"It gets worse, Concetta. They haven't even bothered to repair the condition that *led* to your assault."

"You mean the lock's never been fixed in the room I stayed in?"

"That's right. And the screen door is still torn where it was slit with a knife and nobody seems to have cared that this event ever took place." I hesitated a long while.

"Okay, Richard, do whatever it is you have to do."

June 8, 1976
United States District Court
Brooklyn, New York

"Welcome back, Connie, we love you," cried the large mob of spectators and onlookers standing at the entrance and in the corridors of the courthouse.

"Hey, Connie, *canta Italiano!*" shouted a spectator.

"Why are you bringing this case, Miss Francis?" asked one reporter.

"Concetta, autograph this for Billy, will ya? I'm from Brooklyn, too."

What had once been common occurrence in my life

felt almost strange and alien to me now. For a long while I'd felt like such a private person, hiding completely behind the safer cloaks of obscurity and seclusion.

The carnival-like atmosphere of the negligence trial against the Howard Johnson's motel chain lasted for four trying weeks, weeks during which I relived the nightmare of Westbury as I had done so many nights before, but this time for the world. Weeks during which I broke down repeatedly on the witness stand during days of grueling and badgering questioning by the defense.

Early on in the case, Richard Frank succeeded in having Judge Thomas Platt, a very able and kind judge, bar the press for the remainder of the trial in order to try to protect me from the daily glare of publicity the case had stirred up. But his decision was overturned by the United States Court of Appeals when the New York Press Club and the National Lawyers' Guild brought a proceeding to compel Judge Platt to open the courtroom to the press and spectators.

The unusual and novel aspects and events of this case would, in and of themselves, make a very interesting book. It is truly a landmark case, a watershed in personal injury litigation against the owners and operators of places of public and private accommodations—including apartment houses—all premises where people are allowed to pass through and congregate.

Richard Frank was nothing short of brilliant, and on July 1, 1976, after four weeks of trial, I was awarded $2.5 million by an all-male jury—by far the largest jury verdict ever given for an act of sexual assault.

Richard Frank called me recently and told me, "Connie, because you had the guts to pursue it, you have become an important name in legal history—and that's not nonsense!"

The trial took a big toll on an already eroding marriage. Joe is an extremely successful man and he's gregarious within the confines of his business. But he's a very private man about his personal life. During the trial, when he read headlines like "Connie Has the Sex Blahs" in the *Daily News,* he became even more withdrawn than he had been of late.

Shortly after the trial, when Joe and I went to dinner at a small candlelit restaurant in New York, we both had an unexpected surprise for each other. I was going to tell him that I was expecting a baby; he, instead, told me that although he was trying to work it out with professional help, he simply didn't enjoy "being married anymore."

Almost instantly I developed intense abdominal pains. I came within twelve minutes of losing my life from ileitis when the doctors performed emergency surgery, because they thought I was suffering an ectopic pregnancy. Ten days later I lost this baby, too. And three months afterward Daddy was operated on for cancer of the colon.

On an evening in December 1976 Joe and I were discussing whether or not I would have the ability to return to work and face the public again. I discussed something else with him that night.

Ever since 1967 when I had nasal surgery performed to narrow my nose, I found it impossible to sing in air-conditioned rooms without losing my voice almost instantly, and without developing serious and debilitating throat infections. At one point during that time I remember ingesting sixty-five pills a day, mainly antihistamines.

For the first time in my career I was forced to cancel a Las Vegas engagement midstream—that was followed by a series of such canceled engagements. To cancel an engagement is serious business—always one of the most difficult things to do. In a place like Las Vegas where a performer knows that big, big dollars are riding in the casino on whether she appears or not, the responsibility is particularly awesome. For the first time in my life of show business, it ceased to be a joy to me.

That's why I was so eager to tell Joe that if I was, indeed, thinking of returning to work, there was new nasal surgery I'd heard of that could help me with this frustrating problem that had taken so heavy a toll on me.

February 15, 1977
Columbia Studios
New York City

"Hey, fellas, give me a break, will you? Somebody shut off the air conditioning!" I shouted to the control booth after the first few bars of the first take.

"There *is* no air conditioning, Connie," said Pat Niglio.

Ten days following the nasal surgery I was back again in a recording booth. A compilation of some of my earlier Italian records were going to be offered in a TV promotion, and since my voice was stronger and surer than it had been when I first made those Italian LPs so many years before, I wanted to re-record them.

"You're wrong, fellas! The air conditioning's gotta be on! Didn't you hear my voice? I sound like Joe E. Lewis after those guys slit his throat in Chicago. Check it again," I told Frank Laico, the engineer.

"It's off, Connie," he said. "You're just a little rusty. Try it again."

During the second take, sounds emanated from my throat that were completely foreign to me, and my blood froze inside me. "MY GOD! I CAN'T SING! OH, MY GOD!" I had lost my voice completely.

For many months I frantically visited doctors all over the world and most of them said I'd never sing again. It seems that the scar tissue that had formed after the surgery had caused major physiological changes, and that was why my sound was altered so dramatically.

The shock I experienced when I discovered I could no longer sing was something from which I would not recover for a long time. I was a woman consumed by that one fact. I gave my record collection away—both my performances and everybody else's. I could not go to see other performers work or even watch variety TV. I didn't laugh anymore. For four years I never tuned to a music station on the radio. I didn't want to hear beautiful songs I could no longer sing.

I paid a vocal coach (the first in my life) $1500 each weekend all winter long to fly from New York to my home in Florida so that I could vocalize with him. My voice was unrecognizable—so bad that I'd stay in bed for two days each time he left with the kind of unrelenting depression that, I fervently hope, very few people will ever experience.

Joe was powerless once more. Were it not for Joey, I would have taken my life. After the rape I barricaded myself in my home; after the loss of my voice I barricaded myself in my bedroom. Except for Joey, there seemed to be no real reason for living anymore. I dreaded the mornings when I awakened and rejoiced when the day was through.

It's a sad admission, but gone with my voice was my already badly damaged self-esteem. Even though after the rape I was unable to face the public, I always knew in my heart that someday when I put my life back together again, singing was always an option for me—the only option, really.

I felt like a surgeon who had lost his hands. I felt like a stranger to myself. I felt like some other woman. Indeed, I had become another woman. I was certainly not the girl Joe married; I hadn't been that girl for a very long time. Two months after I lost my voice, Joe, a true, good, and patient man, left me.

September 1978
Essex Fells, New Jersey

"You have to do the show, Connie," pleaded Dick Clark long distance. "Are you going to blow the next ten years the way you blew the last ten years?"

"Dick, you don't seem to understand. I *can't sing!*"

"Yes, you can. It's all in your head."

"Dick, believe me. It's not. I can't sing one song straight through. I'll show you the medical reports from London, New York, L.A., Boston—all the doctors I visited. I've had three more operations, and I still can't sing!" Dick Clark was the only person in show business to whom I told the whole truth.

"Look, we'll pre-record your voice. No one will ever know. You can do a medley of your hits. Do a hundred takes if you want to."

And a hundred takes I did. With a range of only seven notes, I put together a medley, singing only those portions of the songs containing notes I could reach, recording only one line at a time, until I could hear a reasonable facsimile of what I used to sound like.

November 29, 1978
Burbank, California

"Sixteen Top Ten records. The world's number one female vocalist when she elected to stop performing," said an enthusiastic Dick Clark. "Everybody in the world has begged this lady to come back and frankly, she turned us all down. But tonight's the night, she is back! Ladies and gentlemen, Miss Connie Francis."

As I entered the stage to begin my song and the audience rose to its feet and cheered wildly, and it was heavenly *déjà vu.* The lip synchronization was almost perfect. Dick was right. Nobody knew.

At the conclusion of the medley, I felt humbled as the audience stood once more, crying out a thunderous chorus of "Mores" and "Bravos." Dick Clark, with tears brimming in his eyes, walked over to where I was standing. And it was a moment in television history as I embraced the man who has been there for every crisis of my life, my dearest friend in show business. Dick found it most difficult to speak.

"Why did you . . ." he sobbed, openly choking on the words.

"Aren't they wonderful? Aren't they. . ." I barely managed, so overwhelmed and so grateful that they remembered.

"Why did it take you so long?" Dick cried again.

"Well, Dick," I said, avoiding his question, "I know you don't like to hear these things, but I owe all of this to you, everything that's ever happened to me in my life in show business. And not for anyone else in this world would I have gotten up on stage tonight. I want to thank you. I want to thank everybody. It's a beautiful feeling."

On the plane ride home with the wild applause and cries of the audience still ringing in my ears, instead of the exhilaration I should have felt, a feeling of loneliness and despair, pain and frustration, consumed me as never before. I felt like a fraud, and I wanted to die.

December 1, 1978
Hallandale, Florida

As I stared in deep contemplation at the bottle of sleeping pills in my hand, there was a rap on my bathroom door.

"Mommy?" I slipped the bottle of pills into a drawer.

"Come in, sweetheart. What is it?"

"Mommy, I know how much you hate football," Joey said hugging me tightly. "So I wanna thank you for letting me play. I love you, Mommy."

When Joey left, I opened the drawer and flushed the pills down the toilet.

August 30, 1981
Essex Fells, New Jersey

"I received a tape in the mail today . . . from a

fan," I said very wistfully to Ed Schnitt, my friend and
companion from Florida who was visiting me."

"What's wrong?" Ed asked intuitively. "What kind
of tape was it?"

"It's the best thing I ever did, Ed," I said excitedly.
"All those fabulous Cole Porter songs—'I Concentrate on You,' 'It's All Right with Me,' 'At Long Last
Love'—wow! It's a medley Joe Mazzu, my conductor,
and I wrote—I sang it on the Sullivan show sitting
atop a piano."

In these past few years I had always avoided like the
plague any discussion of "when you used to sing."

"I have always had a tremendous amount of respect
for Mel Torme as an artist. He's the best," I continued
enthusiastically. "And once he told me that when he
saw my show in Vegas, he thought the medley was
brilliant. It inspired him to write a tribute to Fred As-
taire. That made me very happy."

"So play it, already."

"I don't think I can, Ed. I started to a dozen times
today, but if I did, it would be too painful."

"Look, Connie, whenever you sing a little now—
which is rare—you sound pretty good to me. Besides,
I never heard you sing live, only on records. Play it."

Ed has always been like five psychiatrists for me.

"C'mon, Connie. We'll listen to it together," urged
Ed. "Besides, it's about time." We both listened intently.

Mr. Porter:
YOU'RE THE TOP, and you always will be
YOU'RE THE TOP, how your songs can thrill me
They have heart and rhyme and tunes that time can't stop
Through your songs you'll live forever
YOU'RE THE TOP

I was totally overwhelmed by the avalanche of emotions that came bursting forth—all kinds of emotions—happy, sad, nostalgic, melancholy—all kinds.
And for the first time since I lost my voice, I began

sobbing uncontrollably. Ed embraced me and with tears in his eyes said, "Oh, my God, Connie. Now I understand what you meant. You're right. You don't sound the same."

"Thank you, Ed," I cried in relief. "You *do* understand, don't you?"

"Connie, I think if I'd had a talent such as yours and lost it, I would have committed suicide."

In an effort to comfort me, my friends would invariably say one of two things to me. "You don't sound *that* bad," or else, "You've made the money. You've had the acclaim. Now put it to rest."

And each time they did, I felt as if no one in the world could understand the depth of my loss; I existed all alone on a very private island.

When I finally stopped crying, I felt as if a tremendous weight had been released from my shoulders. I felt freer, more optimistic than I had felt in a long time. I didn't feel alone anymore.

The next morning Ed and I were driving into New York to keep an appointment. For the first time in four years, I tuned the radio to a music station. (It was ordinarily set on WINS News.) The song "What I Did for Love" began playing. It has always been a real favorite of mine, but it was written after I lost my voice, so I could never sing it.

But now, as I began to sing it very softly to myself, my body started to tingle and quiver. For the first time in four long years, my voice was clear and true. And although the day was a scorcher, I had chills that lasted for hours.

When Ed and I arrived in New York and began walking toward our destination, very quietly I began singing another song and another, until I was sure that the whole thing wasn't my imagination. Then in the middle of a busy intersection, I stopped abruptly, threw my arms about Ed, and shouted. "I CAN SING! I CAN REALLY SING!"

Later I realized that the third corrective operation I'd undergone had been a success. But because it was so agonizing to sing, I simply stopped and never realized it had healed properly. (Incidentally, thank you again, Dr. Richard Webster of Brookline, Massachusetts, a fine gentleman and a superior surgeon.)

I could hardly wait to return to the car to begin playing the Cole Porter tape I'd heard the evening before, and when I began singing along, each and every note was vibrant and clear.

"Pull to the side of the highway, Ed! Get me to a telephone booth."

The first call I made was to Daddy; the second to George Scheck.

"George, I can sing again! . . . I don't know how— it's a miracle from God, but it's true! Book me at Carnegie Hall. I want to do a benefit for the Cancer Fund! . . . Of course, I'm sure!"

At first George Scheck was incredulous. Then he asked, "When do you want to go back to work?"

"Yesterday, George, yesterday!"

When I arrived home, George called me.

"Carnegie Hall is unavailable right now," George hesitated. "I don't know if you're interested, but . . ."

"What is it, George?"

"Well . . . Westbury is."

Since November of 1974 the very word Westbury evoked vivid and terrifying memories—Westbury appeared in many of my nightmares. In one recurring dream, I would enter the stage and when I looked out into the audience everyone had the same face—the face of the man who'd raped me.

I hesitated for the longest moment before saying, "Okay, George, book it."

                                        November 12, 1981
                                        Westbury, New York

With outstretched arms I circled the theater, embracing the audience and they me, ending seven agonizing years of self-doubt and heartbreak. There was the same old love affair between us, just the way it had always been since my career began a millennium ago. It was a night of never-felt-before-exhilaration—of coming home again—of reaching out almost desperately to touch the hands and hearts of the people. Then I sang my final song.

In my heyday young men wrote to me
Everybody seemed to have time to devote to me
Everyone I saw all swore they knew me, once upon a song

Main attraction, couldn't buy a seat
The celebrity celebrities would try to meet
I've had every accolade bestowed on me, and so you see

IF I NEVER SING ANOTHER SONG, it wouldn't bother
     me
I've had my share of fame, you know my name
IF I NEVER SING ANOTHER SONG, or take another
bow
I could get by, but God knows how

Always posing but you love it all
Though you have to learn to act like you're above it all
Everything I did the world applauded, once upon a star
Golden records hang on every wall
There are scrapbooks full of quotes, I can't recall it all
There were times I felt the world belonged to me,
     and so you see

IF I NEVER SING ANOTHER SONG, it wouldn't bother
     me
I've had my share of fame, you know my name
IF I NEVER SING ANOTHER SONG, or take another
bow
I could get by but God knows how

Yes, I've had fame, you know my name
And upon this stage tonight you've made me know
     where I belong

Thanks to you I'll get by
Even IF I NEVER SING ANOTHER SONG

"I guess you've probably suspected by now that
tonight is a very, very special night for me," I said,
with bouquets in both arms and tears streaming down
my face. "You know everybody likes to hang around a
celebrity. Everybody likes the glamour and the glitter
and the excitement of opening nights, but I shall never
forget those people who were there for me—I mean,
really there for me over the past seven years when
there were no opening nights. I'm proud to call you
my friends. I told you to hang in there, guys. Thank
you for waiting."

DISCOGRAPHY

U.S. RELEASES

Single Record Releases

K 12015: "Freddy"/"Didn't I Love You Enough?"

K 12056: "(O Please) Make Him Jealous"/"Goody Good-bye"

K 12122: "Are You Satisfied?"/"My Treasure"

K 12191: "My First Real Love"/"Believe in Me (Credimi)"

K 12251: "Forgetting"/"Send for My Baby"

K 12335: "My Sailor Boy"/"Everyone Needs Someone"

K 12375: "I Never Had a Sweetheart"/"Little Blue Wren"

K 12440: "No Other One"/"I Leaned on a Man"

K 12490: "Faded Orchid"/"Eighteen"

K 12555: "The Majesty of Love"/"You My Darlin' You"

K 12588: "Who's Sorry Now?"/"You Were Only Foolin' (While I Was Fallin' in Love)"

K 12647: "I'm Sorry I Made You Cry"/"Lock Up Your Heart"

K 12669: "Heartaches"/"I Miss You So"

K 12683: "Stupid Cupid"/"Carolina Moon"

K 12713: "Happy Days and Lonely Nights"/"Fallin'"

K 12738: "My Happiness"/"Never Before"

K 12769: "If I Didn't Care"/"Toward the End of the Day"

K 12793: "Lipstick on Your Collar"/"Frankie"

K 12824: "You're Gonna Miss Me"/"Plenty Good Lovin'"

K 12841: "Among My Souvenirs"/"God Bless America"

K 12878: "Mama"/"Teddy"

K 12899: "Everybody's Somebody's Fool"/"Jealous of You (Tango della Gelosia)"

K 12923: "My Heart Has a Mind of Its Own"/"Malagueña"

K 12964: "Many Tears Ago"/"Senza Mamma e Innamorato"

K 12971: "Where the Boys Are"/"No One"

K 12995: "Breakin' in a Brand New Broken Heart"/ "Some-one Else's Boy"

K 13005: "Atashi-no"("Where the Boys Are"—Japanese) "Swanee" (Limited release)

K 13019: "Together"/"Too Many Rules"

K 13039: "(He's My) Dreamboat"/"Hollywood"

K 13051: "When the Boy in Your Arms"/"Baby's First Christmas"

K 13059: "Don't Break the Heart That Loves You"/"Drop It Joe"

K 13074: "A Second Hand Love"/"Gonna Git That Man"

K 13087: "Vacation"/"The Biggest Sin of All"

K 13096: "I Was Such a Fool"/"He Thinks I Still Care"

K 13116: "I'm Gonna Be Warm This Winter"/"Al Di La"

K 13127: "Follow the Boys"/"Waiting for Billy"

K 13143: "If My Pillow Could Talk"/"You're the Only One Can Hurt Me"

K 13160: "Drownin' My Sorrows"/"Mala Femmina"

K 13176: "Your Other Love"/"Whatever Happened to Rosemarie?"

K 13203: "In the Summer of His Years"/"My Buddy"

K 13214: "Blue Winter"/"You Know You Don't Want Me"

K 13256: "Looking for Love"/"This Is My Happiest Moment"

K 13287: "Don't Ever Leave Me"/"We Have Something More"

K 13303: "Whose Heart Are You Breaking Tonight?"/"C'mon Jerry"

K 13325: "For Mama (La Mamma)"/"She'll Be Comin' Round the Mountain"

K 13331: "Wishing It Was You"/"You're Mine (Ho Bisogno di Vederti)"

K 13363: "Forget Domani"/"No One Ever Sends Me Roses"

K 13389: "Roundabout"/"Bossa Nova Hand Dance (Deixa Isso P'rá Lá)"

K 13420: "Jealous Heart"/"Can I Rely on You?"

K 134 : "When the Boys Meet the Girls"/"Exodus"/"Hava Nagila" (Withdrawn)

K 13470: "Love Is Me, Love Is You"/"I'd Let You Break My Heart"

K 13505: "It's a Different World"/"Empty Chapel"

K 13545: "A Letter from a Soldier"/"Somewhere, My Love"

K 13550: "A Nurse in the U.S. Army Corps" (Promotional)

K 13578: "So Nice (Summer Samba)"/"All the Love in the World"

K 13610: "Spanish Nights and You (Noches Españolas)"/"Games That Lovers Play"

K 13665: "Another Page"/"Souvenir D'Italie"

K 13718: "Time Alone Will Tell (Non Pensare a Me)"/ "Born Free"

K 13773: "My Heart Cries for You"/"Someone Took the Sweetness Out of Sweetheart"

K 13814: "Lonely Again"/"When You Care a Lot for Someone"

K 13876: "My World Keeps Slipping Away"/"Till We're Together Again"

K 13923: "Why Say Goodbye"/"Addio Mi Amore"

K 13948: "Somebody Else Is Taking My Place"/"Brother Can You Spare a Dime?"

K 14004: "The Welfare Check"/"I Don't Want to Play House"

K 14034: "The Wedding Cake"/"Over the Hill Under-
    ground"
K 14058: "Gone Like the Wind"/"Am I Blue?"
K 14089: "Invierno Triste Azul" ("Blue Winter"—Span-
    ish)"/"Noches Españolas (Spanish Nights)"
K 14091: "Zingara"/"Mr. Love"
Latino Series: "Noches Españolas y Tú"/"Invierno Triste"
    (LA)

Several big hit singles were also made available on the
Golden Circle Series by MGM and Polydor in different couplings.

Ivanhoe label: I-508: "Don't Turn Around"/"I Don't Want
    to Walk Without You" (First mix)
GSF Records: GSF 6901: "The Answer (Should I Tie a
    Yellow Ribbon?)"/"Paint the Rain"
Polydor Label: K 14853: "I'm Me Again"/"Comme ci,
    Comme ça"
810 087: "There's Still a Few Good Love Songs"/"Let's
    Make It Love Tonight"
813 980-7: "Where the Boys Are"/"My Heart Has a Mind of
    Its Own"

EP Releases:
X 1599: *Connie Francis*
X 1603: *Who's Sorry Now?* Vol. I
X 1604: *Who's Sorry Now?* Vol. II
X 1605: *Who's Sorry Now?* Vol. III
X 1655: *My Happiness*
X 1662: *If I Didn't Care*
X 1663: *The Exciting Connie Francis* Vol. I
X 1664: *The Exciting Connie Francis* Vol. II
X 1665: *The Exciting Connie Francis* Vol. III
X 1675: *My Thanks to You* Vol. I
X 1676: *My Thanks to You* Vol. II

X 1677: *My Thanks to You* Vol. III
X 1688: *Connie's Greatest Hits* Vol. I
X 1689: *Connie's Greatest Hits* Vol. II
X 1690: *Connie's Greatest Hits* Vol. III
X 1691: *Rock 'n' Roll Million Sellers* Vol. I
X 1692: *Rock 'n' Roll Million Sellers* Vol. II
X 1693: *Rock 'n' Roll Million Sellers* Vol. III
X 1694: *C & W Golden Hits* Vol. I
X 1695: *C & W Golden Hits* Vol. II
X 1696: *C & W Golden Hits* Vol. III
X 1703: *Valentino*
X 1706: *Don't Break the Heart That Loves You*

LP Releases

E 3686: *Who's Sorry Now?*
E/SE 3761: *The Exciting Connie Francis*
E/SE 3776: *My Thanks to You*
E/SE 3791: *Connie Francis Sings Italian Favorites*
E/SE 3792: *Christmas in My Heart*
E 3793: *Connie's Greatest Hits*
E/SE 3794: *Connie Francis Sings Rock 'n' Roll Million Sellers*
E/SE 3795: *Country and Western Golden Hits*
E/SE 3853: *Connie Francis Sings Spanish and Latin American Favorites*
E/SE 3869: *Connie Francis Sings Jewish Favorites*
E/SE 3871: *Connie Francis Sings More Italian Favorites*
E/SE 3893: *Songs to a Swinging Band*
E/SE 3913: *Connie at the Copa*
E/SE 3942: *More Greatest Hits*
E/SE 3965: *Never on Sunday*
E/SE 3969: *Connie Francis Sings Folk Song Favorites*
E/SE 4013: *Connie Francis Sings Irish Favorites*
E/SE 4022: *Do the Twist* retitled *Dance Party*
E4023: *Fun Songs for Children* (repackage of L 70126)

E/SE 4048: *Connie Francis Sings Award Winning Motion Picture Hits*

E/SE 4049: *Connie Francis Sings ("Second Hand Love") and Other Hits*

E/SE 4079: *Country Music, Connie Style*

E/SE 4102: *Modern Italian Hits*

E/SE 4123: *Follow the Boys*

E/SE 4124: *Connie Francis Sings German Favorites*

E/SE 4145: *Greatest American Waltzes*

E/SE 4161: *"Mala Femmina" and Connie's Big Hits from Italy*

E/SE 4167: *The Very Best of Connie Francis*

E/SE 4210: *In the Summer of His Years*

E/SE 4229: *Looking for Love*

E/SE 4251: *Connie Francis & Hank Williams, Jr., Sing Great Country Favorites*

E/SE 4253: *A New Kind of Connie*

E/SE 4294: *For Mama*

E/SE 4298: *Connie Francis Sings All Time International Hits*

E/SE 4334: *When the Boys Meet the Girls*

E/SE 4355: *Jealous Heart*

E/SE 4382: *Movie Greats of the 60s*

E/SE 4399: *Connie's Christmas* (re-release E/SE 3792)

E/SE 4411: *Live at the Sahara in Las Vegas*

E/SE 4448: *Love, Italian Style*

E/SE 4472: *Happiness: Connie Francis on Broadway Today*

E/SE 4474: *Grandes Exitos del Cine de los Años 60*

E/SE 4487: *My Heart Cries for You*

E/SE 4522: *Hawaii: Connie*

SE 4573: *Connie & Clyde*

SE 4585: *Connie Francis Sings Bacharach and David*

SE 4637: *The Wedding Cake*

SE 4655: *Connie Francis Sings the Songs of Les Reed*

L 70129: *Connie Francis Sings Fun Songs for Children*

GAS 109: *Greatest Golden Groovy Goodies*

LES 903: *Connie Francis and the Kids Next Door*

MATIMOR 802: *Sing Along with Connie Francis*

M/MS 519: *Connie Francis*

M/MS 538: *Connie Francis Sings Folk Favorites*

M/MS 571: *Songs of Love*

M/MS 603: *The Incomparable Connie Francis*

91145: *My Best to You* (Capitol Record Club)

LAT 10, 014: *Connie Francis Sings Spanish & Latin American Favorites*

LAT 10, 105: *Grandes Exitos del Cine de Los Años 60*

SG-60: *Connie* (Sessions)

LH-8019: *Connie: Italiano* (Laurie)

LV 8098: *Connie: Italiano* (CBS Special Products)

E6PS-2: *A Connie Francis Spectacular* (5-Record Set)

M6-1-5406: *I'm Me Again*

AR1-1023: *Merry Christmas: Connie Francis* (Sessions)

M6B 5410: *Connie's Greatest Hits*

M6B 5411: *Connie's Greatest Jewish Hits*

M6B 5412: *Connie's Greatest Italian Hits*

Foreign Releases

It would be impossible to list every single, EP, and LP issued in foreign countries because of the prolific recording career of Connie in each individual country. A full discography is available from: Ron Roberts, 34 Basing Hill, Wembley Park, Middlesex (London) HA9 9QP England.

Below we will mention a few of Connie's biggest sellers in a sampling of the major countries:

Japan (in Japanese): "Someone Else's Boy," "Too Many Rules," "Pretty Little Baby," "Vacation," "Don't Ever Leave Me," "I'm Gonna Be Warm This Winter"

Germany (in German): "Barcarole in der Nacht," "Wenn Du Gehst," "Paradiso" (Italian), "Die Liebe Ist ein

Seltsames Spiel," "Napoli" (Italian), "Du Musst Bleiben
Angelino," "Schöner Frehder Mann"

Italy (in Italian): "Tango della Gelosia," "Chitarra
Romana," "Violino Tzigano," "Aiutami a Piangere,"
"Mama," "Qualcuno Mi Aspetta," "Ho Bisogno di
Vederti," "Una Notte Così," "Dove Non So," "Canta
Ragazzina," "Dammi la Mano e Corri"

Spain (in Spanish): "Gracias," "El Novio de Otra," "La
Paloma," "Linda Muchachita," "La Gente"

Latin America (in Spanish): "Invierno Triste," "No Pueda
Olvidar," "Tanto Control"

Mexico: "Mi Tonto Amor," "Gracias," "Malagueña"

Brazil (in Portuguese): "Deixa Isso P'rá Lá," "Al Di La"
(Italian), "Torero," "Mama"

France (in French): "Jamais" ("La Paloma"—French),
"C'est Lui que Je Veux," "Valentino"

Canada (in French): "Jamais," "Danke Schön" (German),
"Paradiso" (Italian), "Chitarra Romana" (Italian),
"Décidément"

Israel: "Chitarra Romana" (Italian), "My Yiddishe
Momme" (Yiddish and English), "Baby Roo" (English)

England: "Robot Man," "Who's Sorry Now?" "Carolina
Moon," "My Heart Has a Mind of Its Own," "My Child,"
"Vacation"

Scandinavia: "Pretty Little Baby" (Swedish), "Mr. Twister"
(Swedish), "Lara's Theme"

Philippines: "Wishing It Was You," "Spanish Nights and You," "Somewhere My Love"

Holland: "Everybody's Somebody's Fool," "My Happiness," "Napoli," "Blue Winter," "Lipstick on Your Collar," "Someone Else's Boy" (Dutch)

High adventure and intriguing secrets aboard a 1920s luxury ocean liner

MAIDEN VOYAGE

GRAHAM MASTERTON

"Written with dazzling *panache*....High quality entertainment from start to finish...."
—*Publishers Weekly*

"Indisputably entertaining—with spiffy chat, mucho naughtiness, and sybaritic delights...."—*Kirkus*